Praise for *Lies My Therapist Told Me*

"Few books combine theological precision with practical wisdom as skillfully as *Lies My Therapist Told Me*. Dr. Greg Gifford's careful analysis cuts through the fog of contemporary mental health discourse to show why the Bible's teaching about the mind remains our surest guide. Rather than merely critiquing secular approaches, this book provides a robust, hope-filled biblical alternative for those seeking true transformation rather than symptom management. Gifford demonstrates that God's Word speaks authoritatively and sufficiently to our deepest inner struggles, showing us that Christ offers more than coping mechanisms—He offers true renewal of the mind. This is an essential resource for navigating mental health issues with biblical faithfulness."

—**Jonny Ardavanis**, pastor of Stonebridge Bible Church, Brentwood, TN; and author of *Consider the Lilies: Finding Perfect Peace in the Character of God*

"The church has needed this book for decades. With compassion, sympathy, and, above all, biblical clarity, Greg Gifford demonstrates that in so many cases, what we are suffering from are not psychological ailments, but spiritual ones. And we go on suffering because we fail to turn to the Great Physician. *Lies My Therapist Told Me* offers a courageous and convincing case that God's Word is the balm that heals the deepest afflictions of the mind."

—**Megan Basham**, culture reporter for the *Daily Wire*, and *New York Times* bestselling author of *Shepherds for Sale: How Evangelical Leaders Traded the Truth for a Leftist Agenda*

"We live in a day that talks incessantly about 'mental health' and 'mental illness' while still not understanding these issues clearly or deeply. Greg Gifford writes with clarity, compassion, and depth as he points the way back to real hope and help. And thankfully, Greg doesn't just write *about* the people who've been trapped in this secular model; he writes *to* them with a pastor's heart that longs for them to experience something better. This book is not simply about what he's against. It's a biblical foundation and framework for something he believes can transform your life. Buy it. Read it. Give it away to others."

—**Brad Bigney**, pastor of Grace Fellowship Church, Florence, KY; host of the *Thrive* marriage and family podcast; and author of *Gospel Treason: Betraying the Gospel with Hidden Idols*

"Equating the brain and the mind is one of the greatest errors of this present time. Such confusion has ramifications upon how we assess the world, parent our children, perceive the Christian life, and understand the need and nature of salvation. *Lies My Therapist Told Me* recovers the distinction between the brain and the mind. While certain issues can stem from the brain, Gifford—with wit, clarity, and pastoral care—reminds us that Christians can renew their minds, be transformed, and have true freedom instead of being enslaved to sin, just as the Bible commands. In an age of mental health and therapy, this is a must-read for Christian discernment."

—**Abner Chou**, president of The Master's University and Seminary

"People visit therapists because they want change. But below the surface are important questions about definitions of problems and methods of effecting change. With competence and compassion, Greg Gifford skillfully identifies distinctions between solutions offered by various therapeutic methods and the answers in the Bible. Whether or not you come to this discussion with faith, you should consider the important comparisons found in this book. Modern psychiatry can seem mysterious. Having the curtain lifted will help you understand the nature of the problem so that you can move toward the best solutions."

—**John Crotts**, pastor of Faith Bible Church, Sharpsburg, GA; host of the *Integrated* podcast; and author of *Hope: Living Confidently in God*

"*Lies My Therapist Told Me* offers a bold and thought-provoking critique of the secular mental health paradigm. It's incredibly helpful and will undoubtedly be a great resource for many. The world may have limits on what it can heal, but Jesus has none."

—**Shelbi Cullen**, assistant professor of biblical counseling and women's ministries at The Master's University and cohost of the *Women's Hope* podcast

"In this age of science and medical intervention, there is much confusion in the culture, and unfortunately in the church, on the topic known as 'mental illness.' Dr. Gifford offers much-needed wisdom on the topic. His thoughts are well-balanced to the truth of Scripture and the issues of science. This book is a must-read to better understand being human, both body and soul."

—**Lee Edmonds, MD**, associate clinical professor of medicine at Columbia University College of Physicians and Surgeons (Retired) and chief of pulmonary and sleep medicine at Bassett Healthcare Network (Retired)

"*Lies My Therapist Told Me* will be the definitive book on the problems with secular psychology. Greg Gifford not only exposes the barren wasteland of secular therapy, but he also provides the cure. He points to Jesus Christ and His sacred Word as the rich soil out of which all faithful counseling grows."

—**Heath Lambert**, senior pastor of First Baptist Church, Jacksonville, FL; and author of *The Great Love of God: Encountering God's Heart for a Hostile World*

"This book explains how therapy has often become a substitute for Biblical teaching about sin, repentance, and the renewing of the mind. Rather than experiencing the power of the Holy Spirit, Christians today frequently rely on humanistic solutions that offer no real help for the soul. Be prepared to take a deep dive into some controversial issues that relate to the distinction between the mind and the brain and how our reliance on drugs can at best cure only the symptoms of a deeper malady."

—**Erwin W. Lutzer**, pastor emeritus of Moody Church, Chicago, IL

"Spiritual infirmities cannot be cured with psychotropic drugs. The guilt and dysfunction with which sin has marred the human soul is not fundamentally a medical issue. Those are truths that the atheistic, materialistic worldview that now dominates our culture cannot comprehend. But it is a fact that spiritual issues lie at the root of most mental and emotional disorders—depression, crippling fear, post-traumatic stress, and other supposed 'mental health' maladies. Dr. Greg Gifford unpacks these truths in careful detail, with extraordinary clarity and biblical insight, in *Lies My Therapist Told Me*. This is an extremely helpful answer to the so-called mental health epidemic. I highly recommend it."

—**Phil Johnson**, executive director of Grace to You

"Gifford cuts through the confusion raging over the mind and brain while demonstrating how the treasures of wisdom and knowledge found in our Lord Jesus Christ are sufficient and strong enough to rescue us from deep and dark affliction. *Lies My Therapist Told Me* will grow your discernment in a confusing world. This book will be helpful, and we need a hundred more like it!"

—**T. Dale Johnson Jr.**, executive director of the Association of Certified Biblical Counselors (ACBC); professor of biblical counseling at Midwestern Baptist Theological Seminary; cohost of the *Transformed* TV series; and host of the *Truth in Love* podcast

"We are surrounded by a therapeutic culture that represents one of the most dangerous and seductive powers of this age. We should be thankful for convictional voices who are pressing back on the regime of the therapeutic and the ideologies of the self in order to direct Christians to the only source of true wisdom and wholeness: the gospel of Jesus Christ and the unsearchable riches of Scripture. I'm thankful to Greg Gifford for pressing back and pointing forward in just this way."

—**R. Albert Mohler Jr.**, president of the Southern Baptist Theological Seminary

"This well-researched book makes an important contribution to the biblical counseling movement. Greg Gifford seeks to help Christian counselors correctly identify the spiritual issues behind their counselees' struggles along with biblical solutions. I highly recommend this book and plan to commend it to my students."

—**Jim Newheiser**, professor of Christian counseling and pastoral theology at Reformed Theological Seminary, Charlotte, NC; and executive director of the Institute for Biblical Counseling and Discipleship

"Truth-telling has become a rare occurrence in an era that has made deception fashionable. Lies continue to thrive and abound because their father is still going to and fro on the earth and walking back and forth on it. And since he is the prince of the power of the air, the spirit who now works in the sons of disobedience, there is no shortage of willing servants to help propagate his insidious lies. Greg Gifford is an avid lie-hater and truth-lover, and he has gifted the planet with an extraordinary lie-stopper and truth-dispenser. *Lies My Therapist Told Me* is more than just a book; it is a thoroughly biblical masterpiece and a must-read for anyone seeking clarity and God-glorifying sanity in a world gone mad."

—**Emeal "E.Z." Zwayne**, president of Living Waters and author of *Fight Like a Man: A Bold, Biblical Battle Plan for Personal Purity*

Lies My Therapist Told Me

ALSO BY GREG E. GIFFORD

Helping Your Family Through PTSD
Heart & Habits: How We Change for Good

Lies My Therapist Told Me

Why Christians Should
Aim for More Than Just
Treating Symptoms

GREG E. GIFFORD
Foreword by Todd Friel

BROADSIDE BOOKS

Parts of chapter five have been adapted from the author's paper "Does the Body Keep the Score?" The manuscript is in the *Journal of Biblical Soul Care* 7 (Spring 2024).

FIRST EDITION

Library of Congress Cataloging-in-Publication Data

Names: Gifford, Greg E., author.
Title: Lies my therapist told me : why Christians should aim for more than
   just treating symptoms / Greg E. Gifford.
Description: First edition. | New York, NY : HarperCollins Publishers,
   [2025] | Includes bibliographical references and index.
Identifiers: LCCN 2024051500 (print) | LCCN 2024051501 (ebook) | ISBN
   9780063416734 (hardcover) | ISBN 9780063416758 (ebook)
Subjects: LCSH: Counseling—Religious aspects—Christianity. | Thought and thinking—
   Religious aspects—Christianity. | Mental health—Religious aspects—Christianity.
Classification: LCC BR115.C69 G54 2025 (print) | LCC BR115.C69 (ebook) |
   DDC 261.8/322—dc23/eng/20241206
LC record available at https://lccn.loc.gov/2024051500
LC ebook record available at https://lccn.loc.gov/2024051501

25 26 27 28 29 LBC 8 7 6 5 4

To The Master's University, for Christ & Scripture

The natural person does not accept the things of the Spirit of God, for they are folly to him, and he is not able to understand them because they are spiritually discerned. The spiritual person judges all things, but is himself to be judged by no one. "For who has understood the mind of the Lord so as to instruct him?"

But we have the mind of Christ.
—*1 Corinthians 2:14–16*

Contents

Foreword

A name game is being played, and the spoils of victory are substantial and very, very personal. Here's how it works.

In 1980, a fidgety kid would have been diagnosed with AIYP: Ants In Your Pants. The cure was a healthy dose of exercise and extra chores.

Today, a kid with ants in his pants is diagnosed with ADHD: attention-deficit hyperactivity disorder. The cure is a prescription for expensive psychotropic medication.

Soldiers who returned from the Civil War with severe anxiety were said to have "soldier's heart." World War II soldiers who experienced night terrors were called "shell-shocked." These men were given time, love, support, encouragement, and counseling.

Today, if a soldier returns from war and struggles with anxious thoughts, nightmares, and flashbacks, he is diagnosed with post-traumatic stress disorder and offered a cocktail of medications.

The list goes on and on:

- Melancholy is now called clinical depression.
- A person with any sort of fear has a phobia.
- A lunatic or madman is now labeled a psychopath.
- Scrupulosity has been replaced with obsessive-compulsive disorder.

While the evolution of words is a natural phenomenon, the entire category of words that once described human experiences and emotions has been intentionally replaced with clinical and scientific terminology. While financial incentives are a part of the explanation for the name game, it does not fully explain the recent explosion in mental health diagnoses. The mental health industrial complex dominates Western civilization's understanding of emotional and behavioral issues. Clinical and therapeutic language is merely a fruit of our cultural shift from a Christian explanation to what we are told is a scientific surety.

Perhaps you have heard the joke, albeit in bad taste, that "we are all on the spectrum." That comment reveals that the proliferation of mental health diagnoses is so pervasive, it has become a cliché.

This would all be rather innocuous if it weren't so personal. If you are reading this book, it is probably because you, or a friend or family member, have been formally diagnosed with something from the American Psychiatric Association's ever-expanding *Diagnostic and Statistical Manual of Mental Disorders*. That is most certainly true for my family.

It's funny how a phone call from a school authority can instantly transform a fully functioning adult into a tremulous child. Even though my wife and I had graduated from elementary school three decades earlier, when our daughter's third-grade teacher called, we both felt like we were being summoned to the principal's office ourselves for being naughty.

"Mr. and Mrs. Friel, I would like to meet with you to discuss your daughter." When we asked what transgression our oldest child had committed, we were told, "There are just some things I would like to share with you." That was not the truth, the whole truth, and nothing but the truth. Her tone revealed that she wanted to discuss something wrong with our daughter.

The meeting took place in our daughter's classroom. As we sat in chairs designed for eight-year-olds, the teacher tried her level best to sound genuine when she said, "You have a wonderful daughter." We both knew we were about to hear a conjunction. And we did.

"But," she said as she reached into her desk drawer and pulled out well-worn pink and blue laminated documents, "I think your daughter might need some help if she is going to succeed in school."

She refiled the blue document and began to march us through the symptoms of female ADHD. It turns out that our daughter:

- Struggled to sit still for an entire hour
- Seemed more interested in talking than listening
- Looked out the door when someone walked down the hallway

According to the pink laminated document, these were clear signs our daughter had ADHD. After asking us if we would like a business card of a doctor who could help us, we said, "Thank you. We will think this over." That too was not the truth, the whole truth, and nothing but the truth. We were stunned.

An elementary school teacher, without medical or psychological training, wanted to give our precious little girl mysterious medications that would accomplish one goal: make a third-grade teacher's job easier. It seemed to us the problem wasn't a child with a psychological disorder; the problem was a teacher who couldn't hold the attention of fidgety eight-year-olds.

Millions of parents have endured similar meetings. Like us, they sense something isn't quite right, but they don't know what. Lacking medical or psychological training, they are inclined to trust the experts. And who can blame them? It's hard to resist a prescription that promises to bring peace to the home and fewer phone calls from frustrated teachers.

I recently received an email from one such parent who feels pressure to medicate his short-attention-spanned pubescent son.

I used to think my son (11) was just an immature boy. He is highly active and plays every sport we can fit into his schedule, so it seemed normal that a highly active boy would have trouble sitting still through lectures all day at school.

As he has gotten older and into middle school, I'm starting to have second thoughts about not using medication. I'm curious if you think there is a point where these types of medications should start being considered.

Unfortunately, it isn't just ADHD that is diagnosed at disconcerting levels. The University of Michigan reports that antidepressants for twelve- to twenty-four-year-olds is up a staggering 66.3 percent since 2016.[1] The kids are not alone: one in five adults are currently on psychiatric medications.[2]

Have we all lost our minds?

While I love a black-helicopter theory as much as the next guy, it is undeniable that something is afoot. Either we are all losing our minds, or the metrics for diagnosing mental health disorders is evolving to the point we are all "on the spectrum."

If you or someone you love has been diagnosed with a disorder, you have been thrust into the choppy waters of "mental health" and you are reeling. You owe it to yourself, or to your family, to read this eye-opening book.

Not only will you discover that the Mental Health Emperor has no clothes, but you will also be offered a biblical explanation that forces secularists to concede, "The Bible explains our emotions better than secular psychiatrists do."

- Do I really have a mental disorder?
- Does the DSM-V really explain my loved one's behavior?
- Are psychotropic medications the solution to what ails us?

If you are asking any of these questions, I implore you to read *Lies My Therapist Told Me*. Dr. Greg Gifford will help you make sense of your emotions, feelings, behavior, and fears. He will also navigate you through the choppy waters of a mental health diagnosis.

Dr. Gifford is exceptional in many ways. Not only is he whip-smart, but his bedside manner is impeccable. I saw Greg in action dozens of times as he counseled people on our *Transformed* TV series. He is kind, gentle, slow to speak, and wise. Very wise.

There is a reason *Transformed* is one of the top podcasts worldwide. His warm, biblical, and loving way of speaking to hurting souls exudes wisdom beyond his years.

The decisions you make about a mental health diagnosis are big. Dr. Gifford understands that and has taken the time to write a book that will prove invaluable to you as you seek to make a wise and godly decision. Not a word is wasted.

When you complete *Lies My Therapist Told Me*, you will be well equipped to make a decision that will impact the rest of your life. You might also see secular psychiatry in an entirely new light.

Best of all, you might discover that you and your loved ones can live a life without the numb.

Todd Friel
Host of *Wretched TV* and *Wretched Radio*
Executive Director of Fortis Institute

Introduction
Secular Therapy Isn't Working

> The psychiatrist must first search my heart and yet he
> never plumbs its ultimate depth. The Christian brother
> knows when I come to him: here is a sinner like myself,
> a godless man who wants to confess and yearns for
> God's forgiveness. The psychiatrist views me as if there
> were no God. The brother views me as I am before the
> judging and merciful God in the Cross of Jesus Christ.
> —*Dietrich Bonhoeffer*[1]

As I sat across from the school psychologist with my wife and sixth-grade son, I knew the system was broken. "We want him to be tested," she said. But it sounded like she really meant "We are looking to diagnose him."

When COVID-19 struck, California's public schools were closed for up to a year and a half, and students were learning online. So, when my son finally returned to the classroom after doing fourth and fifth grades from home, he was regularly not getting his homework done, getting distracted in a class of thirty-five (with no student teacher), and telling the teacher he "didn't know how." But now the school psychologist would "test him" to determine if he had what is often called a "mental illness," such as an anxiety or mood disorder, or if he had another condition, such as ADHD or a learning disability. This would allow him to receive "treatment" and "school resources," also known as medication and a tutor.

But something seemed off. Are we really comfortable with prescribing medication to an eleven-year-old, specifically a medication that is meant to influence behavior by altering their brain's chemistry, all based on a paper examination and not one brain scan or vital sign? Would the label "learning disability" or "ADHD" haunt him for years to come? He had spent the last two grades doing school online and being isolated from his friends. Would medications deal with the roots of his issues?

This moment for my family demonstrated just how saturated our society is with a secular, therapeutic culture. And when I say saturated, I mean it's *everywhere*.

Not just in schools. Billboards, advertisements, and the entire month of May in America is dedicated to spreading awareness about the importance of mental health. A growing number of employers provide workers with mental health days. Therapy-based businesses are now so pervasive, you can get an online counselor within minutes. Pharmaceutical companies inundate us with advertisements about antidepressants. Therapists like Frasier Crane have been major characters in popular novels and television shows, while men like Dr. Phil McGraw and Dr. Jordan Peterson enjoy celebrity status on television and the internet. Books like *The Body Keeps the Score* are massive bestsellers. We have more psychology majors graduating from colleges and graduate programs;[2] more government, nonprofit, and corporate resources going toward "mental health" efforts; and more drugs on the market to treat "mental illness" than ever before.

This therapeutic culture has been growing for decades now, but rather than eradicating anxiety (like smallpox was eradicated by vaccination) or cultivating a nation full of mentally healthy citizens, something very different has happened.

A Surge of Mental Illness

According to the Centers for Disease Control and Prevention (CDC), approximately 20 million American children between the ages of three to seventeen have a mental illness.[3] The most common mental illnesses are seen as ADHD, anxiety, depression, and behavioral disorders. Children who are diagnosed in their childhood with anxiety and depression, according to the CDC, have "increased over time."[4]

Children can be diagnosed with a mental illness before they get to kindergarten. Can you imagine being told since you were five years old that you had a mental illness? How would that affect you?

The CDC would add that if you were diagnosed as a child with a mental illness, you will experience other issues as well. For example, if you have anxiety, then you often also have behavioral problems.[5] Some of our kids have been told since they were young that they have *multiple* mental illnesses, and now their behavioral issues are couched in the language of mental illness as well. Under the guise of mental health care, they are being diagnosed, medicated, and treated for these so-called mental illnesses—and the number keeps growing.

The number of diagnoses is increasing not only for kids, but also for adults. According to the National Institute of Mental Health, 22.8 percent of Americans over eighteen years old suffer from a mental illness.[6] This can be anything from mild to severe impairment in daily functioning. Of all the work friends, church friends, and family friends that you have, more than one in five might have been diagnosed with a mental illness. That could be anxiety, depression, ADHD, or one of many, many other labels.

Just by way of further context, 22.8 percent of American adults is an estimated 57.8 *million* people. That's staggering. The World Health Organization stated, "Mental health conditions are increasing worldwide. Mainly because of demographic changes, there has been a 13% rise in mental health conditions and substance use disorders in the last decade (to 2017)."[7] Within the US, Mental Health America stated there was a year-over-year increase between 2020 and 2021, up from 45.6 to 47.1 million people who were "living with a mental health condition."[8] This is a 1.5 million increase. Again, these numbers are astounding.

Once many Americans receive arbitrary-sounding medical labels, secular therapists typically refer them to psychiatrists to assign medication for these so-called mental illnesses. As the number of mental illness diagnoses grows, so does the number of those taking psychotropics. The American Psychological Association estimated in 2008 that one in ten Americans were taking psychotropic medication, but as of 2021, that estimate is now one in four.[9]

Now, before we go any further, I want to be clear: if you're one of those Americans taking medication for a mental illness, you should listen to your doctor, and stay on your medication. My message here is not that medication has no role in helping people. It can be beneficial to address issues of the body. And quitting without your doctor's guidance can be dangerous.

What I *am* saying, though, is that our secular, therapeutic approach isn't making things better. If it was, we wouldn't have an increasing number of people on psychotropics. There's a deeper problem with our current therapeutic approach, and it's fundamentally a *worldview* problem.

Blurring the Lines Between the Mind and the Brain

The phrase *mental health* is somewhat new to the modern English speaker. It originated from the phrase *mental hygiene,* and both have been coined within the past one hundred years or so. The American Psychological Association defines mental health as "a state of mind characterized by emotional well-being, good behavioral adjustment, relative freedom from anxiety and disabling symptoms, and a capacity to establish constructive relationships and cope with the ordinary demands and stresses of life."[10] Originally the term was used to help focus on preventing insanity, and now it's used for just about anything, as you can see in the APA's definition—relationships, responding to stress, behavior, and emotions.

However, to use the term *mental health*, you have to accept the significant assumption that we are talking about genuine *health* issues, the realm of bodily functions like immune systems, digestion, broken bones, or nutrition. The term, as we will discuss more later, has a carte blanche authority in modern culture to describe the reality of "health" as it pertains to the mind, yet we haven't come to terms with what we mean by "health."

So now we often talk about the *mind* and the organ of the *brain* interchangeably. But if we were to say that they are the same, then that is fundamentally a materialistic and atheistic assumption—one that, as a Christian, I don't make.[11]

The Bible and the Mind vs. the Brain

One person esteems one day as better than another, while another esteems all days alike. Each one should be fully convinced in his own mind. (Emphasis added)

—ROMANS 14:5

According to the Bible, the mind is not the brain, and the brain is not the mind. The Bible tells us to set our "mind [or, to think] on things above" (Col. 3:2), to have a "renewed mind" (Eph. 4:23), and that God has given up certain individuals to a debased "mind" (Rom. 1:28). Other terms, such as "outer man," or "body" (2 Cor. 4:16–18; 5:8), would best capture the external organ of the brain. The mind, according to the Bible, is immaterial, while the brain would be material. You cannot touch the mind. It isn't biological. It will continue to exist after your body perishes. And it cannot get sick with a pathological illness.

Some have never heard this, and I want to help bring clarity in this book to something that has affected your life in many ways. The Bible treats the mind and the brain as different, and if you treat them as the same, it will hinder any genuine and lasting help you would offer to people—or any help you would receive personally. We would never treat our lungs like a kidney. Nor would we treat our stomach as a broken bone. If you get the *diagnosis* wrong, you will get the *prognosis* wrong. Yet some of us have mistakenly treated our mind as if it were a biological/material reality, thus missing some of God's plans for the mind. We can thank the secular therapeutic culture for much of this confusion.

Many experts in different fields have brought their critiques of secular therapy culture and their proposed solutions to this crisis. Some, like Jonathan Haidt, have pointed out the correlation between the rise in anxiety and depression in young people and the proliferation of smartphones.[12] Others rightly point out that the decline in family life, with fewer adults getting and staying married, and fewer kids growing up in two-parent homes, is a major contributor to the rise in diagnoses. Meanwhile, there is no shortage of political commentators—from Matt Walsh to Abigail Shrier—who can point out how today's confusion over sexuality and cynicism about our political outlook can lead to despair. And of course, people who study the brain, like Daniel Amen, argue that lifestyle changes that contribute to a healthy brain, such as optimal habits of sleep, diet, and exercise, *are* key to fighting the issues we call mental illness. "Get your brain right, and your mind will follow," he says—more on that later.[13]

Each of these critiques has some merit. But all of them overlook the real reason our crisis isn't abating: modern therapy is based on flawed, unbiblical ideas. The theories that undergird modern therapy often have wrong assumptions about *anthropology*. That is, they're rooted in false beliefs about how people work, and specifically about the mind and the brain. The Bible offers a superior alternative to understanding people. You can read all the secular literature in the world regarding mental illness/health, but you still won't learn God's solutions to these problems in His Word.

As you'll see in the following chapters, what is being put forward as hard science in psychological evaluations, mental illness descrip-

tions, and the prescription of psychotropics is anything but hard science. It is largely soft science, and it is even recognized as such by
the medical community. Perhaps psychiatry is more akin to a game of
"hot and cold" where a person describes when they're close to a target
by saying "hot" and farther from a target by saying "cold." Did that
medicine help? No. Did that medicine help? Somewhat. Things like
vital signs, blood levels, scans, or other empirical means of evaluation are often overlooked. Rather, a psychiatrist verbally assessed you,
gave you some surveys, and then made a diagnosis.

Still others recommend nonphysical treatments for mental illness,
such as cognitive behavioral therapy (CBT), yoga, mindfulness, new
friendships, vacations, and self-care. Yet pause to answer this—if a
person's mind is thinking thoughts that are fundamentally untrue,
angry, lustful, nihilistic, envious, or futile, what will yoga do for *that*
mind? A person can be more mindful of really bad things. And does a
worldview that is all about "self-care" really help people?

As a biblical counselor, I start with the premise that God is our de-
signer, and therefore, He knows how our minds work and has given us
answers for when they go wrong. Those answers are in the Bible, and I
have seen them transform the lives of many struggling with so-called
mental illnesses. They can transform your life too.

While the majority of Americans still identify as Christians, I
understand many who read this may not. If that's you, thanks for
hearing me out, and I trust you will still benefit greatly from this
book. If you're interested in learning more about why I believe the
Bible is true in the first place, I would point you toward resources
such as *Why Believe the Bible?*, by John MacArthur; *The Ultimate
Proof of Creation*, by Jason Lisle; *The Case for Christ*, by Lee Strobel;
the websites of Fortis Institute and Answers in Genesis; and Voddie
Baucham's message, "Why I Choose to Believe the Bible."

In this book, my goal is to let the Bible frame our perspective
of people, to correct our secular anthropology. Once I've established
this, I'll connect the dots to mental illness. However, I want you

to spend time checking my math regarding the Bible and how God views the human mind. Because if you agree with my work on what the Bible says about the mind, it will help us speak the same language when we talk about mental health and mental illness. My aim is to let the Bible speak for itself, and then offer biblical categories for understanding people. Categories that will be more helpful in the end, because "he has made us, and we are his" (Ps. 100:3). We need better options, options that the secular therapeutic culture simply is not giving us.

A Word of Hope

Some of you who are reading this book have been caught in a vicious cycle of mental health treatment. You've been referred to every doctor, psychiatrist, psychologist, and therapist that exists only to find a label and some medications at the end of each of those paths. Sometimes multiple labels and even multiple medications. You have heard this since you were young, and now mental health/illness is a large part of who you are and the way you function in your daily life—including your self-conception.

I don't want to minimize any of that. I know that your struggles are real, and not only real, but painful. Part of the pain is that no one has been able to *actually* identify what you're experiencing and then offer a solution, rather than "ways to cope."

Bear with me, because this book was written for you. Sure, I'd like academics to work through what I'm writing. Yes, I'd love clergy and educators to learn more about the mind and the brain. But I want you to hear what the Bible says about who God made you to be. Your suffering may not be removed by understanding God's perspective of you, but it will be alleviated. In time, your mind can be transformed. When you understand who you are through the lens of the Bible, you can then know how to respond to any circumstance or suffering. Not only does God have answers, but He created you. He knows His creation. His answers are always best.

Consider the words of the Apostle Paul, who knew more about suffering than just about anyone: "Oh, the depth of the riches and wisdom and knowledge of God! How unsearchable are his judgments and how inscrutable his ways!" (Rom. 11:33). God's ways are so much better than man's ways. His wisdom is infinite and inexhaustible. He alone possesses all knowledge, all insights, and all wisdom.

When we consider God in light of understanding ourselves and our problems, He "enlightens our eyes" (Ps. 19:8). When we view ourselves through the lens of the Scriptures, we see things as they are . . . as God has made them. The Bible is not a patchwork of verses intended for memorization. It is the lens through which we view the world.[14] Our goal is to think God's thoughts—as best as we are able—by thinking biblically, even when we think about "mental health."

Let's allow God, through His Word, to frame how we view ourselves. Let's cultivate self-conceptions that are accurate according to the Bible, to include a reframing of mental health and mental illness.

When my wife, son, and I left the meeting with the school psychologist, we decided to not get my son tested. I asked the school psychologist what testing would *actually* provide for my son, to which she replied, "It will allow for us to get him the resources that he might need." My follow-up question to her was, "Why don't we just get him the resources that he might need without testing?" That's what we did.

It is not any parent's goal to withhold helpful resources from their children. We want our children to thrive in their lives and provide resources to help them do that. But my wife and I decided to simply get tutors. After two years of math tutoring, our son was making A's again. You can actually help your kids without the mental health baggage that is being promulgated through public schools. It is my honest opinion that the label of "ADHD" or "learning disability" can do more harm than good, not to include the reality that those diagnoses are often surprisingly arbitrary.

What if instead of medicating eleven-year-olds and slapping a disorder label on them, we listened to them, learned about them, and sought
to help as best as is possible? What are their strengths and weaknesses?
Through the God-ordained maturing process and some additional
resources, most of our kids will be just fine. As a discerning Christian,
I want you to listen to God's Word first, then the school psychologist—
not vice versa. Don't accept wholesale what a school psychologist
might say. In many cases, the secular therapeutic enterprise just simply
doesn't know the truth about people.

But our God does. He knows the number of stars in the universe,
the number of grains of sand on the earth, and the number of hairs
on our heads. He has granted to us all things that pertain to life and
godliness through a more sure, inerrant Word that equips us for every
good work. For His glory and our good, let us now pursue biblical
clarity, and expose the lies of secular therapy.

PART I

The Mental Health Industrial Complex

CHAPTER 1

A Modern Mental Health Epidemic

Our topic is who is sick and who is not . . .
pretty soon everybody is going to be sick.

—ALLEN J. FRANCES[1]

Depression is one of the most common, if not *the* most common mental disorder/illness. In order to be diagnosed, a person needs to demonstrate depressive symptoms for over two weeks. Symptoms include depressed mood, diminished interest in many things, weight loss, insomnia, psychomotor agitation, and fatigue, among a few others.[2] Honestly, I could not tell you how many people I've counseled who said depression was a part of their struggle, and were already taking antidepressants. There have been just too many.

One man in particular does stand out, though. He was a single man, in his twenties, when we met for counseling. To protect his identity, let's call him Michael.

At the time, Michael's parents were extremely concerned for their son. He was very spacy, missing work, not sleeping, stuck in this rut of dark thoughts, along with reckless living. They called the counseling center asking if we would meet with Michael after office hours due to the urgency of the situation. I do my best to be available when self-harm is part of a counseling case, so I agreed to meet with them.

The parents were conservative Christians, who genuinely did love their adult son (this detail will be important to recall in a moment).

Michael was simply stuck. He had been diagnosed with depression, and also prescribed medication. He didn't want to take the antidepressants for fear of being addicted to them, and also said his antidepressants were not helpful.

When we met for the first counseling session, I was deeply concerned about Michael. He was very distanced. It was hard to get him to focus on conversation. He was obviously under-rested, and like a zombie to talk to. He would space out while talking and then come back to the conversation.

What he did tell me was alarming, even all these years later. He would ride his motorcycle as fast as it would go—100 plus miles per hour—down the interstate. He would stay in his house for days and even painted art—with his own blood as the paint. Not a day would go by that he didn't have thoughts of self-harm. It was quite concerning.

We started meeting twice a week due to the urgency of the circumstance, while I also worked with Michael's parents and his pastor. Michael's parents would check in on him at his apartment and his pastor would look for him at church services and worship-band practice. As we met for counseling we began to dig for the root of what was happening in Michael's heart and how he understood God. The easiest way to say it is that Michael always thought that he was doing something wrong before God and thus felt guilty *all the time*. Michael's view of God was that God was wrath and justice first, and then maybe God would be love . . . maybe.

I find that many who come from really conservative Christian backgrounds can have a high view of God's wrath and justice, to the detriment of other attributes of God like His wisdom, goodness, love, or mercy. It's the equivalent of having an angry father at home, when all you understand about God is one of His more severe attributes. Instead of focusing on the depression, we focused on the character of God in His goodness and love. Michael's understanding of God, or lack thereof, was producing this weight of guilt that was unwarranted. In all honesty, if you meditated on your sins all day and just considered one aspect of God's character—His wrath—then you too would be similar to Michael. But once Michael's understanding of God changed according to the Bible, his guilt lifted. His thoughts were transformed. His mood changed.

The feelings of heavy sadness were not the root issue, but the fruit of what was going on in Michael's heart. And in this instance—although not true in every circumstance—depression was connected to a wrong view of God.

What does Michael's situation teach us? Depression wasn't the real issue. It often is not. Depression is often symptomatic of the real issue. Yet the secular therapeutic culture wants to simply diagnose with arbitrary criteria for so-called mental disorders, like Michael had already received. In fact, I would be surprised if you didn't know someone like Michael who has been told they have depression even though depression isn't *really* the issue.

Due to loosening diagnostic criteria, we have diagnostic inflation. Instead of helping, the secular therapeutic culture is often iatrogenic.

Iatrogenesis and the White House Conference on Mental Health

Perhaps you've heard the term *iatrogenesis*? It means that there is harm brought to a patient by their caretaker that was not a natural result of their condition. For instance, if a medical doctor erroneously conducts a surgery, causing more pain to the patient, that would be iatrogenesis. Just to be clear, iatrogenesis often isn't malicious. A patient can incur greater harm through negligence, accidents, and other unintentional damage. In either case, though, greater harm has been done regardless of the caretaker's motivations.

Mental health treatments in America are often iatrogenic in nature.

It is causing more harm than good by confusing the mind and the brain and thus treating the immaterial mind with material solutions, leading to a mental health epidemic. Despite the motivations of those offering care—and I personally believe many are well-intended—when more harm is done, we are talking about iatrogenesis. This is important to keep in mind. It is very possible for people to be well-intended but still be patently unhelpful.

Consider the following examples:

- A study on those bullied at school found that students who went to CBT after being bullied internalized their symptoms more. The journal article says, "this is evidence of iatrogenic harm."[3]

- Manhattan Institute fellow and *Free Press* editor Abigail Shrier writes in her book *Bad Therapy*, "Police officers who responded to a plane crash and then underwent debriefing sessions exhibited more disaster-related hyperarousal symptoms eighteen months later than those who did not receive the treatment."[4]

- Dr. Miriam Grossman, a board-certified psychiatrist who was featured in Matt Walsh's documentary *What Is a Woman?*, has been widely critical of so-called medical professionals, counselors, and therapists as actually contributing to the problem of iatrogenesis. She testified before Congress about the iatrogenic nature of therapists who support transgenderism, suggesting that secular therapeutic culture is lying about transgenderism leading to further harm to teenage patients.[5]

I'd encourage you to do your own research on the negative effects of the mental health movement. You don't have to get far to see that many unbelievers and medical professionals are quite skeptical of the mental health movement's alleged benefits. Iatrogenesis will inevitably happen when diagnoses are arbitrary, and when everybody starts to receive a mental illness diagnosis.

On June 7, 1999, the White House Conference on Mental Health opened with remarks from First Lady Hillary Clinton, whose words would signal things to come:

> This is a historic conference, but it is more than that; it's a real signal to our nation that we must do whatever it takes not only to remove the stigma from mental illness, but to begin treating mental illness as the illness it is on a parity with other illnesses. And we have to understand more about the progress that has been made scientifically that has really led us to this point.[6]

Clinton, and the experts at the conference, put mental illness on "parity with other illnesses." Pneumonia. Bronchitis. Lung cancer. Heart disease. Mental illness?

While it is commendable to remove the stigma of mental illness, it is significantly erroneous to state that it is on parity with other illnesses. Why is that such a problem? Because the mind is immaterial, not physical. You can examine lungs. You can see an ear, nose, and throat specialist. However, you cannot physically examine the mind.

This particular White House conference brought in experts from varying mental health institutions, many of which were founded by one man, Clifford Beers, whom we'll learn more about in a later chapter. The National Institute of Mental Health (NIMH) sent its director to this conference—then Dr. Stephen Hyman. Hyman currently teaches at Harvard and was formerly its provost. He was the director of the NIMH from 1996 to 2001 and has led just about every meaningful organization within the mental health field in modern times. Hyman is a top expert. He's like bringing your older, stronger, facial-hair-possessing brother to your third-grade dodgeball game. "Can't touch this."

At the conference, Hyman shared the staggering numbers for people affected by mental illness. He cited some 19 million suffering from depression, 2 million from schizophrenia, and the way the World Health Organization has recognized the role of depression in affecting disability worldwide.[7] And those numbers represented the problem decades ago. Today they have significantly increased.

Then Hyman added his basic summary:

> We have also learned some very important facts about these
> illnesses, and if I can just encapsulate them briefly, it's
> that these are real illnesses of a real organ—*the brain*. Just
> like coronary artery disease is a disease of a real organ—
> the heart. We can make diagnoses, and these diseases are
> treatable.[8] (Emphasis added)

So, 1999 signaled something—and no, I am not talking about Y2K. Even the leading "experts" in mental health lost track of what is the mind and what is the brain. More than a simple oversight, the leaders in the national organizations on mental health have argued for the conflation of the two, treating the mind as if it were the brain. "Real illnesses of a real organ—the brain." Would that not be a brain disease? Things like Alzheimer's, dementia, and so forth. We already have a term for diseases of the brain: *brain disease*!

Let me ask you this: If the director of the NIMH is unclear about the mind versus the brain, don't you think there will be a lack of clarity for the everyday person? And if your doctor cannot make a correct diagnosis, is that helpful, or potentially iatrogenic?

The secular therapeutic culture created a problem and then attempted to prescribe the solution. However, the very nature of the problem is unclear. Hyman, the director of the NIMH, confused whether we are talking about the brain or the mind. Imagine if he were preparing for surgery and did not know which organ he was preparing to operate on. "Wrong one, sir, that's the liver!" You do not have to imagine too much to see that what Hyman represents is confusion regarding the nature of people. This has and will continue to lead to iatrogenesis. Call the brain the mind or the mind the brain and watch a host of arbitrary diagnoses begin to swell. That is exactly what has happened with the DSM.

Who *Isn't* Mentally Ill? The DSM-V Chaos

If you have worked in mental health, visited psychologists or psychiatrists, or interacted with mental disorders, then you have heard about the *Diagnostic and Statistical Manual of Mental Disorders*, or DSM. It is a publication of the American Psychiatric Association (APA).

Since the third edition of the DSM, it has grown in popularity to the point that the DSM-IV became the industry standard after its release in 1994. From then until 2013 it was the gold standard for diagnosing the mental illnesses and disorders supposedly within our society.

Allen J. Frances is professor emeritus and former chair of the Department of Psychiatry and Behavioral Sciences at Duke University. He's no chump, and he is also not a Christian. Importantly, he was a key author, contributor, and proponent of the DSM-IV. Frances has been extremely skeptical of the diagnostic inflation happening within our culture, because with each publication of the DSM, people appear to get more and more sick. And the very nature of sickness changes.

Psychiatry has exploded in popularity. There are currently around 25,000 psychiatrists licensed to practice within America and about 12,000 mental health institutions.[9] The DSM has undergone multiple revisions. And, as if that were not enough, we have online counselors, psychiatrists, and medical doctors who often incorporate that psychological language when treating us for medical issues: "chemical imbalances, traumatic injury, moral wounds." Growing numbers of Americans are taking some form of psychotropic medication; 13 percent are said to be on antidepressants.[10] That means at least one out of every ten people you know is on psychotropic medication. Suffice it to say,

---

The West is facing a modern mental health epidemic that started over a century ago and has reached a turning point. We treat the mind as if it needs medical solutions— thus "medicating the mind"—but fail to see that the mind is not the brain. Now we have created our own problems and called them "mental disorders/illnesses." Furthermore, we have created the solutions to those problems resulting in a modern-day epidemic.

Drs. Allen Frances and Robert (Bob) Spitzer were both leading psychiatrists in the late 1980s and '90s who facilitated bringing the DSM-IV to completion. Note: neither of them was a Christian. Frances was also instrumental to the development of the DSM-III, which was published in 1980. These men were leading experts in their field, and both had a vested interest in the publications. Some accused Spitzer of having too much of a vested interest because he apparently received royalties from the DSM-III.[11] Needless to say, they were both men of repute and helped to define the field of mental health.

Yet both doctors also adamantly oppose the DSM-V for stigmatizing normal behavior.

In a fascinating lecture titled "The Overdiagnosis of Mental Illness," given in May 2012, Frances articulates how the mental health field is burgeoning with diagnoses. He opens with this statement:

Our topic is who is sick and who is not . . . pretty soon
everybody is going to be sick.[12]

Frances is referring to *diagnostic inflation*. It means that, if the
crafters of the DSM aren't careful, new categories of mental illness
could result in healthy people being diagnosed as sick. Frances
said that thousands went to bed without an illness but upon publication of the DSM-V they woke up sick.[13] Regarding the DSM he
said, "These things all have in common the idea of medicalizing
the distress of life, turning things that are often social problems
into medical problems, and overdiagnosing them with accompanying stigma, often with accompanying medication that's going to be
more harmful than helpful."[14]

American psychotherapist and professor Eric Maisel said this regarding the changes in diagnostic criteria:

The very idea that you can radically change the definition of
something [i.e., mental illness] without anything in the real
world changing and with no new increases in knowledge
or understanding is remarkable, until you realize that the
thing being defined does not exist. It is completely easy—
effortless, really—to change the definition of something that
does not exist to suit your current purposes.[15]

Maisel isn't arguing for a biblical worldview. He is a licensed
family therapist who was highly skeptical of the changes to the
DSM-V, writing about many of these concerns on the Mad in America website.[16] These men were highly skeptical of the changes in the
DSM because of their arbitrary nature, first of all, but also because
of the diagnostic inflation that would inevitably follow.

There are many examples of how the DSM has increased mental disorders. (However, I would encourage you to explore this idea
more, particularly how we are creating more and more disorders.)

Asperger's syndrome, prior to the DSM-V, was part of the DSM-IV, but after the DSM-V it was included in what has now been termed *autism spectrum disorder*. Instead of having Asperger's or autism, a person has different levels of autism. Change the label, stigmatize the healthy, according to Frances. It should not be a surprise that autism diagnoses almost doubled from publication of the DSM-V in 2013 to 2018.[17] Over an eighteen-year period, new diagnoses of autism spectrum disorder have almost quadrupled.[18] Some claim that the increase is because "clinicians are getting better at spotting what was always there."[19] The problem with that logic is the diagnostic criteria aren't more verifiable. Rather, the DSM changed diagnostic criteria based on symptoms.

The result is that some, like the Cleveland Clinic, are rejecting the idea of ASD being a mental disorder altogether, instead calling it a "neurodevelopmental disorder." ASD is a developmental "disability caused by differences in your child's brain."[20] Does this mean autism does not exist? No, it doesn't mean that at all. But it does speak to diagnostic inflation when criteria for autism changed.

Another example is attention-deficit hyperactivity disorder (ADHD). The DSM changed certain criteria for a person to be diagnosed, opening up diagnoses from those seven and under to those twelve and under. Furthermore, if you're an adult, then the reduction of symptoms to establish a diagnosis also changed.[21] In other words, you can experience fewer symptoms and still be diagnosed with ADHD.

So what is the result of the changes in diagnostic criteria? With children under seventeen, ADHD diagnosis has roughly doubled since 1997, according to the CDC.[22] One in ten minors are expected to be diagnosed with ADHD. In another interview, Frances said, "The best predictor of attention deficit disorder is when you're born. If you are born in December as opposed to January, it doubles the risk. The youngest kids in the class are being diagnosed with ADHD and given medicine."[23] A runaway train is picking up steam, and ADHD diagnostic inflation for young boys is just one example.

The diagnostic requirements for generalized anxiety disorder (GAD) were also changed in the DSM-V. GAD is said to be "excessive anxiety and worry (apprehensive expectation)."[24] GAD can involve any issue and has roughly six criteria, three of which must be met for someone to be diagnosed with it.

1. Restlessness or feeling keyed up or on edge
2. Being easily fatigued
3. Difficulty concentrating or mind going blank
4. Irritability
5. Muscle tension
6. Sleep disturbance (difficulty falling or staying asleep, or restless unsatisfying sleep)[25]

As Frances notes,

Generalized Anxiety Disorder (GAD) merges imperceptibly into the worries of everyday life. And the DSM-5 will make that diagnosis not only much more unreliable (it's very hard to get agreement on it) but it will open up the floodgates so that anyone who has the slightest bit of worry has a mental disorder of GAD.[26]

What would have been classified as worry prior to the DSM-V's diagnostic criteria for GAD is now called a disorder. As Christians, we recognize anxiety as a spiritual and a moral issue. There are many verses on anxiety—most famously Philippians 4:4–8—and they don't describe it as a medical issue. The DSM-V has taken the moral issue of anxiety and turned it into a "medical" one. The reality is that most people experience some level of worry in their life, and under the new terminology the DSM-V would say the person who experiences anxiety has a mental disorder.

A final example is binge-eating disorder (BED).[27] Binge-eating episodes are associated with three or more of the following:

1. Eating much more rapidly than normal
2. Eating until feeling uncomfortably full
3. Eating large amounts of food when not feeling physically hungry
4. Eating alone because of being embarrassed by how much one is eating
5. Feeling disgusted with oneself, depressed, or very guilty after overeating[28]

Eating more rapidly than normal? Feeling uncomfortably full? I don't want to brag, but I've done that at least twice this week—maybe three times. (There's an all-you-can eat sushi place in town that knew my family until it closed. RIP.)

The criteria have become so fast and loose that many of us would be diagnosed with BED if we were to see a psychiatrist.[29] Again, the runaway train of the DSM-V has stigmatized healthy individuals. The lines are blurring in the West between what is normal and what is abnormal. For this reason and others, both Drs. Frances and Spitzer admit that the DSM-V has not helped with a reliable diagnosis of mental disorders.[30]

As if that saga were not concerning enough, Dr. Thomas Insel, then director of the National Institute of Mental Health, rejected the DSM-V upon its publication in May 2013. His reason? "It lacks validity."

The strength of each of the editions of DSM has been "reliability"—each edition has ensured that clinicians use the same terms in the same ways. *The weakness is its lack of validity.* Unlike our definitions of ischemic heart disease, lymphoma, or AIDS, the DSM diagnoses are based on a consensus about clusters of clinical symptoms, not any objective laboratory measure. In the rest of medicine, this would be equivalent to creating diagnostic systems based on the nature of chest pain or the quality of fever. Indeed, symptom-based diagnosis, once common in other areas of medicine, has been largely replaced in the past half century as we have understood that symptoms alone rarely indicate the best choice of treatment. (Emphasis added)[31]

In other words, there were no ways to prove that someone actually has a specific mental disorder. According to the National Alliance on Mental Illness (NAMI), "Unlike diabetes or cancer there is no medical test that can provide a diagnosis of mental illness. A health care professional can do a number of things in an evaluation including a physical exam and long term monitoring to rule out any underlying medical conditions that may be causing symptoms."[32]

So mental illness diagnoses are based on symptoms. And how are many of these symptoms identified? Through *our* verbal description of them. We describe our interpretation of what is happening, and then a medical doctor (that is, psychiatrist) labels us with a mental disorder. No proof. No X-rays. No blood work. As highly cited psychology and mental health researcher Pim Cuijpers wrote in *World Psychiatry* in 2019, "It is . . . still not clear what these disorders exactly are. There are no objective tests or measures to establish the presence of a mental disorder, nor are there clear thresholds for when a patient has a disorder and when not."[33]

There is a labyrinth of mental disorders in the DSM-V and yet recent articles have revealed that certain diagnoses have been doled out in as few as ten minutes.[34] That may be an extreme example, but it reflects an important fact: We have used the DSM to create arbitrary illnesses that lack verifiability. Then we treat people based on these illnesses, and now we see that everyone is becoming sick. The result is a therapeutic culture in which so many aren't getting better. It shouldn't surprise anyone, then, that when you increase the number of mental illnesses, reduce the criteria required to be diagnosed, and lack any empirical way of validating symptoms, you now have an epidemic of mental illnesses. The easier question to answer is "Who *doesn't* have a mental illness?" if these are the criteria we are going to use.

Did you know that homosexuality was considered a mental illness up until 1973? I'm serious. According to the American Psychiatric Association, "In the context of Psychiatry, APA removed homosexuality from the DSM in 1973 based on the new scientific studies, opening the way for new understanding and treatment [of] LGBTQ."[35] So in other words, before 1973 the ever-so-authoritative DSM called homosexuality a mental disorder. According to the American Psychiatric Association, before that homosexuality was considered a "sociopathic personality disturbance."[36]

Yet in 1973 there was a change in the diagnosis based on "scientific studies." Despite findings that there is no medical evidence of homosexuality being linked to genetics, the DSM removed homosexuality from the list of mental disorders.[37] Where are the scientific studies that were conducted? Oddly enough, the American Psychiatric Association didn't provide those.

In fact, Robert Kinney III, holding a PharmD from Purdue, reviewed the proposed studies that moved homosexuality from the category of mental illness and found that "instead of supporting their claim with scientific evidence, those major medical associations arbitrarily label homosexuality as normal."[38] In other words, the American Psychiatric Association says that homosexuality is no longer a mental disorder based on "medical and scientific studies," yet it doesn't provide those very studies. Furthermore, geneticists still say there is no genetic marker for homosexuality.[39] How can a mental disorder be so empirical, and then be debunked?

To be clear, I am not saying that homosexuality is a mental illness or disorder. Rather, I am showing you that what was called a mental illness can arbitrarily be changed to no longer being a mental illness when it is convenient.

The history of gender dysphoria is instructive. The American Psychiatric Association has conveniently redefined the nature of what it means to have gender identity disorder (GID). In the DSM-IV-TR (Text Revision), GID is diagnosed when a person has a "strong and persistent cross-gender identification (not merely a desire for any perceived cultural advantages of being the other sex)." The criteria for GID:[40]

1. A strong and persistent cross-gender identification
2. Repeatedly stated desire to be, or insistence that he or she is, the other sex
3. In boys, preference for cross-dressing or simulating female attire; in girls, insistence on wearing only stereotypical masculine clothing
4. Strong and persistent preferences for cross-sex roles in make-believe play or persistent fantasies of being the other sex[41]

When the DSM-V was released in 2013, which mental disorder was no longer present? Yes, GID.

Did the "scientific studies" demonstrate that this was no longer an illness? Of course not. The concerns of stigmatization of an already "marginalized people group" led to the reclassifying of GID.[42] In other words, before 2013 you would have been diagnosed with the mental disorder of GID, but after the DSM-V was published, GID was no longer a mental disorder? Yes, that is exactly what happened. One secular therapeutic historian said, "This change further focused the diagnosis on the gender identity-related distress that some transgender people experience (and for which they may seek psychiatric, medical, and surgical treatments) rather than on transgender individuals or identities themselves."[43]

Just like that, a mental disorder changed. In 2012 GID was a mental disorder, and one year later that was no longer the case.

The DSM-V did, however, introduce "gender dysphoria." Since 2013 it has been increasingly considered insulting, perhaps even transphobic, to call all transgender people "gender dysphoric."

According to the American Psychiatric Association, a person who is transgender is someone "whose sex assigned at birth (i.e., the sex assigned at birth, usually based on external genitalia) does not align their gender identity (i.e., one's psychological sense of their gender)."[44] Just because you are transgender, that doesn't mean you have gender dysphoria, according to the APA. You can be comfortable with your so-called gender identity not matching your gender at birth, and as long as that doesn't create psychological distress for you, if that's true, the APA would say you are not experiencing gender dysphoria.

But did you notice that what was called GID in the DSM-IV-TR is strikingly similar to that of transgenderism? Here's a comparison:

DSM-IV-TR Definition of Gender Identity Disorder	APA's Definition of Transgender Person
"A strong and persistent cross-gender identification (not merely a desire for any perceived cultural advantages of being the other sex)."[45]	A person "whose sex assigned at birth (i.e., the sex assigned at birth, usually based on external genitalia) does not align their gender identity (i.e., one's psychological sense of their gender)."[46]

Hmm. How about that? The American Psychiatric Association would have called it GID in 2012, but now it's called transgender, and only when it creates psychological distress would it be a mental disorder.

Since the DSM-V, GID has been jettisoned and the new kid on the block is gender dysphoria, defined as "psychological distress that results from an incongruence between one's sex assigned at birth and one's gender identity."[47] *Scientific American* published an article titled "Where Transgender Is No Longer a Diagnosis," which stated,

> A new condition called "gender dysphoria" was added to diagnose and treat those transgender individuals who felt distress at the mismatch between their identities and their bodies. The new diagnosis recognized that a mismatch between one's birth gender and identity was not necessarily pathological, notes pediatric endocrinologist Norman Spack, a founder of the gender clinic at Boston Children's Hospital.[48]

You can watch gender dysphoria inconspicuously get relegated to the "psychological distress" category, which, as Spack admits, has no clear pathological genesis. So, conveniently, transgenderism is not a mental illness, like GID was in 2012, but now gender dysphoria is only for those who experience "psychological distress." *Does this feel like a circus ride because of how dizzying it is?*

This is not to argue for seeing the sinfulness of homosexuality (Rom. 1:24–27), nor to address the sin of transgenderism (1 Cor. 6:9–11). Both are sins according to the Bible, that can be met with forgiveness graciously offered in Jesus Christ. And other biblical counselors, pastors, and theologians have provided resources to help those struggling with these issues.

My point is this: mental illnesses change because there is often no biological evidence they are indeed illnesses. They are often symptom-based diagnoses that change according to the zeitgeist of the moment. Homosexuality is first a mental disorder according to the American Psychiatric Association, then it's not. Gender identity disorder is a mental disorder according to the APA, then it is not. Because there is no medical evidence that the pathology of what is being called a mental illness is from your body, these so-called mental illnesses are arbitrary, lacking medical verifiability, and ever-changing.

No wonder Dr. Insel says the DSM lacks validity . . . because it does. I'm not stating these to suggest that homosexuality or transgenderism are so-called mental illnesses, but rather to demonstrate the lack of reliability of the DSMs.

It is not hard to see how the DSM can be held in disrepute by those who are familiar with its development and categorization of certain human behaviors. It made many normal behaviors an illness. It wasn't verifiable. The DSM couldn't help but morph into a catch-all of disorders because there were no empirical diagnostic criteria, so each edition will be subject to the worldview of the editors of that edition—not to mention those underwriting its development. But now the mind and the brain have been conflated into one entity, thus leaving us with no choice but to treat an immaterial issue as a medical issue. If you see the mind and the brain the same, then the DSM is a means of treating the insane of the world using medical treatments for immaterial problems. But biblically the mind and the brain are not the same thing, so this has led to diagnostic inflation of those who are not actually insane.

Diagnostic Inflation

Perhaps you've heard the term *diagnostic inflation*. To be fair, I personally don't use it much. (Imagine a dinner party: "So let's get down to business and talk about diagnostic inflation.") What it means is that the definitions of mental illnesses have been broadened so that more people meet the criteria for diagnosis.[49]

There are many reasons why this can occur—and we'll discuss a few—but it's one of the reasons why, instead of seeing treatment help people and thus witness a decline in disorders, America is buzzing with mental illnesses, even with all of the first-world advances of psychology and psychiatry.

The National Alliance of Mental Health publishes statistics about mental health in America to help communicate that "You Are Not Alone." In 2022, 20 percent of adult Americans were said to have a mental illness and 17 percent of teenagers.[50] Johns Hopkins Medicine estimates the number to be a little higher, stating mental illness affects 26 percent of American adults.[51] If either of those is correct, we are talking about one in five Americans being affected by mental illness. The diagnosing hasn't gone down—it's gone up.

The DSM is a key reason for such "disordering" because it has served as *the* diagnostic overlord, maybe even an evil overlord at that. If a general practitioner wants to make a mental illness diagnosis they'll consult the DSM. If an attorney wants to argue for the mental instability of their client, they'll do the same. The DSM has been the dark overlord (forgive my Star Warsian terms) ruling the diagnostic galaxy of mental health. (Insert Darth Vader Stuffy Breathing.)

If you change the diagnostic criteria for *any* medical issue, you'll see an effect on the nature of the illness itself. That's what happened with the DSM in diagnosing so-called mental disorders. The 2012 changes occurred and a flurry of concerns arose, all stating that this would segue into a modern-day mental health epidemic. *And it has*. Change the diagnostic criteria and by loosening them you'll instantly stigmatize normality. In various ways the DSM has done just that.

The DSM has mystified what we understand about people, clouding it with ambiguous, unverifiable diagnoses. I'm not here to doubt the motivations of those who made such changes, but I want to show you that the DSM has confused a right anthropology (i.e., belief about people) resulting in an Oprah-esque phenomena of "you get a mental disorder" and "you get a mental disorder."

Diagnostic inflation is inevitable with the most upright of medical professionals because of the loosening of diagnostic criteria. But mix into that financial motivation by private medicine and I get increasingly skeptical. Not "build a bunker stocked with food" skeptical, but cautious of accepting the mental health so-called diagnoses by so-called medical professionals. Let me be clear: not all mental health professionals are diagnosing to get money. That would be an unfair generalization. Yet, as we'll see in the next chapter, financial gain is part of the equation in diagnostic inflation.

CHAPTER 2

Incentivizing Insanity

Now there is in Jerusalem by the Sheep Gate
a pool, in Aramaic called Bethesda,
which has five roofed colonnades.
In these lay a multitude of invalids—
blind, lame, and paralyzed.
One man was there who had been an
invalid for thirty-eight years.
When Jesus saw him lying there and knew
that he had already been there a long time,
he said to him, "Do you want to be healed?"

—JOHN 5:2–6

I was preparing to end my time in the US Army in 2012. One of the great honors of my life was to serve as an active-duty Army officer from 2008 to 2012, finishing my time in service as a captain. While I never wanted it to be a career, I believe in the US military and was glad to serve. As you may know, you serve according to the "needs of the Army"—the Army will give you an opportunity to offer input for your preferences, but the needs of the Army are what will drive decision-making. The result of that for me was that I was sent to South Korea for most of my time in the military. Out of my four and a half years in the service, two and a half were in South Korea.

The Iraq and Afghanistan wars were still raging, which meant that post-traumatic stress disorder (PTSD) was being diagnosed quite rapidly for service members. PTSD is considered a mental illness/ disorder and the diagnosis was formerly reserved mostly for combat veterans. Now, however, it is being assigned even to those who have never seen combat. The US Department of Veterans Affairs estimates that "[a]bout 6 out of every 100 people (or 6% of the U.S. population) will have PTSD at some point in their lives."[1] That is not only combat related, but those who experience any traumatic moment that results in PTSD.

When I was leaving the Army, it was standard procedure to go through a physical screening to assess any injuries that might qualify someone for disability. Injuries that happen while serving in the US military can potentially qualify you for a financial stipend for the rest of your life. In my outprocessing, a slimy peer captain told me to "just tell the doctors you have nightmares and they'll diagnose you with PTSD. Then you can collect disability."

I was appalled at that statement, even as a twenty-five-year-old first lieutenant. Seriously. Finish your time in service by telling the doctors you have nightmares—which I didn't have—so you could receive a disability check. I never claimed to have nightmares and in fact never did my outprocessing physical screening. I simply was discharged and moved on with my life.

What if our culture actually incentivizes diagnoses that are arbitrary? What if certain resources—whether they are financial, educational, or simply work accommodations—necessitate an arbitrary diagnosis? Is it as easy as telling the doctors I had nightmares would have been to get diagnosed with PTSD after leaving the military? Our culture has shifted from helping people who genuinely are struggling to now employing arbitrary diagnostic criteria to diagnose a person, and after receiving an arbitrary diagnosis, then providing resources.

I am not saying that PTSD and other so-called mental disorders are not real in some way. What I am saying is that they are loosely diagnosed, with loose criteria, and that there are financial benefits from receiving a diagnosis like PTSD (which I will cover in a later chapter).[2]

In this chapter I want to show you that there are actually incentives to receiving a mental illness diagnosis. Some of those are financial and others are couched in the language of "resources" to help. So you have diagnostic inflation through the DSM's loose diagnostic criteria, and now you have incentive diagnosing through resources. "Just tell them you have nightmares," so to speak.

The diagnostic criteria for a mental illness are increasingly arbitrary. Yet there are times when a diagnosis is necessary. Sometimes a person needs to receive one in order to have access to certain government and medical resources. In an attempt to help prevent people from illegitimately couching their struggles in mental illnesses, various organizations have said that a mental illness diagnosis from a medical doctor is required in order to access certain resources. Thus a person needs the formal diagnosis to get "help."

For instance, a school counselor needs a diagnosis to assign your student a tutor. The unemployment office needs a diagnosis to get you paid for disability. Or the Social Security Administration says, "We need objective medical evidence from an acceptable medical source to establish that you have a medically determinable mental disorder. We also need evidence to assess the severity of your mental disorder and its effects on your ability to function in a work setting."[3] All of these institutions, as will be demonstrated, are caught in the slippery diagnostic criteria of mental illnesses.

Add to that the complications of social media, which allows us to share—perhaps even overshare—our struggles. By highlighting our problems, we can receive extra attention from those watching and even extra follows, likes, and subscribes. Although there are long-term dangers, the short-term concept of being transparent is seen as being courageous and helping others know they are not the only one who struggles. The reality, regardless of the motivation, is that a person is attempting to use their so-called mental illness to receive support and attention.

Hooked on Our Own Hardships

Generationally, we are seeing the Gen Zers and post–Gen Zers open up about their personal struggles in unprecedented ways. A baby boomer is rarely going to talk about their personal struggles in a public format, especially social media. Those issues are private, after all, and you don't want everyone to know your business.

But the new mantra of the younger generations is transparency. While boomers often get help privately and work on any personal issues with their pastor or counselor, Gen Zers are public and very communicative about their issues.

One of the interesting things I've noted in counseling is that older generations also tend to wait until there are significant problems before they reach out to receive help. Counseling those who are fifty and up often means that things have gotten pretty bad for them to reach out to me for help. In contrast, I have found that many from younger generations see me like a nutritionist. They might not have any significant problems, but they still want to simply meet with me for overall wellness. Regarding certain problems, a former generation might say "suck it up." But the younger generations feel that is phony and hurtful.

However, this mentality is often accompanied by a lack of discernment. It can become a proverbial instance of the blind leading the blind. We would never encourage someone to receive counsel from a friend who is not doing well. If you are lacking direction in your life, don't ask others who are also lacking direction in their life! But in this "age of authenticity," to use philosopher Charles Taylor's words, younger generations want to talk about their problems with just about anybody who will listen.[4]

And more than that, in the age of YouTube and TikTok, young people have discovered that going viral can get you fame, and even money. And one of the best ways to build viewership is by sharing increasingly personal, taboo, or shocking content. For many there are no limits to what they will share. They'll post about their marital problems and sexually explicit material. They'll share about their health, or lack thereof. They'll share crazy takes on politics or religion. As long as it gets them views.

Enter "sadfishing." Now an audience can be found by creating sad content. No longer do you need credentials, education, experience, or some other investment of preparation to build a public following. What you need to do now is simply talk about your problems. You don't even need to know the solution.

Garnering a social media following by sadfishing is inevitably a flash-in-the-pan way to build a social media platform. However, this incentivization is enough for some teenagers to seemingly glorify their issues rather than seek to change. It's an odd way of rallying together, by finding others who can identify with you and provide support to you online. This new online colony of individuals with so-called mental illnesses perpetuates the problem it is attempting to correct. This online attention is inclining teenagers to lean into their diagnoses rather than question them.

In 2022, Oxford University Press released an analysis of a strange new social media phenomena: young people were stating that they had Tourette's syndrome, which is thought to be a nervous system disorder that often causes a person to make involuntary sounds and movements, or "tics."

Like most mental illnesses, Tourette's is quite arbitrary; the criteria for diagnosing are all symptomatic. No labs. No X-rays. Simply observing if there are tics and if so, what types of them there are. In Germany, a YouTube channel called *Gewitter im Kopf—Leben mit Tourette*, which translates as "Thunderstorm in My Head—Living with Tourette's," has been a social phenomenon.

What the authors of the Oxford article say is that while the creators of this YouTube channel possibly have a mild form of Tourette's, much of what is being put forward as involuntary movements doesn't in fact resemble actual Tourette's syndrome. The authors said this was obviously a socially constructed Tourette's because 1) there are long sentences with words and phrases, which is unknown in Tourette's; 2) the swear words and insults are countless, unlike typical Tourette's; and 3) the "presented symptoms change on an almost weekly basis."[5] In other words, this isn't what Tourette's actually looks like. It really is a fascinating phenomenon to consider.

Thus the authors argue that this is not actually Tourette's but instead a "mass sociogenic illness (MSI) (also known as 'mass psychogenic illness,' MPI) that in contrast to all previously reported episodes of MSI is spread solely via social media."[6]

Yep, you read that correctly. People are impersonating fictional Tourette's symptoms—not even actual symptoms—based on the influence of social media. To put it another way, when it's popular to have Tourette's, more people have Tourette's.

My point is not to argue for the validity of Tourette's as an actual neurological problem, nor its criteria, but more to demonstrate the incentivizing of the diagnosis. What is noteworthy here is that incentivized diagnosing for *Gewitter im Kopf* means more subscriptions on YouTube and—you may have guessed it—a merchandise shop where you can buy the clothing with all the phrases that these guys use. Not to mention speaking engagements, notoriety, and a social media platform that reaches millions.

This same article suggested that certain Tourette's-related foundations actually distanced themselves from the channel, seeing their behavior as "misrepresentations and disrespect to people with Tourette syndrome."[7] Yet secular therapeutic culture has no framework to claim when a person is being fraudulent. Because these are arbitrary so-called illnesses that are diagnosed based on symptoms, the mental health epidemic keeps blazing on.

Doctors Receive Resources Based on Diagnoses

For those of us not in the medical field, it's important to know that doctors must diagnose you in order to bill your insurance for reimbursement. For those of you who are medical doctors, I don't envy the ethical decisions you must make for coding within your practice. Coding makes things increasingly complicated.

This is true in mental health situations as well. For a patient to have their first visit covered, there needs to be proper insurance coding that a mental health professional submits to the patient's insurance company for reimbursement. That coding is based on three different diagnostic mechanisms, one of which is the DSM-V.[8]

According to Psychiatry.org, "For the clinician, the key to appropriate insurance reimbursement lies in accurate procedure coding. Coding errors can lead to delayed payments or rejections of submitted claims."[9] These codes are known as Current Procedural Terminology (CPT) and "CPT coding tells insurance payers what you would like to get paid for."[10]

In North America, this is the crux of financial compensation for medical doctors. Again, it would be an overgeneralization to say this is a nefarious system practiced by those bent on destruction. There are, in fact, ethics of coding, some of which are even regulated for health care providers. But are you sensing the fragility of the diagnostic methods? You cannot prove I have the mental illness in any empirical way. The doctor needs to find a diagnosis in order to bill this, and I can be diagnosed with a mental illness in under an hour—perhaps even under thirty minutes. That seems a little precarious at best. It doesn't always work that way, where a psychiatrist needs a diagnosis and thus codes for the sake of billing. But if insurance is used and you are not a cash patient, you can bet that it works this way for you.

When asked about the pressure insurance companies put on clinicians to rapidly find a diagnosis, Dr. Allen Frances said,

> Well, first off, the [insurance] system is crazy. Insurance companies do this because they think it will restrict costs, but it has the perverse effect of forcing people to make premature decisions that often will result in more costly treatment. . . . The system is counterproductive; the more time we spend upfront with people in the evaluation process, before diagnosis and before treatment, the fewer diagnoses will be necessary, the less lifetime treatment will be needed.[11]

Unfortunately, pragmatism often reigns as a doctor needs to see other patients, finds the coat-hanger category, tells you that you have this disorder, leaves, and then their secretary bills the insurance for your diagnosis. This is incentivization with a capital *I*.

The Individuals with Disabilities Education Act (IDEA)

Doctors and schools get governmental resources based on diagnoses of students and patients. The Department of Education passed a law in 1975 that allowed proper educational access to children with disabilities. Some see this as a foundational matter of civil rights, providing access to education no matter the student's background or ability. It was intended to provide fairness in educational opportunities and access to education for all students of all abilities.

"The Individuals with Disabilities Education Act (IDEA) is a law that makes available a free appropriate public education to eligible children with disabilities throughout the nation and ensures special education and related services to those children," according to the IDEA website.[12] It's really quite remarkable to consider that students with special needs can now have access through their local, public school at no additional cost to the family. Those with physical mobility issues, eyesight issues, hearing issues, and other disabilities can access an education. Most schools have either dedicated individuals or even whole teams who serve as educational specialists for students with special needs.

But what are the diagnostic criteria for a student with disabilities?

Here's where it gets interesting. Consider some of the criteria for identifying those with a disability. This is a summary of the list, but you can find the exhaustive list on IDEA's website:

- Intellectual disabilities
- Hearing impairments
- Visual impairments
- *Serious emotional disturbances*
- Orthopedic impairments
- Traumatic brain injuries
- *Learning disabilities*
- Other health impairments
  (Emphasis added)[13]

Most of these seem right and good, because they are obvious physical or physiological issues. If a student cannot climb the stairs, there should be accommodations for them so that the student is not hindered from receiving a proper education. Yet "serious emotional disturbances" and "learning disabilities" are a bit more subjective. How do you verify a student has a learning disability? Is it by how fast they read? And who are you comparing the student's performance against to determine if it is abnormal? Are we willing to say that a mental health issue is the same as deafness?

In Section 504 of the Rehabilitation Act (RA) of 1973, there is further delineation of how schools are to utilize funds received for IDEA. The Rehabilitation Act was designed to hold organizations accountable for any federal funding they might receive, ensuring there is no discrimination. In the RA, a person who is to be protected against discrimination must "have a physical or mental impairment that substantially limits one or more major life activities; *or* have a record of such an impairment; *or* be regarded as having such an impairment."[14]

Again, terminology that is introduced such as "mental impairment" becomes increasingly subjective to diagnose. When clarifying what constitutes a mental impairment, Section 504 includes mental illness/disorders.[15]

Now, I personally believe these acts to be mostly beneficial in America, so that all students have access to the education they deserve, which I agree is a fundamental civil right. Yet here is the linchpin of these two laws: *in order to receive these federal funds and specialized care for students there must be a diagnosis.* Not just any diagnosis, but one that fits the criteria for IDEA. Now come mental impairments and learning disabilities. Are we sure that a mental illness and deafness are on equal playing grounds regarding diagnoses? How do you truly verify that a student has a mental illness?

Let me share with you my experience as a parent.

I have the privilege of being a father to three sons. At the time of this writing, two have been in public schools in California and the youngest is still too young for school. As with all of us, each of my boys expresses a different level of interest in school. I'm pretty sure my oldest loves school because he gets to be with people all day.

Yet, upon returning to sixth grade after two years of online school due to COVID-19, he was struggling academically. He was in a class with thirty-five students and one teacher. Often he would not get his work done; he would rush to try to finish his work and leave school most days with half of the actual homework assignment written down. That meant he would fail to complete half of his homework on almost a daily basis.

This led to a request from his teacher to "get him tested with the school psychologist." As a trained biblical counselor, professor, and mental health nerd, I was intrigued to see what this entailed. I consented to a meeting with the teacher, and she said she would like the school psychologist to attend along with the assistant principal. I went to the meeting with the assistant principal, teacher, and educational specialist—the school psychologist was not at the first meeting. As I sat there, the teacher showed multiple assignments of my son that were admittedly terrible. Embarrassingly so. He had written poorly, and only half-finished the assignments. He had stated that he didn't know how to do fundamental tasks. His educators were genuinely concerned for him—as they should have been.

After the teacher shared her concerns, the educational specialist suggested that my son may have special educational needs and that the school had resources for him. She recommended getting him tested with the school psychologist to see if he would qualify for those resources. I believe she meant to imply that he might have a learning disability.

In all fairness, I didn't scream "Anathema!" and run out of the room . . . "Get behind me, Satan." I simply asked what she meant by testing. How would that be conducted? And what would they be testing for? How do they know what "right" looks like? She stated that there are standardized tests, but she wasn't familiar with the exact nature of those tests. However, "You can speak with the school psychologist and they would be glad to answer your questions." After being silent most of the time, the assistant principal asked me if I'd be willing to get my son tested. I responded respectfully, "I'd like to speak with the school psychologist about the nature of the testing and then we can go from there."

After a bit of telephonic tag, we coordinated a meeting together.

It was the school district psychologist, the teacher, my wife, and myself. The school psychologist came because the teacher wanted her to come—that was obvious in her demeanor and the brevity of our meeting. The psychologist recommended testing in order to provide help. When I asked about the methodology for testing, she told me how the testing would proceed, not exactly what they were testing for. It was a paper-based test, with no vital signs, brain scans, or other empirical means of measuring his brain's ability to comprehend. The school psychologist was a friend, not a foe, but I found her answers *unhelpful*. She spoke of things like time management, focus, and learning in a group environment. Things more like life skills. I asked questions like, "What difference does the diagnosis make?" and "Shouldn't we just identify my son's weaknesses and help him learn to grow without any labels?"

Soon enough the semester ended, and my son graduated to junior high. He never got tested, to my knowledge, and I never heard any more about it from his teachers.

In situations like these, can we say that the age of a student will affect their performance in the classroom? When the girls in the class are literally one foot taller than the boys, when the class has thirty-five kids and one teacher, and when no individualized help is available, are we willing to say it's the *student* who must have an issue and thus needs to be tested?

The neglect of these other factors is quite significant. One study published in *BMJ Open* said, "Interestingly, children born just before the school-entry cut-off date (i.e., the youngest pupils of a classroom) are at higher risk of being diagnosed with ADHD compared with children born just after the cut-off date. Noteworthy, this *month-of-birth* effect tends to disappear with increasing absolute age."[16] Instead of resourcing the family without a diagnosis, schools are embracing diagnoses and doing so prematurely without considering other factors. I often wonder about those who would have gone along with the recommendation for testing and accepted a diagnosis.

It is my perspective that these educators are mostly well-intentioned but lack a thorough understanding of the mind and its distinction from the brain, and the true arbitrary nature of so-called mental illness. Seemingly good motivations, but poor execution. Perhaps I could say iatrogenic in nature?

You might be wondering here if I am an overly protective father. "No one can condemn my perfect little angel." And I suppose that is something I need to always keep in consideration. But I'll ask you what I asked the school psychologist: "If there is no empirical way to prove my son has this impairment, wouldn't it be best to simply learn what works best for him and do that as opposed to trying to find a label for him?" She agreed that would make sense. That's where we left it. And my son continued to mature, got a tutor, and has had no more academic issues. What a shocker, right?

That whole experience was a result of IDEA and how students receive resources based on diagnoses at school. I'm sure many of you have experienced something similar with your own child. For greater clarity and nuance, I'd encourage you to read Chapter 13: Questions, Objections, and Clarifications at the end of this book to address how you might personally engage in these delicate conversations.

Workers' Compensation and Disability

Workers' compensation and Social Security disability benefits are also available for people with a mental illness diagnosis. The California Employee Development Department states: "Disability is an illness or injury, either physical or mental, which prevents you from performing your regular and customary work."[17] Each state has its own labor laws, which allow for the state to regulate legal and fair working conditions. Thus most employers pay some type of fee to cover compensation when their employees are injured on the job. These are known as workers' compensation cases. These injuries are obvious for some: car accidents, lifting a box that's too heavy, falls due to unsafe environments, and so forth. In addition to physical injuries, a worker can also claim that they have incurred a work injury through the psychiatric damage incurred from their workplace.

Psychiatric damage is something that an employee would incur due to work-related stress. In order to demonstrate a workers' comp case, an employee would need to demonstrate that the psychiatric damage started on the job or was worsened by their job's conditions.[18] The California Labor Code states, "A psychiatric injury shall be compensable if it is a mental disorder which causes disability or need for medical treatment, and it is diagnosed . . . using the terminology and criteria of the American Psychiatric Association's Diagnostic and Statistical Manual."[19] What would be the criteria for understanding what qualifies as a psychiatric injury? The good ol' DSM.

Work stress could be from circumstances like an unreasonable boss, unfair treatment for legitimate work conduct, stressful deadlines, and so forth. If a person can demonstrate they had a stressful work environment, and their mental illness was instigated or worsened, they could file a workers' comp claim. One claim might be that a person crushed their hand under a car; another might be that working for a certain boss caused post-traumatic stress disorder.

Again, workers' compensation is desirable within the West of ensuring fair, safe, and sustainable work environments. But it is now increasingly tricky because a person cannot verify through empirical means that psychiatric damage has occurred, nor can they verify that it occurred at their work. But if they receive a diagnosis, then they are paid for *not* working.

Does that mean that everyone who receives workers' comp for psychiatric reasons is just trying to be lazy? Of course not, although in some cases they obviously are.

Disability work regulations are similar. Most employees pay into Social Security, which is meant to prevent widespread poverty. Whatever you think about the value of Social Security, it is a helpful mechanism to ensure that certain people are protected.

The Social Security Administration's criteria for determining disability eligibility are roughly as follows:

> The law defines disability as the inability to engage in any substantial gainful activity (SGA) by reason of any medically determinable physical or mental impairment(s) which can be expected to result in death or which has lasted or can be expected to last for a continuous period of not less than 12 months.[20]

Similar to workers' comp, disability permits the inclusion of mental impairments in the criteria for determining eligibility for this benefit. Obviously, like I mentioned above with IDEA and educators, these rules are not crafted by some system that is seeking to expose and hurt people. No, I honestly believe the SSA protects from rampant poverty in America. The only issue that I see is utilizing nebulous measures to identify whether a person is in fact unable to "engage in any substantial gainful activity."

This would include nonverifiable so-called mental illnesses. It is tempting for a person to claim that they are unable to work when not having to work could bring a steady means of income. How do you know if you have a mental impairment? Again, the DSM is the standard for defining these mental impairments.

This feels like one of those carnival rides, where we move very fast, get nauseous, and don't go anywhere. The SSA says you cannot work because you have a nonverifiable mental illness. And the way we know you have a nonverifiable mental illness is from a book that has stigmatized normal behavior and destigmatized abnormal behavior.

The subtle and insidious incentives to find diagnoses are intended to protect people who have been injured. This isn't the dark working of some Illuminati-type organization, but it is a shaky place to be standing nevertheless. Disability, for which a person is paid to not work, is given to those who can get a mental illness diagnosis. If you were in this situation, and had honest questions about why you were struggling at work, wouldn't it be tempting to accept a mental illness diagnosis that seemed to explain why you struggle the way you do? Not to mention that you could potentially get paid a reasonable wage that would allow you to not work.

If you weren't clear on the mind versus the brain, so-called mental illness, and the arbitrary diagnostic methods of the DSM, then I have no doubt there would be an openness to receiving a diagnosis.

Medical Companies Making Money on Mental Illness

I'm sure you're aware of the cost of medicine in America. You've gone to the pharmacy in the past year or so, right? So it should be no surprise that psychotropic medication is a cash cow in North America.[21] Psychotropic meds are antidepressants, antianxiety medications, stimulants, mood stabilizers, and a few that are also neurological or epileptic meds. And these medications are raking in the dough for psychopharmaceutical companies. Here is a list of the top three antidepressants and antianxiety meds according to the Mayo Clinic:[22]

Medication	Maker	Annual Revenue[23]
Antidepressant for MDD:		
Celexa	Forest Laboratories	$3.6B
Lexapro	Forest Laboratories	$3.6B
Prozac	LillyMedical	$30B
Anti-anxiety for GAD:		
Lexapro	LillyMedical	$30B
Cymbalta	LillyMedical	$30B
Buspirone	Bristol Myers Squibb	$45B

Note a few things from this chart and general treatment of mental illnesses titled "Generalized Anxiety Disorder" (GAD) or "Major Depressive Disorder" (MDD). First of all, certain medications can be prescribed for both. Lexapro is an example of this. It serves as a sedative and can help with those who are experiencing feelings of depression or anxiety.

Next, notice the revenue for these companies. The *B* represents "billions"! The revenue at stake here is that of a small country. These companies are making money off arbitrary diagnoses. Trust me, I'm not a conspiracy theorist. I have no basement. I don't stock up on ammunition. But do you believe that those private companies are really concerned with the proper diagnosing of mental illnesses, to include the proper use of their meds? Do you believe these companies are concerned about diagnostic inflation and more people being prescribed their meds than should really be taking them?

When Lexapro was released in 2009 after being accepted by the Food and Drug Administration (FDA), a scathing review by the *New York Times* soon followed.[24] In this review, *Times* reporter Gardiner Harris demonstrated how Forest Laboratories spent massive marketing dollars to help people buy the more expensive Lexapro when other generic versions were proven to be equally effective. Harris wrote,

> The document, "Lexapro Fiscal 2004 Marketing Plan,"
> is an outline of the many steps Forest used to make
> Lexapro a success. Because of concerns from Forest, the
> Senate committee released only 88 pages of the document,
> which may have originally run longer than 270 pages.
> "Confidential" is stamped on every page.
>
> But those 88 pages make clear that one of the principal
> means by which Forest hoped to persuade psychiatrists,
> primary care doctors and other medical specialists to

prescribe Lexapro was by finding many ways to put money into doctors' pockets and food into their mouths.[25]

Wait a minute! Schmoozing doctors so that they will use your medication when prescribing medication to their patients? Yes, private medicine runs marketing ads and schmoozes doctors so they use their medicine. Surely this can't really be a shock to you! (To which you reply, "It's not. And don't call me Shirley.")

Whether or not the *Times* got it 100 percent right (and you should read the Senate's Financial Review, published on August 12, 2009), you can easily see that there is much financial gain for pharmaceutical companies that have doctors who prescribe their medication.

I would remind you that the billing system for treatment requires a diagnosis of a mental illness. Disability and workers' comp need a diagnosis of a mental illness. Public school programs, such as IDEA, all need a diagnosis to help provide resources to students. So, in other words, most agencies need a diagnosis of a mental illness to provide resources. Then in come the "ever-so-helpful" pharmaceutical companies to provide biological treatment for immaterial "diseases" at stupefying profit levels. If this doesn't make the hair on the back of your neck stand up, I'm not sure what will.

Incentivized Diagnosis Is Fueling the War for America's Mental Health

By medicalizing the immaterial mind and incentivizing diagnoses, the secular mental health care system is, for many, creating a crisis. People are now more likely to be diagnosed with so-called mental illnesses that didn't exist a few decades ago, and for these alleged illnesses, people are being given options for medication that in many cases they've not been truly proven to need.

But while these incentives and diagnostic inflation are partially to blame, they're not the ultimate cause. People are not committing suicide at record rates because of invented or arbitrary labels. Many people *are* truly suffering.

The root cause is deeper, at the foundation of modern mental health theory. Let's go back into history to see where that theory went wrong, and what the secular therapeutic is missing.

CHAPTER 3

A Confusing New Religion

Has evangelical religion sold its birthright for a mess
of psychological pottage? In attempting to rectify their
disastrous early neglect of psychopathology, have the
churches and seminaries assimilated a viewpoint and
value system more destructive and deadly than the evil
they were attempting to eliminate? As a psychologist
and churchman, I believe the answers to these questions
is in the affirmative. If so, the time is upon us of a
searching reappraisal and a new plan of action.

—O. HOBART MOWRER[1]

History is important, but if I'm candid, not all history is equally interesting. I live in California and often visit different historical and
maybe-not-so-historical sites within the Golden State.

The location where gold was first discovered. Woo-hoo!

The end of Route 66. Wowzers!

Frankly, though, many of the California historical sites are quite bor-
ing to me. Some are about ranchers who lived a hundred years ago—
yawn—and others are about the movie industry and its influence across
the world—snoozefest. "Do they sell coffee around here?"

But there are times when understanding history really helps me to
understand the present. When I first learned about "taxation without
representation" (thank you, *School House Rock*), it was clear why the

American colonies wanted their independence. When I read about the history of the Taliban, it made sense why they are a global threat.

So in this chapter I want to look at how Clifford Beers, the father of the mental health movement, sparked a *revolution* that would morph into an *epidemic*.

Clifford Beers Goes Crazy . . . Literally

For Life depends on Light,
And Light on God,
Who hath given to Man the perfect knowledge
That Grim Despair and Sorrow end in Light
And Life everlasting,
In realms Where darkest Darkness becomes Light.
—CLIFFORD BEERS[2]

As I mentioned in the introduction, Clifford Whittingham Beers is the godfather of mental health. He was born in Connecticut in 1876 and was one of five children.

Some families seem to be riddled with varying demons, and that was true of the Beerses. History tells us that most of his siblings would face serious issues. Some—including Clifford—would also be hospitalized for their emotional distress. It makes you wonder what his family life was like, and especially who his father was.

But before you form any judgments about Beers, just know that he graduated from Yale in 1897. Six days after graduating from Yale, he began work for the city of New Haven's tax collector.[3] Beers served in New Haven until landing his dream job in the financial district of New York City. He was making money and chasing the American dream. Beers admits in his autobiography that his ambitions were for wealth, and the power that comes with it.[4] Unfortunately, through time, Beers found that his health was declining. He labeled himself a "neurasthenic," which is really an umbrella term to define things like fatigue, headaches, irritability, and so forth. In modern times, we might use terms like "chronic fatigue" or "burnout" to describe what Beers was experiencing.

He had a breakdown at work in New York in June 1900. He acted erratically, found old articles from the *Yale Bulletin* to shred them, hopped on a train to go home, and began what he thought would be a period of rest and restoration.[5]

However, Beers had a stubborn fear of developing epilepsy. It wasn't unfounded, because his brother developed epilepsy later in his adult life and Beers's thought was, "Now, if my brother who had enjoyed perfect health all his life could be stricken with epilepsy, what was to prevent my being similarly afflicted?"[6] This fear would prove to be a heavy-handed taskmaster, never allowing Beers to rest or find any reprieve.

Things spiraled downward so quickly that Beers went from fearing that he would have epilepsy to authentically believing he *was* epileptic. His fears conquered him, and now he felt it necessary to end his life before he had a seizure and his family would stumble upon him in the middle of it. Frantically, he started rehearsing the means by which he could end his life, and through the process of elimination, he decided it best to jump from the fourth-story window of his parents' home.

One day at dawn, he stood in the window, leering out over a sure death. Below him was concrete, iron fences, and broken glass.

But he couldn't do it. He climbed back into bed, only to have his mother offer him lunch around noon. Acquiescing, Beers knew that if he didn't jump then, there would be no other opportunity. He had approximately the time it took for his mother to climb three flights of stairs to jump. So finally, he did.

Beers jumped from the window, breaking bones in both of his feet and shattering those in his right hand. He was sent to Grace Hospital to begin treatment for both the outer man and the inner man. Beers said, "[I] was placed in a room which soon became a chamber of torture."[7] This was the beginning of a long treatment for his perceived insanity. Within three days after his suicide attempt, the stress of that and the hospitalization led to delirious behavior and thinking. At one point Beers thought the Yale baseball game, taking place at a field just around the corner from Grace Hospital, was actually a rally of citizens who were coming to "grab him, drag him to the lawn, and tear him limb from limb."[8]

For three years, except for the intermittently few times when he was sent home, Beers was committed to an insane asylum. On some days he was delirious, other days suspicious, some days violent, and on others he inflicted self-harm. By any definition, Beers was insane. He was put into a straitjacket for hours on end, transferred from different facilities, and at one point restricted from all communication with his family. To Beers's chagrin, at one of the last facilities he attended he was classified as a "raving lunatic."[9]

How does a person accused of being crazy prove they're not crazy? It seems almost impossible, and that was the case for Clifford Beers. He changed from a patient needing help to a "violent patient" who was mistreated, accused, and unable to validate his own sanity. In this period, the superintendent of an asylum often served as prison warden of sorts. Superintendents could limit liberties, discourage contact from families, require isolation, and remove creature comforts—like warmth, writing utensils, and clothing. Beers may have been a "raving lunatic" but part of his goal throughout his time in the asylums was to reform this type of mistreatment upon his release. Beers promised the superintendent of one asylum that he would report the superintendent's negligence to the governor of Connecticut, something he actually followed through on.

Beers wasn't released until September 10, 1903. He spent just over three years bouncing from one institution to another. Asylum to asylum. The final destination was one that allowed him freedom to begin to roam about the city and visit with friends and family. These conversations were part of what helped restore Beers to a place of sanity. He was convinced that his time surrounded by the insane had only worsened his condition and lengthened his time in an asylum. All of this led Beers to push for reform. Reform of the way patients were treated. Reform of the way crazy people were classified as crazy people. Beers wanted it to change. And here was his approach: start talking about "mental hygiene."

From Insanity to Mental Hygiene

It is worth noting that if Beers lived in modern times, he would still be committed to a behavioral health unit (BHU) of just about any hospital, but there would be a noticeable difference in treatment of patients and their rights. Nevertheless, if you act crazy, you still go to the BHU. You cannot jump from a fourth-story window, believe that your alma mater is trying to kill you, and accuse your family of being detectives who are spying on you without at least being suspected to be insane. Beers would have been considered insane in 1900 and that would also be true today.[10]

But Beers's journey through the asylum system positioned him like no one else to speak to the reforms that were needed throughout the system. Here is a snapshot of what he said was necessary:

1. Individual sympathy and participation in protecting the insane
2. For individual citizens to mail their individual names to institutions, societies, associations, and committees to petition for the need of such organizations
3. A federal investigation of insanity
4. An agency with a primary focus on mental hygiene with the recommended title of "National Committee for Mental Hygiene"
5. The establishment of psychiatric hospitals[11]

Beers believed that the only way to prevent the kind of mistreatment he experienced was to summarily raise awareness and start to
focus on mental hygiene. His recommendations would be published in
1908 in his autobiography, *A Mind That Found Itself*. Beers would go
on to pioneer four separate organizations to focus on mental hygiene,
which we will visit a little later in this chapter. His work would be
received by three powerhouse individuals: Adolf Meyer and William
Welch of Johns Hopkins, and William James, a professor at Harvard
and the father of American psychology. For Beers, to have these three
men endorse his work meant momentum and resources. Beers became
the poster child of crazy people who were able to get help.

William James said of Beers's book, "It is the best written out 'case'
that I have seen; and you no doubt have put your finger on the weak
spots of our treatment of the insane, and suggested the right line of
remedy."[12] James became a fan of Beers and soon the ideas of mental
hygiene spread in America. Starting at Harvard and disseminating to
other institutions, mental hygiene societies, committees, associations,
and psychiatric hospitals were exploding with resources and publications. Beers for the win!

Mental Hygiene's Solution? Moral Treatment

So, what is mental hygiene, anyway? Well, to be clear, Beers described
the purpose of the National Institute of Mental Hygiene as being "the
spreading of a common-sense gospel of right thinking, in order to
bring about right living, knowledge of which is needed by the public
at large if the populations of our asylums is to be controlled and eventually decreased."[13]

As a Christian, when you see the terms *Gospel, right thinking*, or
right living it should give you goose bumps, and I don't mean the positive kind. How do we help the insane? Teach them how to live right
and act right, according to Beers.

It's interesting that Beers doesn't start with medical treatment and the treatments that he first found to be helpful. This type of medication or that type of straitjacket. It seems that there are multiple things that Beers could point to within his own three years in the asylums that was of help to him. He could have said, "When using the straitjacket, ensure that the clasps aren't too tight so it's easier to sleep." But rather than focusing on medical and brain treatment, Beers starts by suggesting that to bring about the necessary reform, there should be a "spreading of a common-sense gospel of right *thinking*, in order to bring about right living." There is no medical treatment in that suggestion.

Beers wanted to help the insane, and rightfully so. Yet he moved away from medical treatment to moral, even spiritual, treatment. What does right thinking and living have to do with a medical issue?

How did Beers make the leap from medical treatment, establishing psychiatric hospitals, learning from insane patients to treat them with the scientific treatment they deserve to, finally, moral suggestions? Beers was able to do this because he confused the mind and the brain.

Classic blunder. C'mon, Beers.

As a Christian, I find Beers's mission quite interesting: preventing insanity by helping people think rightly and live rightly. The Bible clearly delineates how we should think and how we should live. There is a connection to insanity and living against God's standards for our lives. In all reality, to live against God's will is the epitome of insanity. "The fool says in his heart, 'There is no God'" (Ps. 14:1). Yet the conversation of mental hygiene was born in the confusion over the mind and the brain. Our boy, Beers, conflated the two and called it "mental hygiene." This anthropological confusion is at the crux of the mental health crisis. Mental illness is treated as if it were a brain illness.

The Mind and Brain Conflated by Beers and His Organizations

When I say the mind and brain have been conflated, I mean that they have lost their conceptual distinctiveness. In a later chapter I will offer exact definitions from the Bible of each. However, for now just see that Beers has treated the mind and the brain as the same thing. This fundamental anthropological error limits his helpfulness.

Beers's lack of a clear understanding of people is demonstrated multiple times throughout his work. Perhaps the clearest example is in the appendix of *A Mind That Found Itself*, where he shows the work of an English doctor as helpful for the insane because that doctor "found insanity regarded as a disease of the mind, [but] he left it recognized as a disease of the body."[14]

There are multiple times throughout his writing in which he speaks of the mind as being an inner-person reality—which is biblically correct—but then uses medical terminology to refer to it. He'll say things like "disease, medical treatment, pathological" and use other terms that can really only be true of the organ of the brain. At the same time, Beers uses moral adjectives to describe the mind: "unbalanced, perverted, uncontrolled" and so forth. In offering treatment for the insane, Beers said:

> What is needed in order to reach the root of the problem
> of insanity is the establishing of so-called Psychiatric or
> Psychopathic Hospitals in connection with our Medical
> Schools—hospitals wherein *nervous and mental diseases* may
> be treated in the most scientific manner, not only for the

benefit of the patients, but also for the benefit of physicians and students.[15] (Emphasis added)

A nonassuming reader might blaze right through statements like that and fail to ask, Can the mind get a pathological illness in the same way the nervous system can? Amyotrophic lateral sclerosis (ALS) is a disease of the nervous system that causes muscle atrophy and can ultimately lead to death. Beers is saying that we need to study the mind as if there are clearly identifiable diseases, like that of ALS. This is just one example of how he confused the mind and the brain.

Many of the organizations Beers founded are still active today. For instance, Mental Health America directly connects their genesis to Beers.[16] And like their founder, they are guilty of this confusion, as seen in its description of mental illnesses:

> Mental illnesses are *brain-based* conditions that affect *thinking*, *emotions*, and *behaviors*. Since we all have brains—having some kind of mental health problem during your life is really common.
>
> For people who have mental illnesses, their *brains* have changed in a way in which they are unable to think, feel, or act in ways they want to. For some, this means experiencing extreme and unexpected changes in mood—like feeling more sad or worried than normal. For others, it means not being able to think clearly, not being able to communicate with someone who is talking to them, or having *bizarre thoughts* to help explain weird feelings they are having.[17] (Emphasis added)

"Brain-based" conditions? Brains have changed in some way? Wait, I thought this was Mental Health America, not Brain Health America. At the same time, they are referring to *thinking*, *emotions*, and *bizarre thoughts*. Are thoughts material, like the brain is?

Another organization that Beers started is the World Federation for Mental Health (WFMH). The WFMH was originally the International Committee for Mental Hygiene. In its history the WFMH says this: "In 1947, the ICMH agreed to change their name to the WFMH and accept as a new purpose to promote among all peoples and nations the highest possible level of mental health in its broadest biological, medical, educational, and social aspects."[18]

Not to be a total buzzkill, since the WFMH party looks fun, but the reality is that the WFMH does not know that the mind isn't biological—it's immaterial. The mind is not material. Thus the mind is not ever going to be treated with medicine. Is it possible for the mind to affect the body? Yes, of course—the Bible teaches that the inner man and outer man affect each other (2 Cor. 4:16–18). But the mind is not the brain and the brain is not the mind. The war for America's mental health is being fought by those who don't understand the true nature of people.

Mental Hygiene Becomes Mental Health

It is true that the insane were neglected, mistreated, and deprived of basic human rights. Beers experienced this and offered solutions to treat the insane in ways that would be beneficial. It seems that in an effort to destigmatize insanity, Beers created a structure where more people would be diagnosed with a so-called disorder. Again, in the words of Mental Health America, "Since we all have brains—having some kind of mental health problem during your life is really common."[19]

One time, my kids, their friends, and I went to a candy shop while on vacation in a small California beach town. After grabbing our candy, we went to the public library before heading back to the house.

As we walked through the door of the library, outside on the steps was a crazy person, literally. He was laughing, singing at the top of his lungs, unkempt, and offering odors to the public that were mysteriously bad.

Once we passed him, each of the kids respectfully asked what that man was doing. To which I replied, "Don't worry about him everyone, I think he might be on drugs or insane." I'm sure you've had the same experience (and wouldn't be surprised if it was also at a public library!). Yet here is something that I do want to clarify: an insane person is not the same as a person who is said to have a mental illness.

Yes, the man on the corner singing at the top of his lungs would be given the label of mentally ill, or insane. But the converse is not true, and the confusion of the mind versus the brain has created a diaspora of mental illnesses that has lacked clarity in this regard. Beers wanted to help the insane, but in a way he made more people "insane" through generic classifications. As Allen Frances would say, pretty soon we'll all be sick.[20]

The Full Circle of Lacking Clarity on Mind vs. Brain

President Harry Truman commissioned the National Institute for Mental Health (NIMH) in 1943. In the following decades, America began to unpack what Beers had proposed for mental health treatment. In 1963, President John F. Kennedy addressed Congress and spoke to the issue of mental health. Here is part of the introduction to his speech:

> Most of the major diseases of the body are beginning to
> give ground in man's increasing struggle to find their cause
> and cure. But the public understanding, treatment and
> prevention of mental disabilities have not made comparable
> progress since the earliest days of modern history. Yet
> mental illness and mental retardation are among our most
> critical health problems.[21]

Beers's continued confusion of mental health is evidenced by President Kennedy equating a mental illness to a "major disease of the body." The problem is, again, the mind is not material!

This confusion led to more people being diagnosed with a mental illness. The National Alliance on Mental Illness estimates that:

- 1 in 5 US adults experience mental illness each year
- 1 in 20 US adults experience serious mental illness each year
- 1 in 6 US youth aged 6–17 experience a mental health disorder each year
- 50 percent of all lifetime mental illness begins by age fourteen, and 75 percent by age twenty-four
- Suicide is the second leading cause of death among people ages ten to thirty-four[22]

Secular Pastors

Part of Beers's effort to help the insane was to propose that America take on a similar posture to that of Europe in his day and begin building psychiatric hospitals. Now, to be sure, there were psychiatric "hospitals" before Beers's time. The National Library of Medicine states that the earliest of these hospitals can be traced back to approximately 1752 in Philadelphia, as started by the Quakers.[23] However, these were not medical centers as we might see them today. Rather, they were more like prisons for those who were deemed insane. For instance, the Philadelphia hospital was built with "rooms in the basement complete with shackles attached to the walls."[24] Not exactly the behavioral health units of modern day, even though padded isolation rooms still exist.

It was not until the early 1900s that medical schools in America began to train psychiatrists, even though psychiatry would trace its roots further back to the 1700s. The University of Pennsylvania claims to be the first school to offer psychiatry as part of the training for a future medical doctor, starting in 1912.[25]

Psychiatry was in a tug-of-war with psychoanalysis and Freudianism because Sigmund Freud was a believer in the immaterial aspects of humanity, with concepts like the subconscious, id, ego, and so forth. Yet psychiatry was attempting to use medical sciences instead of psychoanalysis to treat the mind. Psychiatrists today are almost exclusively trained in medicine, and varying therapists and counselors might still practice psychoanalysis. In this tug-of-war, psychiatrists as medical doctors became the new mantra, beating out psychiatrists as counselors.

This is evidenced in work like Jon Franklin's. Franklin won the Pulitzer Prize in 1985 for explanatory journalism because of a seven-part series he had written, titled "The Mind Fixers."[26] When speaking of psychoanalysis, which is the "psychiatrist as counselor," Franklin said:

Since the days of Sigmund Freud the practice of psychiatry has been more art than science. Surrounded by an aura of witchcraft, proceeding on impression and hunch, often ineffective, it was the bumbling and sometimes humorous stepchild of modern science. But for a decade and more, research psychiatrists have been working quietly in laboratories, dissecting the brains of mice and men and teasing out the chemical formulas that unlock the secrets of the mind. Now, in the 1980s, their work is paying off. . . .

As a result, psychiatry today stands on the threshold of becoming an exact science, as precise and quantifiable as molecular genetics. Ahead lies an era of psychic engineering, and the development of specialized drugs and therapies to heal sick minds.[27]

Franklin saw a bright new era of psychiatry that was now stepping into the supposed light of modern science. From the 1980s onward, biological psychiatry—psychiatrist as medical doctor—was to be the path forward.[28]

Others have not been as keen on psychiatrists as medical doctors as Franklin was.

Dr. Marco Ramos is an assistant professor in the History of Medicine and Department of Psychiatry at Yale University.[29] In 2022 he published an article titled "Mental Illness Is Not in Your Head," in which he states what has changed in psychiatry since the 1980s:[30]

> Thirty years later we still have no biological tests for psychiatric disorders, and none is in the pipeline. Instead our diagnoses are based on criteria in a book, the *Diagnostic and Statistical Manual of Mental Disorders* (often called, derisively, the "bible" of American psychiatry). It has gone through five editions in the last 70 years, and while the latest edition is almost 100 pages longer than the last, there is no evidence that it is any better than the version it replaced. None of the diagnoses is defined in terms of the brain.[31]

The hope of the 1980s was that psychiatry would turn to step into the light of modern science, but this has not happened. Rather, the DSM has only gotten larger and with none of its diagnoses relating to the actual organ of the brain.

Medical Doctors Treating *Mental* Issues

Despite this, psychiatrists are far more educated than many others who could fall in the broad category of "mental health expert." They are an elite group of professionals who have gone through rigorous medical training. A psychiatrist would be able to write prescriptions, while a psychologist would not be able to write prescriptions. Both have received extensive training, but psychologists are focused more on the clinical practice and psychiatrists are focused more on the medical treatment for so-called mental illness:

Psychiatrist	Medical doctor who can conduct psychotherapy and prescribe medications along with some medical treatment.[32]
Psychologist	Counselor who specializes in treatment through nonmedical practices[33]
Licensed Professional Counselor (LPC)	Master's-level counselor who is able to counsel, diagnose, and educate regarding mental health[34]

A psychiatrist must have ten-plus years of medical training, then must earn their medical license and pass examinations with the American Board of Psychiatry and Neurology. This certification must be maintained, and a psychiatrist is subject to renewing this certification every ten years. Needless to say, psychiatrists are no chumps in terms of their education and experience.

But what exactly does a psychiatrist treat? Broken bones? Nope. Contagious diseases? Still no. Verifiable illnesses? Again, no. According to the American Psychiatric Association, psychiatrists practice psychiatry, which is "the branch of medicine focused on the diagnosis, treatment and prevention of mental, emotional and behavioral disorders. A psychiatrist is a medical doctor (an M.D. or D.O.) who specializes in mental health, including substance use disorders."[35] The APA defines psychiatry as a branch of "medicine" that focuses on immaterial realities: mental, emotional, and behavioral disorders.[36] That should catch your eye. Let me put my finger directly on the issue: psychiatrists claim to use medicine (material) to treat the mind (immaterial).

In her analysis of the history of psychiatry, Anne Harrington's

2019 book, *Mind Fixers: Psychiatry's Troubled Search for the Biology of Mental Illness,* explores the work of psychiatry in attempting to treat people according to biological findings. From Harrington's perspective, psychiatry was the puppy who lost its way because it started with a focus on the immaterial, utilizing psychoanalysis, and then moved to focus on the pathology of mental illness. Harrington points to the very organizations that Beers helped establish as, surprisingly, the strongest critics of psychiatry. Harrington cites Dr. Thomas Insel—then NIMH director—as highly skeptical of psychiatry's legitimacy. What an irony. Beers would suggest starting mental health organizations, but then those entities would fight tribal wars to determine their legitimacy. Harrington describes Insel as saying "there seemed to be little if any sound biology undergirding the psychiatric enterprise."[37]

In other words, psychiatry is a field of "medicine" (I'm using that term very loosely) that does not have verifiable proof that mental illnesses are medical issues.

It is now increasingly clear to the general public that it [psychiatry] overreached, overpromised, overdiagnosed, overmedicated, and compromised its principles.

—ANNE HARRINGTON

From my understanding, Harrington was not trying to promote a biblical worldview. Rather, she simply pulled back the curtain to show that, as a profession and a science, psychiatry has indeed lost its way. If you want to learn more about this subject, I would encourage you to read *Mind Fixers.*

Beers was instrumental in forecasting the need of such "medical" professionals, regarding psychiatrists. Beers said in his autobiography, *A Mind That Found Itself:*

What is needed in order to reach the root of the problem
of insanity is the establishing of so-called Psychiatric or
Psychopathic Hospitals in connection with our Medical
Schools—hospitals wherein nervous and mental diseases
may be treated in the most scientific manner, not only
for the benefit of the patients, but also for the benefit of
physicians and students.[38]

This was written in 1908, and in the following years, psychiatric
hospitals were in fact built. Two distinct schools developed: those that
focus on neurological issues and those that focus on mental issues.
However, one is organic, biologically based (neurologist) while another is immaterially based (psychiatrist). Medical doctors who focus
on nonmedical issues. That seems like a misnomer, doesn't it?

It sounds absurd to say that we now have trained medical doctors who, according to *their* definition of what *they* practice, specialize in nonorganic issues. *Medical doctors who specialize in matters of
the mind.* Medical doctors who are treating—with organic remedies,
mind you—"mental" issues. A psychiatrist is a medical doctor who
self-admittedly sees their job as treating the immaterial aspects of
people. When Dr. Erica Lubliner, a psychiatrist at UCLA Health, was
asked "What does a psychiatrist do?," she answered:

Psychiatrists are trained physicians who specialize
in mental health. They evaluate, diagnose, and treat
psychiatric disorders according to the American Psychiatric
Association's Diagnostic and Statistical Manual of Mental
Disorders. The treatments they offer include medication,
therapy, and behavioral interventions.[39]

How can reasonable, logical, well-educated doctors not see the
confusing treatment of outer man and inner man? Lubliner goes on

to even say these are "health" issues.[40] Some psychiatrists, like Insel and Frances, seem to understand the limits of what they're doing. Yet others are seemingly oblivious. How can a psychiatrist believe that "mental" means "brain," something so fundamental to their profession? To find the answer, I went to a psychiatrist to see what type of treatment I might be offered. (I felt a bit like an investigative reporter.)

My Personal Visit to the Psychiatrist

As part of my research for this book, I wanted to go to a psychiatrist and see how I would be diagnosed and what recommendations would be given me by simply describing my life as it truly is. In order to conduct this research, I made a few commitments that are important for you to know.

First, I didn't want to misrepresent my life in a way that wasn't true. You know, the "I see dead people" type of comments. When asked, I would respond truthfully. And when asked why I was reaching out for an appointment, I consistently said I wanted a medical professional's evaluation of my life, an appointment to see what the professional's opinion is. I'm a pastor who plans on living in this community for a long time and didn't want to be embarrassed if I saw the psychiatrist at church on Sunday. *"Oh, hello, Doctor . . . I don't see dead people anymore."*

Also, I didn't want to create a circumstance in which the psychiatrist would *have* to respond with a diagnosis and medication. If I dropped the "I see dead people" comment, it could very well mean that they *have to diagnose* me with some mental health disorder. I didn't believe that to be fair to them. (Nonetheless, it is not true!) Thus, I accurately answered the questions—even about employment—and then let the psychiatrist and therapist guide the questions. If they would ask, I would respond truthfully.

I reached out for an appointment in December 2022 and started a two-month process to actually meet with a psychiatrist. I had to pass a phone screening first to ensure I was not suicidal or homicidal. Next I could schedule an appointment with a Licensed Marriage and Family Therapist (LMFT) who would screen me to see if I did indeed qualify to meet with a psychiatrist. Although some can get an online counselor in as little as ten minutes with organizations like Better Help or Talk Space, the time between my phone screening and my scheduling an appointment with an LMFT was about two weeks.

When I met with the LMFT, whom I will call Mr. Smith, it was for only thirty minutes. When the meeting began, he said it would be quick and it was only a screening. He asked me about general things in my life.

After questioning, Mr. Smith said that I showed signs of anxiety and depression, but might not qualify for meeting with a psychiatrist. He was candid and I appreciated the fact that he didn't jump to a diagnosis. As you might guess, there wasn't a laboratory and I didn't need to provide a vile of blood. He didn't take any of my vital signs either. I asked him, "How do I know my symptoms are severe enough and no longer normal?" Mr. Smith said, "When you can no longer function." I know that my symptoms are no longer normal when I cannot go to work. Wow. It was simply when I describe the symptom of no longer being able to function that he'd recommend me to a psychiatrist. This arbitrary diagnostic method is shaky.

I did get an appointment with a psychiatrist, whom I will call Dr. Jones, scheduled for February 14. Dr. Jones was the assigned psychiatrist and I originally scheduled an in-person visit, but the day before my appointment she required a telehealth meeting due to a possible illness on her part. There's an exact play-by-play of the appointment in the appendix but I'll give you a general summary here.

Dr. Jones asked questions for just under thirty minutes. She was very kind and good at asking questions, for which I was thankful.

She asked about personal life, work, emotions, sleep, alcohol, drugs, my community, my goals, and so forth. Although she asked the age of my kids, she never connected some important dots in her data-gathering. For instance, when she asked if I have good sleep, I said, "No, I don't." But she never asked if my then-one-year-old son was affecting that, which he most certainly was.

She also never asked what personally changed in my life last year, only if anything had changed in the past year. The reality is my immediate family had friends stay with us for about five months. So we had my three kids, plus another three kids, for five months.

Dr. Jones made a diagnosis and recommended steps for care. But she missed some significant details in that half hour.

What was the diagnosis? She seemed convinced that my work responsibilities were adding pressure to my life. She said I showed symptoms of depressive disorder, and could either take antidepressants, attend therapy, or perhaps do both. In all fairness to Dr. Jones, she wasn't on a rampage to prescribe medication. She gave me the option as the patient. For the sake of this book, I asked her for her recommendation instead of pushing for meds. I could have easily pushed to see how far it would go, but I felt that would be dishonest and could skew the findings.

She recommended therapy first, then meds if they were still needed. I wonder how another person would respond who was facing difficulty. Would they trust the process of therapy, or would they push for immediate help with medications? While Dr. Jones wasn't medication-happy, would most patients be medication-happy? With Zoloft, the twelfth-most-prescribed medication in the US, and Lexapro, both used for depression, it seems people want a quick fix.[41]

What's interesting is that she was willing to provide an antidepressant after no blood test, no labs, no taking of weight or height, not a single question about my nutrition, and never taking one of my vital signs. Did I have high blood pressure? Dr. Jones had no clue. I had simply asked, "What do you recommend?" To be clear:

> She did no medical work but was
> willing to give me medicine.

I hope I'm not the only one who finds that concerning. In fact, it felt even more odd because I was physically located in a different place. She couldn't even look at my body to see if I was overweight because the camera only showed my face. How can a medical doctor not practice anything medical with my body and offer medication as a remedy?

I will say this, though: she was a great data gatherer. In biblical counseling, we are trained to ask questions, and she did that quite well. Although she rushed and missed obvious facts about my life, she did ask most of the important questions for thirty minutes.

Out of those questions, the interpretation was almost entirely based on her *worldview*. She asked how I respond to anxiety, but she never defined anxiety. Furthermore, she could not describe what functioning should look like, but she asked if I could function daily. Remember, no lab results, no physical examination. Dr. Jones was more like a spiritual advisor with the ability to prescribe medications. That must be part of the draw to psychiatrists in the first place, at least to some.

In the end, as I told a friend, psychiatrists are pastors who can write prescriptions. They make worldview decisions with no medical proof of their decisions and perhaps even prescribe medicine throughout the process. And (*read carefully my next statement*) how could there *not* be a mental health epidemic when we have medical doctors employing arbitrary diagnoses to "help" people while lacking any medical proof?

Psychiatry is as much medical science as is a shaman practicing in their village—perhaps less so than the shaman.[42] At least the shaman will see you in person! What is more surprising to you: that a medical doctor can prescribe medication without practicing any health-related exam (vital signs, weight, labs, X-rays etc.) or that we believe when psychiatrists do this, they are indeed practicing medicine? Both are shocking. Psychiatrists are indeed medically trained, but the reality is that they are not practicing medicine. The only way in which a psychiatrist is practicing medicine is by prescribing medication. I'm sure there are a few inpatient-treatment psychiatrists who will call for lab tests and X-rays, but not the majority of psychiatrists. Psychiatrists use no medicine or empirical means to diagnose but need a diagnosis to treat and bill patients. They arbitrarily assign arbitrary illnesses and are calling this medicine.

False Religion Cannot Heal True Maladies

Psychiatry actually means "healing of the soul."[43] Psychiatrists have usurped the clergy's role as a source of help people go to with the cares of their souls. Really, they are secular pastors. Secular, because many psychiatrists are not Christians, yet what they have to offer is more like life advice with the authority to write a prescription. As one holistic psychiatrist asked, "Are we drug dealers or soul healers?"[44]

It seems the answer is that psychiatrists are drug dealers and have no business being soul healers.

Clergy, who have been the experts in the mind and inner person since the time of the early church, are now marginalized. And who becomes their heir apparent?

The only way it can make sense for a Christian to go to an unbelieving psychiatrist is if that Christian doesn't understand that the brain and mind are not the same thing. Put another way, if a Christian goes to a psychiatrist, they must believe that the psychiatrist is actually using their medical training to treat the mind. Yet the fatal error in this assumption is that the mind is not the brain and the mind cannot be treated with medical remedies.

Psychiatry may represent the cutting edge of modern therapy

approaches in the West, but it is by no means the only secular option on the market. But if this is where the most educated, supposedly most scientific experts are at, what about psychology, cognitive behavioral therapy, and approaches to mental health based on positive thinking or Eastern religious practices?

We will get to each of those later. But for now, here's what I want you to understand: Secular therapy is not based on objective, worldview-neutral ideas. It has religious biases, because ultimately it is rooted in false religion. And ultimately it tries to provide a counterfeit to Christianity.

Consider the words of British-based writer Freya India regarding therapy culture:

> Because where is God, in all this? Who is God? Some say
> therapy culture has no God. I think, more accurately, it's
> us. God is who all this revolves around. All these apps and
> platforms *serve us*.[45]

India, a colleague of world-renowned social psychologist Jonathan Haidt, says that in the secular therapeutic culture, you are the god. It all revolves around you. It affirms you. You are the center of the secular therapeutic universe. The danger of stepping into this world is that you will begin to think it's true. You need to be clear in the Bible and strong in your faith in order to not let secular therapeutic become functionally more authoritative than the Bible, shifting your focus from a God-centered universe to a me-centered universe.

Care for the mind is not the business of medical doctors—it is and will continue to be the work of pastors. Even if you don't like that statement, just remember that medical doctors are trained in medicine—not in the mind. The mind is immaterial. You cannot put it under a microscope. You cannot listen to its breathing. You cannot X-ray the mind.

In light of these ideological shifts, our struggles have remained the same, yet the source of our help has dramatically shifted. Instead of talking to your pastor about sadness, anxiety, and wayward emotions, we now go to our psychiatrists and other therapists with these issues. And what is the net result? Are we seeing improvements? We are not.

No wonder we aren't getting help, because secular pastors are bankrupt when compared to the treasures of God's wisdom that authentic, biblically qualified pastors should be sharing. Instead of talking about the Gospel, grace, forgiveness, repentance, and finding mercy in God through Jesus Christ, secular pastors give arbitrary mental disorders and medications.

E. Brooks Holifield, church historian at Emory University, suggests that "the movement from an ideal of otherworldly salvation to an implicit ethic of self-realization" has taken place within America.[46] It is no longer about salvation, but becoming a better you! Yet God has better plans. We don't need the lukewarm, reheated wisdom of the world. We need the Bible to show clarity to the true nature of people and then we develop ways to help people based on who they really are. All secular pastors are doing for us is perpetuating faulty understandings of people and rampant hopelessness. Consider the way that Clifford Beers ended his legacy.

The Tragedy of Clifford Beers

Despite all he did to increase care for the insane, Beers's symptoms of insanity returned and he went to a psychiatric hospital in Providence, Rhode Island, in 1939.[47] He would stay there for over three years, until he died in 1943, at the age of sixty-seven. Unlike earlier in his life, Beers committed himself to the psychiatric hospital after becoming "overwhelmed and depressed while fundraising for the organization [International Committee for Mental Hygiene]."[48] No one is sure if this was a physical breakdown of his body, as some have speculated that a tumor is what may have ended his life, or the culmination of the treatment and soul struggles that took their toll. Regardless, Beers died in the place he helped create—the psychiatric hospital.

Some see Clifford Beers as a reformer. And he did bring about helpful human rights to those who were deemed insane. However, he created a system that sidesteps an accurate anthropology. Mental hygiene created a category of caring for people that distracts them from the true nature of who they are. The secular therapeutic culture, as medically savvy as it presents itself to be, is bankrupt. God has better answers than what secular therapy has to offer, answers that are found within the pages of the Bible.

PART II

Misunderstanding Humanity

CHAPTER 4

Distinguishing Between the Mind and the Brain

"For who has understood the mind of the Lord so as to instruct him?" But we have the mind of Christ.

—1 CORINTHIANS 2:16

It may sound easy, but nothing can be harder. It will test your head, your mind, and your brain, too.

—DEWEY FINN, *SCHOOL OF ROCK*[1]

One of the main problems in secular approaches to mental health is confusion about the mind and its distinction from the brain. But where the world causes confusion, the Bible offers great clarity.

In this chapter, I'm going to lay out the biblical evidence demonstrating that the brain is not the mind, and the mind is not the brain. You must see it for yourself! The Bible actually has a category for mental activities, cognition, and mental "health/hygiene." Furthermore, what you will see is that the mind is something that God renews through the work of the Holy Spirit (Eph. 4:23). And you are called to also renew your mind by not being like this world (Rom. 12:2). Thus, your mind isn't stuck with so-called diseases that are incurable. Your mind can be transformed through the work of the Holy Spirit. Once you see this, your clarity in understanding people multiplies. God's Word, as always, is the light to our path (Ps. 119:105).

When the Apostle Paul tells the Corinthians that we have the *mind* of Christ, he's not referencing the *brain* of Christ. And to be sure, Jesus does have a human brain! Paul is saying that you have a similar way of *thinking* to that of Christ, or you have the *disposition* of Christ. Paul is not saying that you share in the organs of Jesus.

When Jesus appeared to His disciples, He proved to them that He was real, rather than a spirit (Luke 24:39). They could touch Him, and watch Him eat fish, which could not have happened if He was merely a spirit. This is obviously a revelatory moment for the disciples, and Luke says, "Then he opened their minds to understand the Scriptures" (Luke 24:45). Jesus helped them see the connections between Himself and the Old Testament promises of the Messiah.

Now, when Jesus opened their minds, He wasn't conducting brain surgery or even giving them a drug. He granted them understanding. He explained truths, and those truths finally "clicked" for the disciples. Jesus used the Scriptures to correct the disciples' thinking, thinking that was occurring in their *minds*.

A Biblical Definition of the Mind

"Mind" in the Old Testament

To begin, let's identify a few terms that demonstrate what the mind is and what the authors of the Bible use to define it. In the Old Testament (OT), when you study the mind, there are not many words that are a distinct reference to it. Perhaps the clearest is when Darius sets his "mind" on freeing Daniel (cf. Dan. 6:14).[2] The term בָּל (pronounced "bal") is used as a reference to the mind. This term is only used once, whereas the term לֵב (pronounced "leb") is used 591 times, and the majority of those are a reference to the immaterial heart, with roughly 30 times the word referencing the mind specifically. *Leb* is used to represent "the inner man . . . soul, comprehending mind, affections and will, with occasional emphasis of one or the other by means of certain verbs."[3] This means the term and context will best describe the faculty being emphasized, whether it is the soul, mind, will, and so forth.

However, the terms *bal* or *leb* are a reference to the inner person, not the organ of the brain. Context really dictates the best translation of *leb*, which could easily translate to the term *heart* instead of *mind*. For instance, does the Lord put skill in the *mind* of the craftsmen of the temple or within their *heart* (Exod. 36:2)? Well, both English words—*heart* and *mind*—could be used to translate the term *leb* as long as we clearly say "the inner person in contrast with the outer person."[4]

Another word, שֶׂכְוִי (pronounced "sekwi"), is translated as *mind* in Job 38:36, which says, "Who has put wisdom in the inward parts or given understanding to the mind?" While it seems odd initially, since it could also be translated as "rooster" according to Hebrew scholar Ludwig Koehler, the term *sekwi* is used to represent the mind regarding inner-man intellect and understanding.[5] Who gives wisdom in the inward parts? The Lord does. Where is understanding given? To the mind, according to Job 38:36.

The OT shows us that the Hebrew understanding of the mind is that the mind is an aspect of a person's inner man. It is interchangeable with the immaterial heart, but with an emphasis on the faculty of thought. Genesis 6:5 says, "The Lord saw that the wickedness of man was great in the earth, and that every intention of the thoughts of his heart was only evil continually."

The thoughts and intentions of the *leb* are evil continually. Is this the heart or the mind that is evil continually? The answer is both, because *leb* can be translated as either. The OT authors place the mind within the inner man. It is not the brain. "Whoever trusts in his own mind is a fool, but he who walks in wisdom will be delivered" (Prov. 28:26). A person is not trusting in the organ of their brain; this is a reference to the inner person, to the faculty of thought. If you trust in your own faculty of thought, ultimately you are indeed a fool.

"Mind" in the New Testament

In the New Testament (NT) there are a few words—used in varying forms—that describe the mind. I won't spam you with too many Greek terms, but these words include:

- **νοῦς** (pronounced "nous") is the primary term used to describe the mind, appearing for this purpose twenty-four times in the NT (Luke 24:45; Rom. 1:28, 7:23; 1 Cor. 1:10, 2:16; Eph. 4:17, 23; Col. 2:18). It is pronounced like our English word *noose*. And while there are idioms, like being "out of your mind," most of those idioms are not using *nous*. They are translating some other phrase or term. Just remember: *nous* = mind.

- **διανοίᾳ** (pronounced "dianoia") is only used eight times as a reference to the mind. It's actually a compound word of "through" (*dia*) and mind (*nous*). When Jesus says to love the Lord with all your heart, soul, *mind*, and strength, He uses the term *dianoia*. Paul also says that Christians were formerly hostile and alienated in their *mind*, using the term *dianoia* (Col. 1:21; Eph. 2:3). Just like *nous*, *dianoia* pertains to both the faculty of thought and the thought itself. There are certain uses where *dianoia* is conspicuously referencing the faculty of the mind, like in Matthew 22:37. But other times, it is used to reference the thoughts of the mind and heart as demonstrated in Luke 1:51: "He has shown strength with his arm; he has scattered the proud in the *thoughts* [*dianoia*] of their hearts." Context will dictate whether *dianoia* is a reference to the mind or the thoughts of the mind.

- **νόημα** (pronounced "noema") is used only six times, with a nearly even division between referencing the faculty of thought and the thought itself. Primarily, Paul uses it to reference the hardness of the minds of those who are not Christians (2 Cor. 3:14, 4:4). In this we see that he is referencing the faculty of cognition but later says a Christian is to take their "thoughts captive to Christ" (2 Cor. 10:5), while using the same term—*noema*.

To further clarify these terms, here are some definitions from lexical works:

- **Nous:** the faculty of intellectual perception, way of thinking, mind, attitude, as the sum total of the whole mental and moral state of being, the mental side of man by which he shows himself to be a feeling, willing, thinking being[6]
- **Dianoia:** the faculty of thinking, comprehending, and reasoning, understanding, intelligence, mind[7]
- **Noema:** the faculty of processing thought, mind, understanding[8]

Nous, *dianoia*, and *noema* are not references to different faculties—they are all referencing the same thing, the *immaterial mind*. They are simply different terms to represent the same reality. We do this for varying words in English. I might call a car an automobile, a vehicle, a Camry, transportation, or my sweet ride.

A Summary of the Biblical Terms for Mind

As each of these Old and New Testament terms suggest, the mind is your faculty of reason or thought. It is the sum total of your way of thinking. Thus your ideas, opinions, imaginings, and reasoning come from your mind. Here is a definition of the mind based on the above terms used in the Bible:

The mind is the inner-person faculty of intellectual perception that corresponds to thoughts, reason, attitudes, dispositions, opinions, volition, and morals.

There are generally two positions on the divisions of man, one being *trichotomy* and the other *dichotomy*. A *trichotomist* believes that man is composed of body, soul, and spirit. 1 Thessalonians 5:23: "Now may the God of peace himself sanctify you completely, and may your whole spirit and soul and body be kept blameless at the coming of our Lord Jesus Christ." This means that you are more like a compilation of your body, plus your soul, plus your spirit.

However, the Bible doesn't clearly delineate where the soul and spirit are different. In fact, there are instances where they are used almost interchangeably. Hebrews 4:12: "For the word of God is living and active, sharper than any two-edged sword, piercing to the division of soul and of spirit, of joints and of marrow, and discerning the thoughts and intentions of the heart." God's Word is so precise that it can divide the seemingly indivisible. Therefore, *dichotomists* believe that essentially you are an inner person and an outer person. This is not to suggest dualism of body versus soul, but rather that you cannot divide down the inner person aspects of mind, soul, spirit, conscience, and so forth.

The Bible doesn't say where the soul ends and the spirit begins. Thus a tripartite view of people is a faulty starting point. When Jesus says in Matthew 22:37 to love God "with all your heart and with all your soul and with all your mind," He is referring to a totality of the inner person. "Love God with everything." The mind is an aspect of your inner person, and is distinctly the seat of your cognition. Yes, that is true. But be careful not to slice the mind to be so distinct from the immaterial heart that it is compartmentalized. There is an interplay of other inner-man realities: mind, heart, soul, spirit, etc. For instance, Paul tells us in Ephesians that we as believers are to be "renewed in the spirit of your minds" (Eph. 4:23).

Where Is the Mind Located?

This may seem obvious, but it warrants emphasis: As an aspect of your inner person, your mind is immaterial. It cannot be touched or contained. God gave Solomon breadth of mind (1 Kings 4:29), Jeremiah recalls God's faithfulness to mind (Lam. 3:21), Jesus opens the minds of the disciples (Luke 24:45), God gives certain people over to a debased mind (Rom. 1:28), each person's convictions should be clarified in their own mind (Rom. 14:5), Paul wants spiritual gifts to be used while engaging the mind (1 Cor. 14:14–15, 19), and the mind can be corrupted (1 Tim. 6:5; 2 Tim. 3:8; Tit. 1:15).

Often we associate the mind with the organ of the brain, which in turn leads us to believe that the mind is located within our cranium, where our brain is located. Yet the Bible does not make this a clear distinction, as if the mind were only part of the organ of our brain. Rather, the Bible simply speaks to the mind being an inner-person faculty and does not relegate it to a certain part of our anatomy—like the cranium or brain.

While the Bible is relatively silent on the location of the mind, it is clear that the mind is something inside of you. That is developed in passages like Ephesians 4:23 and Romans 12:2.

> To put off your old self, which belongs to your former
> manner of life and is corrupt through deceitful desires,
> and to be renewed in the spirit of your minds, and to put
> on the new self, created after the likeness of God in true
> righteousness and holiness. (Eph. 4:22–24; emphasis added)

> Do not be conformed to this world, but be transformed
> by the renewal of your mind, that by testing you may
> discern what is the will of God, what is good and
> acceptable and perfect. (Rom. 12:2; emphasis added)

Both verses speak of the mind being personal, for example "your mind." Each person is said to have a mind, even if that mind is corrupted (Tit. 1:15). *You* have a mind and that mind is within *you*, and *you* have a personal call to renew the mind. If your mind leaves your body, that is indicative of you dying (2 Cor. 5:6–9). Paul mentions "whether in body" or "out of body" in 2 Corinthians 12:3, but if you are alive and you think your mind has left, you are actually dreaming. Paul states that in 2 Corinthians 12:1. He didn't leave his body; he had "visions and revelations." Therefore, those who use psychedelic drugs are tinkering with the organ of their brain to *feel as if* they are having an "out-of-body" experience.

Outside of these verses, the Bible does not specify that the mind is something that corresponds to a physical organ—like the brain. It is part of my entire inner person and your entire inner person.

One illustration: In 2 Corinthians 5:1–8 the body is said to be like a tent that is covering your inner person. If you were to drape a sheet over your body, the sheet would be like the outer person and your body would be like an inner person while wearing the sheet. While wearing a sheet, the entire body is covered and the entire body is clothed by that sheet. So you would have an inner person (in this case, the body) and an outer person (the sheet). Paul says in 2 Corinthians 5 that he longs to put off the tent and put on his heavenly tent. In the same way, you have an inner person that is draped by the physical outer person. But that inner person is not relegated to exclusive parts of your outer person (the organ of the brain). As a tent, your body covers the entirety of your inner person. This stands in contrast to seeing that my inner person only inhabits my cranium, for instance. If we were to be consistent with this way of thinking, then perhaps our hands and feet are unimportant because our inner person doesn't inhabit them. But when we think of the outer person like a drape, it helps us not relegate the inner person to a certain part of the outer person, like the brain.

Status of the Mind: Depraved and Darkened or Renewed and Focused

An important theme about the mind that appears throughout the Bible is that it is indeed sick—but not with a physical sickness or mental "disorder." Rather, our minds are sick with sin. The Bible does not represent our minds as inherently clear, objective, and generally reliable. Rather, the Bible shows that our minds are inherently depraved, darkened without the renewing work of the Holy Spirit.

Consider two general descriptions about the status of the mind: a person either has a mind that is *renewed*, which corresponds to being a Christian (Rom. 12:2; Eph. 4:23), or a person has a mind that is *futile*, *sensuous*, and *corrupted* (Eph. 4:17; Col. 2:13; 2 Tim. 3:8). All unbelievers have a mind that is futile, sensuous, and corrupted. It is the mind we are all born with (Ps. 51:5). And within the broad divisions of a mind that is either renewed or corrupted, we do see that there seem to be worse and better statuses.

For instance, the Bible describes false teachers as "depraved in mind" for believing that the Gospel is a means of gain (1 Tim. 6:5). There are even worse states of mind, as seen in 2 Timothy 3:8: "Just as Jannes and Jambres opposed Moses, so these men also oppose the truth, men corrupted in mind and disqualified regarding the faith." A false teacher is the primary example of an individual with a mental corruption. Even their other aspects of their inner person are skewed and corrupted, such as their conscience (Titus 1:15). A false teacher, according to the Bible, has a mind that is in the worst status because they twist the truth, peddle the Gospel, justify wrongdoing, or do some combination of these.

Thus, if there were a spectrum of the "health" of the mind, then an unbelieving mind would be unhealthy, and an apostate/false teacher would be gravely ailing.

Romans 1:28 says this about those who suppress the truth of God's existence and practice sexual sin: "God gave them up to a debased mind, to do what ought not to be done." A debased mind is a mind that is worthless. It cannot be used in a way that is of value. One side of the coin is renewed mind, and the other side is depraved mind.

In general, non-Christians are said to have futile minds (Eph. 4:23). This is *not* a mind that is as bad as it can get, much like that of a false teacher, but is rather a mind that is futile, empty, or useless. The mind isn't functioning as it should. Instead of it thinking correctly, it has thoughts set on earthly things. The non-Christian's mind cannot produce spiritual fruit and/or knowledge. It is not capable of such things.

Yet the unbeliever can understand natural things with accuracy (1 Cor. 2:14). The faculty of the mind works; it simply is broken. I will speak more to this in a later chapter, but the key point to remember is, the mind in its natural state is not good.

The Christian, however, has a mind that has been renewed (Rom. 12:2; Eph. 4:23). A Christian is never said to have a depraved mind. God renews the mind at the moment of regeneration through the work of the Holy Spirit (Tit. 3:5).

This renewal is one of the many effects of salvation, such as God writing His law in our "minds" (Heb. 8:10, 10:16). In this way, a Christian can say that they have the "mind of Christ" (1 Cor. 2:16). No, there was no shared brain transplant with Christ, but rather, the Holy Spirit renewed your mind at the moment of salvation, and thus you began to have the same faculty of cognition as Christ. You can think more and more like Him. And He calls you to do just that.

Paul tells the Roman Christians to be transformed by the renewal of their minds (Rom. 12:2). The put-off and put-on of the Christian life is propelled by renewal taking place in your inner person (Eph. 4:23). In the broader context of verses 22–24, Paul is telling the Ephesian Christians to put off who they were before Christ (v. 22) and to put on their new identity in Christ (v. 24). When you do this, God renews your mind (v. 23). You are to love the Lord with all your "mind" (Luke 10:27) and to take your "thoughts" captive to obey Christ (2 Cor. 10:5).

A Christian receives a renewed mind that is given the capacity to reason, think, observe, and demonstrate logic correctly at the moment of salvation. As he walks with the Lord and progresses in sanctification, his mind is renewed even more. The result is that he increasingly has a mind that is really like Jesus's. A transformed mind. One that can think like Him, reason like Him, demonstrate logic like Him. Paul even says that God will give peace to the Christian to guard their "mind" (Phil.

4:7). Sanctification brings peace of mind. For a Christian, growing in sanctification is to have the faculty of their mind renewed so that he thinks like Jesus, and God guards his mind with His peace.

In Philippians, Paul uses a phrase regularly translated in English as "to feel" (1:7), "same mind" (2:2), "one mind" (2:2), "in humility" (2:3), "have this mind" (2:5), "to think" (3:15), "mind set on earthly things (3:19), "to agree" (4:2), and "concern" (4:10). If we were to read the English only, it would seem as if Paul were referring to the faculty of the mind when he says "have the same mind" or "have this mind." However, the term actually means "to think like" rather than the faculty of thought. That's why some translations, such as the Legacy Standard Bible (LSB), more accurately translate those instances as "to think" rather than "have this mind." Not to be overly and annoyingly technical, but you are called to think certain thoughts within the faculty of your mind. That is Paul's appeal to the Philippians— think like Jesus (2:5).

To "think like" is an appeal to unity of thought, to think of others, or to have thoughts for people in terms of consideration for people. The book of Philippians provides several examples of how you and I are to think in certain ways that honor the Lord. Those thoughts are sourced in our minds, not our brains. To have the mind of Christ, in Philippians 2:5, is to think like Jesus thought and place others before yourself.

Love the Lord with Your Mind

When Jesus is asked by the Pharisees what is the greatest commandment, they were not asking from a place of genuine curiosity. They wanted to pin Jesus down and use His words against Him. So when Jesus quoted Deuteronomy 6:4 in response, it put the Pharisees on their heels.

"You shall love the Lord your God with all your heart and with all your soul and with all your mind. This is the great and first commandment. And a second is like it: You shall love your neighbor as yourself. On these two commandments depend all the Law and the Prophets" (Matt. 22:37–40).

How could they disagree? He cited from *their* law, the passage that would have been recited over and over as a Jew. In doing so, Jesus both answered their question correctly and prevented them from rhetorically trapping Him. Also notice that He said, Love the Lord with your mind.

To love the Lord with your mind is to love Him with your total being, including your thought life. To think the thoughts of the Lord is an act of worship and love. There are obvious implications for this. Consider the following passages that tell Christians to think a certain way or rebuke people for not thinking a certain way:

- **Matthew 16:23:** But he turned and said to Peter, "Get behind me, Satan! You are a hindrance to me. For you are *not setting your mind* on the things of God, but on the things of man.
- **Romans 8:5:** For those who live according to the flesh *set their minds* on the things of the flesh, but those who live according to the Spirit set their minds on the things of the Spirit.
- **Philippians 3:15:** Let those of us who are mature *think this way*, and if in anything you think otherwise, God will reveal that also to you.
- **Philippians 4:8:** Finally, brothers, whatever is true, whatever is honorable, whatever is just, whatever is pure, whatever is lovely, whatever is commendable, if there is any excellence, if there is anything worthy of praise, *think about these things*.
- **Colossians 3:2:** *Set your minds* on things that are above, not on things that are on earth.

In each of these instances, the call is to "think" a certain way. Peter is rebuked for *not* thinking a certain way, those who are unsaved are thinking a certain way, and Christians are to think a certain way. The reality: The thoughts of your mind are not neutral, nor are they only your own. God is interested in your thoughts—He discerns them from afar (Psalms 139:2). Your thoughts are part of faithfulness as a Christian.

What do you think about? What do you fill your mind with? Your answers to these questions indicate your ultimate worship. We are called to love the Lord with all the thoughts of our minds—with our entire minds.

To properly worship the Lord, we give Him total worship from every fiber of our being. The inner man is the control center, and the outer man is the tent that covers the inner man (2 Cor. 5:1–8). As the English pastor J. C. Ryle said, "Guard your thoughts, and there will be little fear about your actions."[9]

Cognition is not an outer-man reality, it's an inner-man reality. Thus Jesus is calling for us to love the Lord with our mind—He could have said "brain," but He didn't. Practically, how could you love the Lord with your brain? Try not to damage it, I guess. Do some sudoku? Wear a helmet? When we understand the mind and the brain, Jesus's statement is as clear as the seawater of Bermuda: Love God with your mind, through your thoughts, as an act of worship.

Finally, no author of Scripture recommends medical treatment for the mind, like they do the body (1 Tim. 5:23; James 5:14). The medical treatment of the mind that we see prevalent today is a result of the secular therapeutic worldview sabotaging a biblical understanding of people. You could argue that the authors of the Bible didn't know that there was medical treatment for "mental" illnesses, but the answer is that they were not writing from their own interpretation, but spoke from God as they were carried along by the Holy Spirit (2 Peter 1:20–21). God is the ultimate Author of Scripture, and He knows how He made us—with minds that are immaterial. And when a mind is darkened and distorted, no medical treatment will fix it. God, through His Word and Spirit, is the only one who can truly heal the mind.

What About the Brain?

While the mind is immaterial, the brain is material, and would correspond to any other component of your body: lungs, kidneys, fingers, blood, bones, etc. The Bible would classify all this as parts of your outer man.

David says that his inner man and outer man are "wasted from grief" (Ps. 31:8); he literally uses the terms *soul* and *body*. While the soul is not the body and the body is not the soul, both are influenced by grief (cf. Ps. 32:3). References to the "outer man" like this appear throughout the Bible. For instance, Paul says in 2 Corinthians 4:16, "So we do not lose heart. Though our outer self is wasting away, our inner self is being renewed day by day." *Outer man* is contrasted with the inner man. Other times, we see the idea of "the body" as a reference to the outer man. "For just as the body is one and has many members, and all the members of the body, though many, are one body, so it is with Christ" (1 Cor. 12:12). It is your body that comprises the different organs (the eye) and members (the foot).

You may not have seen your brain, but technically you could see it. You could have an MRI scan it or a CT image of it. Although we don't desire this, we could have surgery on our brain, or work with a doctor on healing our brain if we received a brain injury, such as a concussion.

The closest place in the Bible where we see the brain spoken of specifically is in Matthew 27:33, which says,

> As they went out, they found a man of Cyrene, Simon by name. They compelled this man to carry his cross. And when they came to a place called Golgotha (which means Place of a Skull), they offered him wine to drink, mixed with gall, but when he tasted it, he would not drink it. (27:32–34)

The term for Golgotha, place of the *skull*, is the Greek term *kranion*. This term is used in four different places in the Bible, all referencing

Golgotha.[10] Modern Bible translations call it the "place of the skull" because Golgotha was a place of death, a place of the dead, or it looked like a skull in some way.

Kranion shows us that the Gospel writers understood the outer-man and inner-man distinctions and would have the ability to appeal to that language if necessary. Thus, when Luke shows us something in Luke 23:33 using the phrase "place of the *Kranion*" and says in chapter 24:45 that Jesus opened their *minds* to understand the Scriptures, it becomes clear Luke had the vocabulary to choose an outer-man term, like *kranion*. But under the inspiration of the Holy Spirit, he used the term *nous* in 24:45. It is possible for Luke to jump back and forth between mind and brain because he understood they were different. And he would have used terms to describe their differences. In this way, we know Luke had the understanding of the difference between the mind and the brain.

But is there an exact word for the brain? There is a word to capture the location of the brain, which is the English term *head* and the Greek term *kephale*.

"The part of the body that contains the brain" is the term *kephale*.[11] It is a term that is used quite regularly to speak of the physical head. However, it can also be used to describe a place of authority, which is why Jesus is the head of the body of Christ (Eph. 5:23). Regarding the use to identify the outer man, note the use of the head:

- "But even the hairs of your *head* are all numbered" (Matt. 10:30).
- "And immediately the king sent an executioner with orders to bring John's *head*. He went and beheaded him in the prison and brought his *head* on a platter and gave it to the girl, and the girl gave it to her mother" (Mark 6:27–28).
- "When Jesus had received the sour wine, he said, 'It is finished,' and he bowed his *head* and gave up his spirit" (John 19:30).

The word *head* is used in the New Testament pretty closely to the way we would use it today. We lay our *head* down to sleep or we bow our *head* in prayer. Jesus assures us that even the hairs of our *head* are numbered by God, which should bring great comfort because of His intimate knowledge and care for us.

Not to be gruesome, but John the Baptist died by being decapitated. When that occurred, his *head* was placed on a platter to be presented as a gift (Mark 6:27–28). For Jesus to get hit on the head by the Roman soldiers would have been His literal head, where His brain is located (Mark 15:19).

There are no instances of biblical authors referencing the specific organ of the brain, but rather the outer man, skull, or head. This insight doesn't leave us empty-handed though, because we know that the authors of the Bible reference the location where the brain would be and then also clearly distinguish that from the mind. Even though the authors of the Bible don't use the term *brain*, they do have an understanding of the difference between the brain and the mind, unlike many in our modern therapeutic age.

So when Paul said that the mind needs to be renewed, he was indeed aware of the outer man. He could have said the outer man needs to be renewed, but he intentionally—and accurately—said mind.

So, what do we do with the understanding of the brain? We must see that it is the outer person. In the next chapter, we will explore more of what the Bible says about the brain and its relationship with the mind. In the meantime, I'd like to take a moment to provide a brief doctrinal statement about the mind and the brain. Just note that some of the conclusions in this statement are based on passages we will look at in the next chapter.

Doctrinal Statement on the Mind and Brain

- The mind is the immaterial component of a person that hosts and initiates thoughts, imagination, choices, reason, and logic.

    This does not mean that mind is uninfluenced by the brain when it functions.
- The natural state of the mind is corrupted, and the Christian experiences renewal of the mind so the mind can focus on the things above.

    This does not mean that an unbeliever's mind is missing, but rather that it is darkened.
- The mind is everlasting. There will be no point in which the mind ceases to exist or function.

    The brain may die and cease to function for a period of time before the resurrection of the dead.
- Regardless of the external treatment of the brain, none of those treatments will change the immaterial mind.

    This does not mean that poor brain health affects in no way the mind. However, brain health cannot cure the immaterial issues of the mind.
- For the mind to be renewed, this takes the work of the Holy Spirit in the life of a Christian who has been born again.

    It is not possible for the unbeliever to have a renewed mind.
- The brain is the outer-person organ of the body and it is located inside the cranium.

    The mind does not always correspond to the physical location of the brain because it is immaterial. It would be inaccurate to say the mind is inside the brain.
- The brain and the mind are intimately connected in their operation.

    Though the mind and brain are interconnected, the mind will outlive the brain because it is everlasting and the brain may cease to function at physical death.

- The brain is not renewed as the mind is, but the brain is affected through the renewal of the mind.

  A renewed mind will affect the physical health of the brain because the renewed mind should be stewarding the outer man with wisdom.
- A person can take medicine and receive physical surgeries to treat the organ of the brain.

  A person cannot take medicine or undergo physical surgeries to address the immaterial mind.
- For a person to be considered "brain dead" generally reflects that there is no physical life within them.

  However, a physically dead brain does not indicate that life has truly ended since the life of the soul is everlasting.
- The brain should receive the proper care and treatment of a medical doctor.

  A medical doctor will not be able to treat the immaterial mind (that is, a psychiatrist).

CHAPTER 5

The Body Creates the Trial

So we do not lose heart. Though our outer self is wasting
away, our inner self is being renewed day by day.

—2 CORINTHIANS 4:16

"Wait a minute," you might be thinking. "My brain has to be *partially* behind who I am and what I do, right? After all, people with dementia or brain damage or trauma behave differently. When people do drugs, or have traumatic brain injuries in combat or on work sites, they act differently and can say crazy things. Isn't their brain the cause of that?"

Those are understandable questions. And there's no shortage of secular therapeutic gurus telling us that much about our personalities, behaviors, and "mental health" status is explained by the state of our brains.

One popular proponent of this view is Dutch psychiatrist Bessel van der Kolk. Known for his massive bestseller *The Body Keeps the Score*, van der Kolk played a significant role in the establishment of the taxpayer-funded National Child Traumatic Stress Network (NCTSN), which has grown to nearly two hundred centers nationwide since it was created in 2000 as part of the Children's Health Act.

Essentially, the thesis of van der Kolk's book is that, through repressed memories, our bodies retain the effects of trauma, and this profoundly shapes our personalities and behaviors. For example, he writes:

> The body keeps the score: If the memory of trauma is
> encoded in the viscera, in heartbreaking and gut-wrenching
> emotions, in autoimmune disorders and skeletal/muscular
> problems, and if mind/brain/visceral communication is the
> royal road to emotion regulation, this demands a radical shift
> in our therapeutic assumptions.[1]

I would argue that van der Kolk has been so influential that his language now infuses our common Western vocabulary, shaping our assumptions about why we do what we do. In a 2023 cover story for *New York* magazine, UCLA professor Danielle Carr described van der Kolk's theory of trauma as "the dominant way we make sense of our lives."[2] Often, his ideas sound scientific, and he even says his "goal in all these efforts is to translate brain science into everyday practice."[3]

But what do those practices look like?

> It is standard practice in many schools to punish children
> for tantrums, spacing out, or aggressive outbursts—all
> of which are often symptoms of traumatic stress. When
> that happens, the school, instead of offering a safe haven,
> becomes yet another traumatic trigger. Angry confrontations
> and punishment can at best temporarily halt unacceptable
> behaviors, but since the underlying alarm system and stress
> hormones are not laid to rest, they are certain to erupt again
> at the next provocation.[4]

Does that set off any alarm bells for you? Van der Kolk is arguing that ultimately our own behaviors, perhaps especially our *bad* behaviors, are best explained (and, I dare say, rationalized) not only by external things that have happened to us, but specifically by functions of our brains, and bodies in general. Indeed, the common issues of anxiety, depression, fear, self-loathing, and other issues of our minds are, according to van der Kolk, rooted in the body, as a result of experiences:

Nobody can "treat" a war, or abuse, rape, molestation, or any other horrendous event, for that matter; what has happened cannot be undone. But what can be dealt with are the imprints of the trauma on body, mind, and soul: the crushing sensations in your chest that you may label as anxiety or depression; the fear of losing control; always being on alert for danger or rejection; the self-loathing; the nightmares and flashbacks; the fog that keeps you from staying on task and from engaging fully in what you are doing; being unable to fully open your heart to another human being.[5]

I often hear ideas based on this from counselees during sessions. One gentleman in counseling said he couldn't love his wife because of his depression. He couldn't help it. His wife was willing to stick it out and to work on things, but he was too depressed. He lacked love. Lacked emotions. His depression was a shield, a rationalization of why he supposedly "couldn't" love his wife. He viewed himself, to a fault, as being incapable of doing what God called him to do.

What a truly hopeless view to have of oneself! Yet that is the conclusion of someone who has bought in to van der Kolk's theory. As van der Kolk himself says, "what has happened cannot be undone." This is in such contrast to what the Bible says, that we always have hope in Christ, and can be transformed by the Holy Spirit, no matter our past. We can always access Almighty God and petition Him in prayer, knowing He sympathizes with our weaknesses, and He will not allow us to be tempted beyond what we are able to bear (Heb. 4:15–16; 1 Cor. 10:13).

Another family I counseled adopted a child who was roughly five or six when they adopted him. He was diagnosed with reactive attachment disorder (RADS) and we met when he was closer to eleven. His father was in the military and his mother was a stay-at-home mom. Because of this diagnosis, the parents weren't sure if they could expect obedience.

What does obedience look like? Someone with RADS absolutely might have learned how to interact with the world differently, but RADS doesn't make them sin. Your body cannot make you be disobedient. The "I can't because I have this disorder" mindset is a common, and convenient, way to try to escape biblical responsibilities.

Secular researchers have found issues with van der Kolk's theories, and they were even controversial at the time he published them.[6] But his assumptions are wrong, ultimately because they are unbiblical. And they only add to our cultural confusion about the mind and the brain.

Still, how does the body, and especially the brain, influence the mind?

The Relationship Between the Mind and the Brain

I was speaking at a biblical counseling conference recently, and after I finished, a gentleman and American Sign Language (ASL) translator came up to ask me questions. Through the translator, the man asked about damages to the brain and how those affect the expression of the mind.

This man was not able to speak or hear due to physical problems, but his mind was quite vibrant. He had learned a new language, ASL, to express through his hands what was happening in his mind. It was a beautiful portrait of how the brain and the mind are interconnected. Yet, as you will see in this chapter, a damaged brain (as from Alzheimer's, dementia, or TBI) does not necessitate a damaged mind.

In the Bible, there is clearly an interconnection between the mind and the brain. And if we're going to understand humanity rightly, we must identify and reckon with this. To say that the mind and the brain are different is not to say that there is zero interplay between the two. It is only to say they are not the same thing.

Theologians would say that the nature of man is a complex unity, or a psychosomatic unity.[7] There is no "dualism" within the nature of man, as if it were the body versus the soul in a battle royale (cf. Col. 2:8).

Is it possible that the mind can actually affect the function of the brain? This question also overlaps with neuroplasticity or brain plasticity, which indicates that the brain can actually restructure itself.[8] Of note, there is a field of therapy called "neuroplasticity therapy" that believes, "When people in therapy learn new coping skills, they are literally building the neural connections that promote resilience. As people learn new habits, their new synapses will replace the connections that prompted unhealthy behaviors and cognitive distortions."[9] In other words, secular therapists believe that therapy based around behavior—which, biblically, begins in the mind—restructures the brain.

I believe that, yes, the mind influences the brain, and I would say there are two theological truths that indicate this:

1. The inner man can affect the outer man, as demonstrated by David and Proverbs 16:24. As part of the outer man, the brain would be included.
2. Generally speaking, obedience to God's commands often results in blessings such as better health. Yes, Christians still can get sick or have health conditions. But a Christian who does not have any illness or health condition may still enjoy better sleep and health if they follow biblical commands regarding stewardship of the body and avoiding behaviors that can harm the body (sexual immorality, illegal substances, drunkenness, etc.).

If the mind is the initiator, then to focus on brain health exclusively when people are suffering from issues like anxiety and depression is to misunderstand biblical anthropology.

Dr. Daniel Amen, a popular author and psychiatrist, has strongly argued in his book *The End of Mental Illness* that if you "get your brain right," then "your mind will follow."[10] This is not correct, according to the Bible. To focus on the brain health as the sole cause of our emotional and spiritual struggles is to put the caboose before the engine. Many of our struggles may not even stem from issues rooted in the brain at all.

For example, a man who gets adequate sleep, regularly does weight training and cardiovascular exercises, and eats healthfully might enjoy some of the benefits of above-average brain health. But if he continues in the sin of pornography, then he will still likely wrestle with anxiety and guilt, which are mind issues. (Granted, his brain will also likely be reshaped around his lusts.[11]) Likewise, anytime we lose a loved one, we experience many of the "symptoms" of mental illness, such as emotional pain and depression, even though none of the lifestyle things we do to maintain a healthy brain (diet, exercise, medications, etc.) might have changed. Biblical care for your mind could promote brain health because the two are connected.

The brain can also affect the mind, although it would be wrong to specifically say that the brain causes the mind to act. This would not be what the Bible teaches. In fact, the better term would be to say that the brain can *influence* but not *cause*. Now of course the brain can cause some actions in your outer man, many of which are vital, such as breathing (especially while you sleep). The brain can cause your muscles to twitch, or even cause uncontrollable movements during a seizure.[12] What the brain *can't* do is control your mind, so that you decide to go to the bar instead of going to church.

Yet you may be thinking that a traumatic brain injury (TBI) can affect the mind, and to that I would say, yes. A TBI can affect the way the brain works so the thoughts of the mind seem different. But a TBI doesn't implant new thoughts into a person's mind. Thus the brain can influence or affect the mind, but it doesn't cause the mind to think on certain things. This is the delicate balance we must maintain because in the end, TBI or no TBI, a Christian is called to believe certain things, to have the mind of Christ (Phil. 2:5–11, 4:8).

This has broader implications for so-called mental health treatments, including the use of medications for those with a "mental illness." If the brain can influence the mind, and the brain is unhealthy, then it is possible for there to be treatments for the brain so that it will better influence the mind.

Don't miss that, dear believer. If you are wrestling with a "mental disorder," you need to work toward renewing your mind to be like Christ's, and having a healthy, functioning brain can make that easier. Yet, while the brain may influence the mind, we would still recognize that we are treating still the brain, not the mind.

I once counseled a gentleman who, years before I counseled him, went off his meds. This had sent him into a tailspin of issues, including hospitalization due to suicidal thoughts and ideation. Thus when he and I met for marriage counseling with his wife, they were interested to hear if I was going to ask him to get off his meds.[13] Yet the meds were helping from his perspective (and his wife's perspective). My recommendation was to not change anything with his meds if there were no problems.

Many of us have known someone who struggled deeply with mood regulation. Some of us have taken antidepressants for years, and those antidepressants are actually treating symptoms of the brain, and appear to be helping the mind express itself, or making it easier to deal with the thoughts in our minds. The outer man does influence the inner person. Some will claim, however, that the body actually causes what the inner person does.

The Body Causes Material Responses

Pointedly, you and I as Christians should ask, "What does the body cause, according to the Scripture?" What "score" does the outer man/the body keep according to the Bible?

The Bible includes the following categories for what the outer man does: 1) physical life, 2) aging, 3) physical health, 4) physical cravings, 5) substances, 6) sensory functions, and 7) death.

Physical Life: The Body and Birth

The beginning of physical life starts at the point of conception, with the formation of a new body in the womb of a mother. The Bible uses significant language to speak of God's active role in this formation during the gestation process: "For you formed my inward parts; you knitted me together in my mother's womb" (Ps. 139:13). The Bible says God "made you and established you" (Deut. 32:6). He created the body and spirit (Zech. 12:1) and gives breath to the people on the earth and spirit to those who walk in it (Isa. 42:5). Jeremiah was called by God in the womb before God "formed" him (Jer. 1:5). The body corresponds to existence and physical life.[14] Preceding the creation of the physical body, we did not exist, and at the moment of conception our brains were created by God. So we can say physical life begins at the formation of the outer man.

Aging: The Development of the Body and the Capacity of the Mind

As we grow from childhood, into young adulthood, adulthood, and old age, our bodies and brains change. And this can affect how our mind interacts with the world. We see this clearly even in the childhood of Jesus. Though He was God incarnate, He still experienced humanity as we do, including the experience of childhood development:

> And the child grew and became strong, filled with wisdom. And the favor of God was upon him. Now his parents went to Jerusalem every year at the Feast of the Passover. And when he was twelve years old, they went up according to custom. And when the feast was ended, as they were returning, the boy Jesus stayed behind in Jerusalem. His parents did not know it, but supposing him to be in the group they went a day's journey, but then they began to search for him among their relatives and acquaintances, and when they did not find him,

they returned to Jerusalem, searching for him. After three
days they found him in the temple, sitting among the teachers,
listening to them and asking them questions. And all who
heard him were amazed at his understanding and his answers.

And Jesus increased in wisdom and in stature
and in favor with God and man.
—LUKE 2:40–47, 52

We see in this passage that Jesus is growing up from being a child to a twelve-year-old. Throughout the first decades of His life, Jesus would have, like all of us, grown taller. He would go through puberty, and His brain would have been developing, all as part of the growth of His outer man/humanity. But the passage also points out that Jesus grew in wisdom, and we see Him as a twelve-year-old learning from teachers while demonstrating understanding. These are all functions of the immaterial mind, but His understanding was affected in its expression by the development of His outer man, including His brain.

We see this also in Paul's famous words from 1 Corinthians 13:11: "When I was a child, I spoke like a child, I thought like a child, I reasoned like a child. When I became a man, I gave up childish ways." When Paul's outer man was in a less developed physiological state (childhood), his *thoughts* and *reasoning*, functions of the mind, were limited in their expression. But as his outer man grew, so also could the expression of his inner man.

Note that I say "could." The development of Paul's inner man was conscious and a choice. When he became a man, he gave up his childish ways. He could have *not* given them up. You can have a developed outer man and still remain spiritually and emotionally immature in your mind (cf. Ps. 119:99; 1 Cor. 3:1–2). We all know men who still act like children (and not in a funny way). Like Jesus asking questions of the teachers in the temple, we have to learn from others and invest in the growth of our inner man, of our mind.

Even though the brain is developing in its abilities, the mind is still morally responsible. Even a child doesn't have the excuse of making bad decisions based on his or her brain development. Rather, if he has been trained up and taught well, he can make wise decisions, even with a less developed brain. Proverbs 20:11 says, "Even a child makes himself known by his acts, by whether his conduct is pure and upright." So, if you're twenty years old and mooching off your parents full-time, not working or going to college, you don't get to blame your irresponsibility on the fact that your brain may still have a few more years of development left.

Physical Health: Pain and Sickness of the Body

We also need to consider the effects of sin on the outer man regarding pain and sickness. As a result of the curse of sin, the outer man has been affected with pain. Specifically, the curse of Genesis 3 highlights the pain of childbirth and pain in work. Pain is promised to be removed in the New Heaven and Earth (Rev. 21:4) but is present for varying reasons until then.

Sickness in the physical body is present throughout the Scriptures, from God removing the Egyptian sickness (Deut. 7:15) for Israel, to Hezekiah getting sick (2 Kings 1:2), to the woman suffering from a condition that caused blood discharges (Luke 8:43–48), Peter's mother-in-law (Luke 4:38–39), and the miraculous healings of the apostles in Acts 19 where the "sick" had their "diseases leave them" (19:12).[15]

The brain is, of course, susceptible to the organic illnesses that affect the body. And so indeed, we find there are in fact brain diseases: dementia, Parkinson's disease, and even infections. The brain can get a tumor, just like other parts of the body. Obviously, a stroke or aneurism could cause serious brain damage.

There are instances of physical sicknesses that elucidate mind responses throughout the Scripture. When Hezekiah was told that he would die, he wept bitterly, appealing for God to preserve his life (Isa. 38:3). The Lord relented of the sickness and delivered Hezekiah.

Hezekiah's body was failing and he responded in "weeping bitterly." It must be noted that his body did not cause the weeping, but as a response to knowing his body would fail, sadness overcame him. Sadness is the response of his inner person.[16] God did ultimately heal Hezekiah, but Hezekiah's body created the physiological trial to which his mind responded in sadness.

Physical Cravings of the Body

Physical cravings also occur in the outer man.[17] These physical cravings include but are not limited to hunger (Matt. 4:2; 1 Cor. 4:11), thirst (Exod. 17:3; John 19:28), tiredness (John 4:6; Rev. 2:3), and sexual expression/ desire (1 Cor. 7:2, 9–10). In each of these instances, a physical craving has an organic origin in the body. Although these physical cravings can become idolatrous, like that of the false teachers in Philippi (Phil. 3:19) or the divisive individuals in Rome (Rom. 16:18), a physical craving is not inherently sinful.[18] It is only a physical craving of the physical body.[19] These physical cravings are part of the rightful and good function of the physical body. In chapter 12, I will address questions related to this, especially as they relate to so-called addictions. For now the point is that the body does develop cravings, and those are not always sinful.

One note: If you are struggling with sexually immoral desires, you cannot blame your body. You are not forced to think sexually immoral fantasies because your body, brain, or genetics "make you" or because you are actually in the wrong body. Because the mind is not the brain, your mind can be transformed and renewed, and is not defined by the body's cravings. I will discuss this more in chapters 10 and 12.

Substances Can Affect the Body in Ways That Affect the Mind

When we consume food, our bodies take the nutrients and substance of the food and break it down into fuel and material for activity, maintenance, and growth. What we ingest affects our bodies, and our bodies, of course, can influence our minds.

We see this most clearly in the biblical descriptions of alcohol.

While the act of ingesting alcohol itself isn't a sin, inebriation is *always* spoken of as being either unwise or sinful. Interestingly enough, the Scriptures vividly warn of how alcohol can negatively affect our bodies to the point that it even affects our minds:

> *Who has woe? Who has sorrow?*
> *Who has strife? Who has complaining?*
>
> *Who has wounds without cause?*
> *Who has redness of eyes?*
>
> *Those who tarry long over wine;*
> *those who go to try mixed wine.*
>
> *Do not look at wine when it is red,*
> *when it sparkles in the cup*
> *and goes down smoothly.*
>
> *In the end it bites like a serpent*
> *and stings like an adder.*
>
> *Your eyes will see strange things,*
> *and your heart utter perverse things.*
> —PROVERBS 23:29–33

The word used for "heart" in the last verse is *leb*, the same OT word used for "mind" that we saw in the previous chapter. The English Standard Version and Legacy Standard Bible translate *leb* as "heart" in this passage, while the New American Standard Bible translates it as "mind."

We see here that the substance of alcohol can affect the outer man in a way that even the senses are no longer accurate ("your eyes will see strange things"). The loss of self-control that occurs with each drink can affect our outer man to the point that you have great difficulty renewing your mind and loving God in your thought life (just as, if you stayed awake for seventy-two hours without any sleep, it would be more difficult to control your mind). Severe substance abuse damages the brain, and in these cases, the brain can make it harder to honor the Lord with your mind, even making the bodily cravings for substances more severe. However, the brain cannot force you to misbehave, even while you are drunk. It is ultimately your mind that is doing that.

These same effects can happen as a result of other drugs besides alcohol. They can cause our brains to malfunction to the point that we even have trouble perceiving reality through our senses. In this way, the body is affecting the mind, but still not causing or determining the mind to do something.

Sensory Functioning and Problems

Our sensory functions have significant implications for the brain, and therefore the mind. These functions include seeing (Gen. 27:1; John 9:6), which happens through the eyes. Blindness is a malfunctioning of the eyes. And while Jesus said of the blind man in John 9, "It was not that this man sinned, or his parents, but that the works of God might be displayed in him" (v. 3), the Bible also makes clear that some physical sicknesses or malfunctions are indeed because of sin.[20]

Hearing is a function of the ears, by which we process sounds to discern information (Gen. 23:10; Exod. 24:7). When our ears fail, we experience deafness. Levitical law protects the deaf (Lev. 19:14), Jesus heals the deaf (Mark 7:37), and Jesus testifies to being the Messiah through the healing of the deaf (Luke 7:22).

Other sensory functions of the body include touch (Luke 8:46), speaking (Exod. 4:14; Luke 1:22), smell (Gen. 27:27; 1 Cor. 12:17), and taste (Exod. 16:31; Col. 2:21).[21] All of the sensory functions are either assumed or stated to possess a physical component. Touch assumes physicality. Taste assumes physicality. In that way, the body is the originator of these varying sensory functions. I would even be comfortable putting the brain toward the top of the list as to why the body does the functions that it does. When our body takes in information through the senses, that information goes through our brain, and our mind responds to it. If you burn your hand on the stove, your senses detect the damage to your body and your brain may cause you to pull your hand back instinctively, but whether you become angry or use profanity is based on the condition of your mind, not your brain.

Physical Death

If the body is the source of physical life, its death is the end of that life, resulting in a state in which the mind is no longer able to interact with the physical world through the body and its senses. This includes the state we refer to as "brain dead."

While death is present in the earliest parts of Scripture as a consequence of sin (Gen. 2:17, 5:5), Scripture teaches that when a person dies, their mind continues to exist. For instance, "We know that while we are at home in the body we are away from the Lord" (2 Cor. 5:6). When Jesus "yields His spirit" (Matt. 27:50), it was the moment of separation of His body from His soul (cf. John 10:18).

In the instances of Joseph's death (Exod. 13:19), King Saul's death (1 Sam. 31:1–12), Jesus's death (Mark 15:43), John the Baptist's death (Matt. 14:1–12; Mark 9:24–28), and others, each is mentioned with their body described in impersonal terms. For instance, the phrases "their bodies" and "their bones" are used. This further indicates spiritual life exists after the cessation of physical life. The body of a person ceases to exist, but the person is not just their body.[22]

Consider how this applies to the brain and the mind: your mind is still fully operational even without your brain, because you will have complete cognition in the intermediary state, awaiting the inauguration of Jesus's return (Rev. 19:11–16).

Consider this: the faculty of cognition
is within your mind and will continue
to exist after your brain is dead.

What do we think about someone who is brain dead?

Well, there are medical criteria to determine brain death. The tests used to evaluate if a person is brain dead or not typically come down to 1) physical examination, 2) apnea test, and 3) ancillary tests.[23] The physical examination evaluates the brain's contribution to reflexes. The apnea test examines the brain's "ability to drive pulmonary function in response to the rise of carbon dioxide (CO_2)."[24] The brain is considered to be dead "if respiratory movements are absent."[25] For us laymen, if the brain is not helping to signal breathing patterns, then it is pronounced dead. Lastly, other tests can be used if the apnea test cannot be conducted.[26] These tests include a cerebral angiogram, transcranial ultrasound, computed tomogram, or radio nuclide brain imaging.[27] Each of these tests evaluates brain activity.

What brain death indicates is that a person's physical life is over, and we know it is at that point that a person's inner person—to include their mind—has left their body. I've had friends even tell me that they could look at their brain-dead loved one and tell that they had died. Their loved one simply didn't look like themselves, in that strange way our bodies appear once our spirits have left. Sometimes we don't need a radio nuclide brain imaging to tell us what we already know. But these tests exist for a more empirical way to verify death in cases of uncertainty.

Issues of the Mind and the Brain Can Be Difficult to Separate

My point in all this is that in none of these instances does the body control an inner person or immaterial response. In other words, the brain does not make the mind *think* something. Thoughts come from the mind, not the brain, even if they are in response to something in the body or brain, whether it be hunger, desire, or an injury that inhibits the senses.

The trickier part—and I simply want to be candid and humble about some of what we (including medical doctors and researchers) know—is that some issues seem to encompass both an outer-man (brain) and an inner-man (mind) issue.

Schizophrenia may be the clearest example of this, and it is one of the regular questions I receive when teaching on the mind and the brain. In all my years of counseling, I've only met with two people who were diagnosed as schizophrenic. One believed that he was running for president of the United States and that the government was sonic-booming his house. Although no one else heard these booms, he was convinced it was true—he even showed me his presidential campaign website that he had created.

It seems like schizophrenia is both a physical and immaterial issue. Many biblical counselors have agreed on this for many years.[28] So, let's frame it this way for the sake of biblical clarity:

1. We know a person can be insane. That takes place when their senses do not comport with reality.
2. We also know that the brain can have an unknown/unidentified problem that influences the inner person.
3. Lastly, we know that the mind can reject truth and become darkened, futile, and calloused. In this way, a mind can reject the truth of reality so that a person becomes self-deceived and delusional.

Based on these facts, it is possible for the body to have unusual issues and the mind to be compounding the problems in its response. Thus schizophrenia is most likely a combination of issues in the mind *and* the brain. (I say "most likely" because this is a hotly debated topic.)

The even more nuanced question that warrants asking is, What causes schizophrenia? Well, we know a person's brain cannot make them paranoid, if by paranoid we mean a way of thinking. However, we do know that a person's brain can encourage them to have fearful thoughts, which they can either take captive to the truth of God's Word, or allow to swell into delusion or panic. In this way, the brain can create the trial to which the mind must respond.

One more body and mind issue: seasonal depression. Also known as seasonal affective disorder, seasonal depression is known to occur among people more during fall or winter months. (The potential causes are a lack of sunshine, increased darkness, and perhaps even the vitamin D that a person gets from exposure to the sun is a factor here.[29]) In this way, the body can create feelings that influence the mind to have thoughts that are sad, listless, hopeless, guilty, not wanting to live, and so forth.[30] Can the brain through lack of vitamins encourage you to have symptoms of depression? Yes. But ultimately, can the brain make you hopeless, as a Christian? No. Christ is our hope no matter what we feel, and no matter what time of year it is.

Still, is seasonal depression a brain or mind issue? It's hard to tell. It seems best to say that the body, including the brain, is encouraging a mind response, but the mind still has all the resources it needs to honor the Lord. Ultimately, the trial created by the body might be helping to reveal what is really happening in the mind.

The Body Creates the Trial

Sensory problems such as hallucinations, of which Rhoda was accused in Acts 12:12–18, misperceptions (Luke 24:36), and faulty functions of the body (John 9:3ff) do not *control* the mind. Rather, these faulty or damaged senses may only *influence* the inner person. A person is still choosing, thinking, and desiring according to their inner person even when their body fails them. In fact, numerous examples exist of those who have bodily problems and yet still believe accurately. The woman who had an issue of blood still believed Jesus could heal her (Luke 8:43–48). A blind man cries out for Jesus to heal him and acknowledges his Davidic lineage (Luke 18:38). Furthermore, the paralytic in Luke 5:17–36 demonstrates faith, along with his friends. One could say that the physical body is damaged but it still does not create or prevent an immaterial response.

If a person is diagnosed with dementia, and they begin to say very lewd and sinful things, the dementia has not put that into their *mind*. Rather, the filter of their brain is damaged and the lewd things they say were an overflow of what was already in their mind (Matt. 12:32).

What about those who have experienced significant brain trauma, and seem to change personalities? Some believe that a traumatic brain injury can create mood and personality changes within a person.[31] For the Christian, this is a nuanced but not overly complicated matter. The Bible recognizes that a person can have physiological influences for your mood to change (cf. Isa. 38:16b). Not to be overly reductionistic, but even smaller physiological influences like sleeplessness, poor nutrition, hormonal changes, and little exercise can affect one's mood. And, please note, a changing mood is not inherently wrong or sinful. If I got into a car accident and my personality was different after it, that would not be inherently wrong or sinful. But it also would not mean the brain was controlling my mind. I still have to choose what I let my thoughts dwell on, and evaluate whether my attitude is biblical.

Jesus uses perhaps the strongest language in the entire Bible to describe the role of the body in inciting the inner person to respond. In Matthew 5:29–30, He says that if "your right eye causes you to sin, tear it out and throw it away," and "if your right hand causes you to sin, cut it off and throw it away."

The phrase "causes you to sin" is reiterated in Matthew 18:6–9. It literally means to "to cause to be brought to a downfall, *cause to sin.*"[32] In an isolated context, Matthew 5 and 18 both seem to suggest that a person can be caused to sin, but Paul reminds the Christian that they are not a slave to sin (Rom. 6:1–6), and that no temptation is beyond a believer's ability (1 Cor. 10:13).[33]

Jesus is saying that the body can cause a stumbling block or enticement to sin, which explains Jesus's words in Matthew 6:22: "The eye is the lamp of the body. So, if your eye is healthy, your whole body will be full of light, but if your eye is bad, your whole body will be full of darkness." The body can encourage inner-man responses that are sinful.

Part of the call of sanctification is to leverage one's "mortal body" toward Christlikeness.[34] While the body can entice us to obey its "passions" (Rom. 6:12), the believer understands sin is no longer able to have dominion in their body (Rom. 6:13; Eph. 2:3). The body's passions must be resisted through self-denial. Paul says he "disciplines his body" (1 Cor. 9:27) for longevity in ministry and usefulness as a minister of the Gospel. The "deeds of the body" must be put to death (Rom. 8:13). This is perhaps the essential understanding of self-control, to deny oneself physical and immaterial cravings and subject them to Jesus.[35]

In the end, the body (including the brain) does indeed entice and influence immaterial responses from the mind, but it does not control the mind. When I say "immaterial responses" it can be both toward greater Christlikeness (Matt. 6:22–23; 1 Tim. 4:7–8) or toward sinfulness (Matt. 5:29–30). In sum:

The brain can *influence* organic issues and also influence mind responses, but the brain does not control the mind.[36]

Though the mind and the brain are intimately connected, the brain cannot cause the mind to think about certain subjects, or ideas, which is the foundation of our behavior. The brain cannot cause impure thoughts. The brain cannot cause angry thoughts. This has significant implications for things like psychotropic medication, understanding traumatic brain injuries, addictions, use of pornography, and suggested research that supports a mental illness framework for understanding our struggles—all of which I will address.

As for Bessel van der Kolk's theories, even secular research is confirming that your past experiences don't define you. "The idea that we carry in our bodies the trauma of our younger selves—much less the trauma of our ancestors—may be a PR campaign in search of a product," writes Abigail Shrier in *Bad Therapy*.[37] Your mind, which determines your personality and actions, might be affected by the brain, but it is not determined (let alone predetermined) by the brain.

Ed Welch, a biblical counselor and author of *Blame It on the Brain*, provides an excellent summary:

> At the level of the brain, this unity suggests that the heart or spirit [i.e., mind] will always be represented or expressed in the brain's chemical activity. When we choose good or evil, such decisions will be accompanied by changes in brain activity. This does not mean that the brain *causes* these decisions. It simply means that the brain renders the desire of the heart [or mind] in a physical medium. It is as if the heart [or mind] always leaves its footprints on the brain.[38]

So, if you are experiencing symptoms of what we refer to as a mental illness, make sure you see a physician and get a blood test. Make sure your thyroid is functioning and that you are getting adequate vitamin D, exercise, and sleep. At the end of this book, I have provided an appendix with suggestions for maintaining a healthy brain, and these could be a part of helping you move past emotional and mental struggles you might have. And in a later chapter, we'll also look at the role medication may play.

But even if it turns out that there is a physiological reason for your affliction, don't use it as an excuse for sin. Don't chalk it up to "trauma" or say "I can't help it because I have a disorder and my brain made me do it." God gives us the responsibility to grow, to obey, and to love Him and others. You might have been shaped by your past, but Christ can still transform you, making you a new creation and working all things together for your good.

In the next chapter, we'll see how He empowers us to do that.

CHAPTER 6

Treatment vs. Transformation

Repentance is purgative; fear not the working
of this pill. Smite your soul, said Chrysostom,
smite it; it will escape death by that stroke. How
happy it would be if we were more deeply affected
with sin, and our eyes did swim in their orb.

—THOMAS WATSON, *THE DOCTRINE OF REPENTANCE*

In a word, if the way to disengage the heart from
the positive love of one great and ascendant object,
is to fasten it in positive love to another, then it is
not by exposing the worthlessness of the former,
but by addressing to the mental eye the worth and
excellence of the latter, that all old things are to be
done away and all things are to become new.

—THOMAS CHALMERS, *THE EXPULSIVE
POWER OF A NEW AFFECTION*

No matter how good a secular therapist might be (and there are some
out there—though not as many as you'd think—who are quite effective
in helping people improve their natural lives), there is one thing that
the Bible offers as help to those struggling with "mental illnesses" that
no secular therapist can provide: eternal salvation.

Don't separate so-called mental health from the role of salvation
in capacitating the mind. According to the Bible, the mind is not un-

healthy, it is *darkened*. It is futile, and in need of renewal apart from salvation by Christ alone. The mind is depraved in its natural state. Opposed to God. Hardened. *Salvation has everything to do with the mind.*

We don't talk about salvation enough, even in church. In our secular age, we are often far more concerned with the issues of this life. With so much modern technology to lengthen our comparatively comfortable lives in the West in particular, it's easy to be worldly minded, as if we will live forever. We fail to see the spiritual significance of our struggles. As historian Christopher Lasch put it decades ago, "The contemporary climate is therapeutic, not religious. People today hunger not for personal salvation . . . but for the feeling, the momentary illusion, of personal well-being, health, and psychic security."[1]

Modern therapy is focused on symptom relief for this life. In contrast, the Bible shows that the roots of many of our issues are spiritual. And indeed, our biggest problem of all is one therapy can't solve.

According to the Scriptures, the biggest problem each of us must grapple with is sin. Each of us is conceived in sin, because the first man, Adam, rejected the perfection of God and plunged the whole world into rebellion, in an act of "cosmic treason," which we also commit every time we sin ourselves.[2] And the wages we earn from our sin? Death (Gen. 2:17; Ezek.18:4; Rom. 6:23).

Not only physical death, but eternal death in the lake of fire, which is the judgment we earn from God every time we sin (Matt. 5:22; Eph. 2:1–3; Rev. 21:8).

How then can we escape from this judgment we've earned?

God Himself, our Judge, took on flesh so that He could receive and satisfy His own wrath—the wrath that we earn—on the cross (Mk. 10:45; 1 Cor. 15:3–8; 2 Cor. 5:16–21; 1 Pet. 2:24; 1 Jn. 2:2). When Jesus died and rose again from the dead, He wasn't only demonstrating His great love for us, but He was paying our debt—*in full!* Thanks be to God!

And so, because God has done all of the work necessary to accomplish our salvation, we are saved by grace, through faith. Salvation is a gift of God, not a result of our works (Rom. 3:28; Gal. 2:16; Eph. 2:4–9). We are not saved by our works, but by trusting in Christ's work. We do not receive salvation by attending church, being baptized, or repeating specific words after a pastor in prayer, but by being reconciled to God through repentance and faith.

And repentance, at the moment of salvation, changes the mind.

Repentance and the Mind

One of the most popular titles of Jesus is the Good Shepherd, which He calls Himself in John 10:11. John's gospel captures instances of Jesus protecting the sheep (John 10:11), dying for the sheep (John 10:15), and restoring lost sheep (John 10:16). It is a beautiful analogy of the love of Christ for His people. He protects them and restores them, which is also how Christian pastors should treat those within their flock (1 Pet. 5:1–4).

Jesus uses the analogy of a shepherd and a lost sheep when speaking about an unbeliever. He says, "What man of you, having a hundred sheep, if he has lost one of them, does not leave the ninety-nine in the open country, and go after the one that is lost, until he finds it?" (Luke 15:4). This is the portrait of Jesus, that He seeks and saves the lost (Luke 19:10).

And when a lost sheep is found: "'Rejoice with me, for I have found my sheep that was lost.' Just so, I tell you, there will be more joy in heaven over one sinner who *repents* than over ninety-nine righteous persons who need no *repentance*" (Luke 15:7; emphasis added).

It is repeated often enough to be a cliché, but it is still true: repentance literally means to "change one's mind." It comes from the Greek term *metanoia*, which serves as a call to think differently. In Acts 2:38,

Peter says, "Repent and be baptized every one of you in the name of Jesus Christ for the forgiveness of your sins, and you will receive the gift of the Holy Spirit."

Repentance in the Christian life has two facets. The first form of repentance occurs at the moment of salvation, as Acts 2:38 states. That is the repentance that brings celebration in Heaven, because it is accompanied by saving faith, which leads to salvation (see Luke 15:7 and Acts 3:19).

In 2 Timothy 2:25, it says that repentance at the moment of salvation leads to "knowledge of the truth." The message of the coming Messiah has been one of repentance (Luke 24:47) as was preached on the Day of Pentecost and later by Paul to the Gentiles (Acts 20:21). As John MacArthur and Richard Mayhue write, "only by repentant faith may a sinner subjectively lay hold of the benefits objectively purchased by Christ."[3] *Repentance, first of all, is a change of mind at the moment of salvation.*

At the same time, there is a second form of repentance, an ongoing repentance, that is necessary for a Christian's right fellowship with God. 1 John 1:5–7 speaks to "walking in the light" as an indicator that we are desirous of honoring God in all we do. John goes on to say, "if we say we have no sin, we make him a liar" (1 John 1:10). In between these verses, John uses the present form of *confess* in verse 9. "If we confess our sins" is present active, suggesting that there is an ongoing aspect to confession and repentance.[4] The Lord's Prayer says, "forgive us our debts, as we also have forgiven our debtors" (Matt. 6:12). And, if we have sinned against another, then we should be willing to go and confess to them in repentance (Luke 17:3–4).

Each of these instances teaches us that repentance begins at the moment of salvation, then continues throughout the life of the Christian. There is not a single Christian who can say that he or she has no need to repent. Rather, "If we say we have not sinned, we make him a liar, and his word is not in us" (1 John 1:10). Repentance has everything to do with the well-being of a person's mind, because it is at the moment of salvation when a person "changes their mind" (has their mind changed) and thus actually starts following Christ.

Yet, even more than just repentance happens at the moment of salvation. Consider some of these glorious theological realities that occur the moment you are saved:

- **Justification:** "A person has been restored to a state of righteousness [as opposed to perfection] through belief and trust in the work of Christ. . . ."[5]
- **Redemption:** "Christ's saving work of 'buying back' sinners out of their bondage to sin and to Satan through the payment of a ransom."[6]
- **Regeneration:** "The work of the Holy Spirit in creating new life in the sinful person . . ." It is also known as being "born again" in John 3:3.[7]
- **Adoption:** "That part of salvation in which God receives the estranged sinner back into the relationship and benefits of being his child."[8]

Each of these theological truths should cause you to put this book down, stand up, and shout, "Oh, the depth of the riches and wisdom and knowledge of God! How unsearchable are his judgments and how inscrutable his ways!" (Rom. 11:33) Hallelujah!

But that's not all (as if these aspects of salvation were not already amazing!). At the moment of salvation, a person receives an entirely new mind. When a person is saved, they don't just receive a few new thoughts, as if their mind was mostly correct and needed a few things altered. Some of us perceive the nature of salvation to be like simply redirecting an already mobile vehicle. We were headed in the wrong direction, had a few dents, but were definitely still operational. Yet that is not how the Bible speaks of your mind before salvation.

> Salvation doesn't take a mind that was "already running" and simply advance it. Salvation, rather, takes a mind that is broken-down— the tires are flat, the engine is missing, and the transmission is busted—and transforms it into something that actually functions.

While you may still have struggles in this earthly life, in Heaven your sanctification will be complete, and you will have a perfect mind. Praise be to God! He justifies, redeems, adopts, and regenerates, and because of this, we can have a mind that actually functions as it was designed to do.

Symptom Relief, or Salvation?

Because modern mental health theory does not have a right understanding of sin, often ignoring it altogether as a source of our problems, secular therapists often focus on either symptom reduction or improving a person's quality of life, often by their own standards.[9] In 2019, Pim Cuijpers wrote in *World Psychiatry*:

> Symptom reduction can be seen as the core target and outcome of psychotherapies. Not only is symptom reduction by far the most common focus of outcome research, especially randomized trials, but qualitative studies also show that it is one of the most important outcomes from the viewpoint of patients (although certainly not the only one).[10]

But God's goal is not for us to merely have better behavior, or to feel better about ourselves. God's goal in salvation is that we be transformed:

> *Do not be conformed to this world, but be transformed by the*
> *renewal of your mind, that by testing you may discern what*
> *is the will of God, what is good and acceptable and perfect.*
> —ROMANS 12:2

> *And we all, with unveiled face, beholding the glory*
> *of the Lord, are being transformed into the same*
> *image from one degree of glory to another.*
> —2 CORINTHIANS 3:18

This is why we receive a new mind.

Why do we need this transformation? Well, when you read the Bible's depiction of the mind of someone who does not know Christ, it ain't pretty.

In 2 Corinthians 4:3–4, Paul says, "And even if our gospel is veiled, it is veiled to those who are perishing. In their case the god of this world has blinded the *minds* of the unbelievers, to keep them from seeing the light of the gospel of the glory of Christ, who is the image of God" (emphasis added). The mind of an unbeliever is said to be blind to the glory of Christ. Paul tells Titus that the unbeliever's mind is "defiled" (Tit. 1:15). The defilement is so pervasive that it affects everything because the mind is the source of thinking.

Ephesians 4 speaks to the unbelieving mind in two distinct phrases. In verse 17, Paul says to the Ephesian Church "that you must no longer walk as the Gentiles do, in the futility of their minds." The term *Gentiles* in this context is not about ethnicity, but about those who do not know the Lord. Many of the Ephesian Christians were themselves Gentiles (cf. Eph. 2:11–13).

Paul tells these Gentile believers to not walk as the unbelieving Gentiles walk. How do they walk? In the futility of their minds. Then, in verse 18, he says that the unbeliever's mind is "darkened." Your Bible might say "darkened in their understanding" but that term *understanding* in the English is a Greek term that is also translated as *mind*.

Here is a list of ways that the unbeliever's mind is described throughout the Bible:

- **"Blind"** (2 Cor. 4:4): "to deprive of sight, to blind"[11]
- **"Corrupted"** (2 Tim. 3:8): "ruin, corrupt"[12]
- **"Darkened"** (Eph. 4:18): "be/become darkened in mind"[13]
- **"Deceitful"** (Jer. 17:9): "deceitful, sly, difficult, insidious"[14]
- **"Depraved"** (Rom. 1:28; 1 Tim. 6:5): "to cause to become morally corrupt, deprave, ruin"[15]
- **"Defiled"** (Tit. 1:15): "to cause the purity of something to be violated by immoral behavior, defile"[16]
- **"Futile"** (Eph. 4:17): "state of being without use or value, emptiness, futility, purposelessness, transitoriness"[17]
- **"Hardened"** (Exod. 7:14): "dull, unresponsive"[18]
- **"Sick"** (Jer. 17:9): "disastrous"[19]

Zoom out and you'll see that the mind, in its unregenerated natural state, is simply disastrous. It's shocking to see the depth of depravity of the human mind apart from the work of salvation! Without salva-tion, we are not in need of slight tweaks here and there. Our need is far deeper than behavior modification, symptom relief, or having fewer "unhelpful thoughts."[20] Rather, we are in dire need of total restoration.

Perhaps echoing Asaph in Psalm 73, you may be thinking, "Wait, I'm a Christian struggling with anxiety and depression, and I see unbe-lievers who don't have these issues." The reality is that an unbeliever may not have these so-called mental health issues, but that is not to suggest their mind is whole. All of the above list is still true of the unbeliever's mind. Thus you can have a "hardened" mind that doesn't struggle with anxiety. You can have a "depraved" mind that doesn't struggle with depression. Conversely, just because you have a renewed mind doesn't mean that you are exempt from certain struggles of the mind.

How can this be? If the depraved mind is darkened in understanding and disastrously sick, how does this actually play out?

First, the depraved mind is inclined toward sin. Colossians 1:21 says we "once were alienated and hostile in mind, *doing evil deeds*." This can include internal deeds, since God sees our minds, and considers things like lust to be adultery of the heart (Matt. 5:21–28). Unlike believers, who are not tempted beyond their ability, unbelievers are slaves to sin (Jn. 8:34; Rom. 6:1–12; 1 Cor. 10:13). And second, the depraved mind cannot understand spiritual realities correctly. Paul writes in 1 Corinthians 2:14, "The natural person does not accept the things of the Spirit of God, for they are folly to him, and he is not able to understand them because they are spiritually discerned." The minds of unbelievers are blinded to the most pressing spiritual questions, which limits their ability to make sense even of the natural world.

Before salvation, your mind wasn't "unhealthy"—your mind was blind, corrupt, dark, deceitful, depraved, defiled, futile, hardened, and sick.

A Christian, however, has a change of mind at the moment of salvation.

Consider 2 Corinthians 4:4 again: "the god of this world has blinded the minds of the unbelievers, to keep them from seeing the light of the gospel of the glory of Christ." The mind before salvation cannot see the glory of Christ, but "when one turns to the Lord, the veil is removed. Now the Lord is the Spirit, and where the Spirit of the Lord is, there is freedom" (2 Cor. 3:16–17).

In this section of 2 Corinthians, Paul is referencing Moses when he spoke with the Lord in Exodus 34:29–35. When Moses would go speak with God on Sinai, he would uncover his face to speak directly with God. And when he descended the mountain, his skin radiated from the glory of God. So he wore a veil.

Paul uses this as an illustration: Before salvation, we have veils over our minds so that we cannot see the glory of God. And yet, at the moment of salvation, the Holy Spirit capacitates you so that you are "free to behold" the glory of God for the very first time. The saved mind can finally "behold the glory of the Lord" (2 Cor. 3:18).

The Holy Spirit gives you the mental capacity to now finally see God for who He is. You can understand the glory of Christ Jesus in a way that inspires awe, wonder, and deep, deep gratitude. You can see what Satan had blinded your mind from seeing, "the light of the gospel of the glory of Christ, who is the image of God" (2 Cor. 4:4).

The saved person's mind is capacitated to see the glory of God!

When unbelievers come to Christ, the Bible says they are reconciled to God (2 Cor. 5:11–21). They are brought into a right relationship with God, and the "terms" of that relationship are what's called the New Covenant. The Old Covenant, between God and the nation of Israel, was meant to show us our inability to access God and please Him on our own merit (Rom. 3:19–20; Gal. 3:23–24; Heb. 10:11–18). In the New Covenant, Christ has kept the law, fulfilled the Old Covenant, and pleased God for us, so that we might be justified by faith and have peace with God (Matt. 5:17; Rom. 5:1; Rom. 8:1).

When Jesus speaks at the Last Supper, He refers to the cup as "the new covenant in my blood" (1 Cor. 11:25). Jesus himself is "the mediator of a new covenant" (Heb. 9:15). Some of the promises made to the house of Israel now even benefit the Gentiles, because now the Gentiles can be grafted in as beneficiaries of the promises made to Israel (Rom. 11:17–18).

So, what does this have to do with the mind?

The New Covenant has promises of not only renewing in the inner person, but actually transformation of the inner person into what it was designed to be all along. In Jeremiah's prophecy regarding the New Covenant, God says, "this is the covenant that I will make with the house of Israel after those days, declares the Lord: I will put my law within them, and I will write it on their hearts" (Jer. 31:33).

The Hebrew word for *heart* is *leb*, which, you'll recall, refers to the totality of the inner person, including the mind (cf. Jer. 11:20). The promise of the New Covenant that God is making with Israel and Judah is that the heart would have God's law written on it. Ezekiel's prophecy reiterates this promise: "And I will give you a new heart [*leb*], and a new spirit I will put within you. And I will remove the heart [*leb*] of stone from your flesh and give you a heart [*leb*] of flesh" (Ezek. 36:36).

In both of these instances, we see a promise that the inner person would be transformed. No longer would it be like stone—dull, inept, incapable, and nonoperative. It would be made alive, like flesh.

What does that mean? Your capacities have changed if you have experienced salvation through Jesus Christ. Your mind was dull and hardened before salvation. After salvation, your mind is now softened, functional, ordered, and able to see the glory of God. As Paul writes throughout his epistles, you were given the "mind of Christ" at the moment of salvation.

Yet, while you have been given the mind of Christ, it is an important nuance that Christ also calls us to sanctification, to grow in Christlikeness (1 Thess. 4:3). God calls us to push forward, with the Holy Spirit's help, in being conformed to the image of Jesus (Rom. 8:29). So to be precise, you have been given the mind of Christ at the moment of salvation, *and* you are called to think more and more like Christ (Phil. 2:5). You have the capacitated mind already, but through progressive sanctification, your thoughts, cognition, intellect, attitude, and way of thinking are to be increasingly like Christ's.

When we speak of progressive sanctification, we are talking about the incremental conformity by which the Christian becomes more and more like Jesus (Rom. 8:29–30). There are a few primary references where we see that Paul is speaking to those who are already saved, yet are still called to be renewed in their minds. The church at Rome is said to be "loved by God and called to be saints" (Rom. 1:7) and Paul tells them, "Do not be conformed to this world, but be transformed by the *renewal of your mind*" (Rom. 12:2; emphasis added). The present-tense use of both *conformed* and *transformed* shows us that these are actions currently taking place for the believer. The mind is presently being transformed.

At the moment of salvation, the work of God is just beginning to conform you to the image of God as seen in Jesus Christ. A Christian's mind still needs to be "transformed" or "renewed," but without the capacitating resurrection that occurs at the moment of salvation, no person's mind will ever be renewed to function as God intended.

At Glorification, the Mind Is Perfected

Glorification is a theological term that refers to the final work of salvation in the life of the believer. John MacArthur and Richard Mayhue define it as "the completion of sanctification and the removal of all spiritual defects."[21] In Romans 8:30, Paul says, "And those whom he predestined he also called, and those whom he called he also justified, and those whom he justified he also glorified." Both the body and the soul will be freed from the presence of sin at the moment of final glorification.[22] In Philippians 3:21, Paul says Christ "will transform our lowly body to be like his glorious body."

When a person is glorified, it means that the effects of sin on the immaterial person are finally eradicated. We are saved and sanctified in our time here on earth, but 1 John 3:2 says, "we know that when he appears we shall be like him, because we shall see him as he is." We will be perfectly conformed to the image of Jesus in both our inner and outer person; in both our mind and our brain.

Consider the progression of the Christian's mind in the chart below:

Before Salvation	At Salvation	During Progressive Sanctification	At Glorification
The mind is corrupt, futile, depraved, and hardened.	The mind is capacitated.	The mind is progressively transformed.	The mind is perfected.

You will never have another covetous, lustful, hateful, selfish, idolatrous, proud, anxious, or untrue thought after God's work has been completed in you at glorification (Phil. 1:6). This is why we *long* for glorification. The mind of Christ that was implanted into us at the moment of salvation, and that we have progressively sought to pursue, will be completed at the moment of glorification. Oh, we look forward to that day!

While I have focused primarily on the mind, I want to briefly show you the wonder of how glorification applies to the brain. Recall that glorification is both of a Christian's outer person and inner person (cf. John 6:39–40; Phil. 3:21). We know that glorification will bring physical restoration to the body, including the brain. Romans 8:23 says that we eagerly wait for the "redemption of our bodies." That means that those who have brain injuries and brain diseases in this life will have their brains restored to perfect physical health at the moment of glorification. They will no longer struggle with memory loss, dementia, or other organic problems of the brain because of the glorification of the physical body! I'm convinced that the older we get, the sweeter this promise is to us: after glorification, true brain illnesses will be corrected through the work of Jesus Christ to redeem both our bodies and our minds. Amen and amen.

Salvation's Implications for Therapy

In light of all this, it is quite noteworthy that, when we go to unsaved psychiatrists and psychologists, we are seeking help for our minds from someone who has a darkened mind.

If I were to give you parenting advice, most likely you would want to know if I have godly kids. If I were to give you home ownership advice, you'd want to know if I successfully owned a home, right?

Yet many Christians go to secular therapists for help with their minds, when the therapists themselves have minds that are distorted, corrupted, futile, and nonoperational. Where is the sense in that?

If you understand the Bible's description of the role of salvation, then those who have not been saved will not be able to solve our real issues, beyond surface-level observations and symptom mitigation. Yes, they do have minds, but even the greatest genius of philosophy or psychology cannot give you the biblical, spiritual truth you need to meet your spiritual needs. They never could have such knowledge unless they believed in the Scriptures and were saved themselves (cf. 1 Cor. 2:14). Yet many Christians have looked to the secular therapist as the "expert" on the mind.

Secular therapists are people with *broken* minds, trying to help us with our minds!

When you go to a secular psychologist or psychiatrist for help with your mind, their solutions will almost always be symptom-focused, rather than causative or focused on the true etiology of the problem. The entire *Diagnostic and Statistical Manual of Mental Disorders* (DSM) is "symptom-based" diagnosing.[23] As evidenced in the DSM, what can an individual whose personal mind is darkened truly offer to others? Band-Aids. That's all.

Some Band-Aids might be more helpful than others, but none will be genuine solutions. The top experts in mental health cannot overcome this, and it is the ultimate reason we have a "mental health crisis" despite more mental health resources than ever before.

Finally, if you meet with a secular psychiatrist or psychologist, just know that most of the solutions will be based on a naturalistic worldview. What naturalistic remedy will you receive when you go to an unsaved psychologist or psychiatrist? Often, medication. More and more psychotropics are being prescribed for anxiety, mood regulation, and depression. This is happening partly because we have unsaved psychologists and psychiatrists who are trying to help people with issues of their mind—inner man issues, which are spiritual—but they themselves have darkened minds. This is literally what Paul was saying—the natural man can only see the natural things (1 Cor. 2:14–16).

We must escape this vicious cycle of going to unbelievers for help with our minds, when unbelievers need the most help for *their* minds. That help comes first and foremost through salvation and the gospel of Jesus Christ. If you go to a psychiatrist or psychologist, at least go to one who is a believer, who has a mind that has been capacitated to see spiritual realities and understand the world biblically.

Secular therapists fail to see how fundamentally and profoundly sin affects us—how it is the root cause of many of our most painful relational conflicts, the source of countless struggles in our motives and thoughts, and the blinder of our eyes to spiritual realities behind so many of our "mental illness" diagnoses. And while some of the symptoms of sin might be treated, sin itself is almost never addressed, because sin cannot be cured by any form of therapy. It is cured through the saving work of Christ and the sanctifying work of the Holy Spirit.

Any conversation about the "health" of the mind must include a conversation about salvation, because no mind will be genuinely and thoroughly well apart from salvation. Salvation is not only about how you stand before a holy and just God to receive forgiveness and the imputed righteousness of Christ (though it is certainly about that!). Salvation is also the beginning of your restoration, in which you are being re-created into what you were designed to be—a clearer and clearer reflection of Christ.

Christ, accordingly, is the True Image in which man was formed at creation and into which by the reconciling grace of re-creation, fallen man is being transformed.

—PHILIP EDGCUMBE HUGHES, *THE TRUE IMAGE*[24]

CHAPTER 7

Mental Health vs. Mind Renewal

Beloved, I pray that all may go well with you and that
you may be in good health, as it goes well with your soul.

—3 JOHN 2

We must work for a welcoming and compassionate
society, a society where no American is dismissed,
and no American is forgotten. This is the great
and hopeful story of our country, and we
can write another chapter. We must give all
Americans who suffer from mental illness the
treatment, and the respect, they deserve.

—GEORGE W. BUSH[1]

Perhaps your curiosity has gotten the best of you, and you have
zoomed through the first chapters of this book to ransack this chapter
for the answer to this question: *Is mental health really what the Bible
calls mind renewal—or a knockoff version of it?*

If that is you, just know I do the same thing all the time! I often
rush through a book for the specific information I'm looking for and
then move on to another book. *Hello, friend.* This is what you've paid
the price of admission to hear. This is the question that so many Christians have been asking:

Is mental health a *legitimate* category for understanding our inner struggles?

The answer to that question is the focus of this chapter. Let's start by briefly reviewing the development of the secular therapeutic culture:

1. A therapist can conflate the brain and the mind.
2. The mind is described with medical terminology (i.e., health, disorder, illness, disease).
3. Treatments often attempt to help the immaterial mind through medical means.

Consider the definition of mental health from the Centers for Disease Control and Prevention (CDC). While you might think that the CDC should focus exclusively on physical illness, they have a section of their website dedicated to mental illness. Here is their definition of mental health:

> Mental health includes our emotional, psychological, and
> social well-being. It affects how we think, feel, and act. It
> also helps determine how we handle stress, relate to others,
> and make healthy choices. Mental health is important at
> every stage of life, from childhood and adolescence through
> adulthood.[2]

The CDC has a very similar definition as the National Institute of Mental Health (NIMH). But think about it: a center for *disease* control is speaking into an immaterial area of life, and is providing a definition of health for our immaterial inner person. Note that this definition says mental health includes *emotional, psychological,* and *social* well-being. Which part of that is treatment of the brain?

Consider the NIMH's definition:

> Mental health includes emotional, psychological, and social
> well-being. It affects how we think, feel, act, make choices,
> and relate to others. Mental health is more than the absence
> of a mental illness—it's essential to your overall health and
> quality of life. Self-care can play a role in maintaining your
> mental health and help support your treatment and recovery
> if you have a mental illness.[3]

The NIMH recommends physical treatment, or self-care for the immaterial mind. Thinking, feeling, and making choices are not part of our body—they are part of our mind. But the NIMH is blurring the lines of the mind and the brain and that leads to this mysterious category of mental health. It is quite odd to use medical terminology and treatment by a leading mental health organization but not realize that the mind is immaterial.

Lastly, consider the American Psychological Association's definition of mental health:

> Mental health is a state of mind characterized by emotional
> well-being, good behavioral adjustment, relative freedom
> from anxiety and disabling symptoms, and a capacity to
> establish constructive relationships and cope with the
> ordinary demands and stresses of life.[4]

Remember, the APA is very influential within the mental health world. But note that the APA's definition *has nothing to do* with physical wellness. Not to mention that the description in the second paragraph is of immaterial things: emotions, thinking, communication, and self-esteem.

Each of these leading organizations has equated mental health with immaterial health. What does this mean? For one thing, it is a signal that even the modern, leading mental health organizations do not have clarity on the very nature of the mind. And what is the resulting standard treatment that they might recommend? Here is a list provided by the federal Substance Abuse and Mental Health Services Administration:

- Stick to a treatment plan.
- Keep your primary care physician updated.
- Learn about the condition.
- Practice good self-care.
- Reach out to family and friends.
- Develop coping skills.
- Get enough sleep.[5]

The problem with this medical terminology is that it fails to capture the biblical reality that the mind is immaterial, and a primary care physician cannot effectively treat your mind.

Mental health has become the secular therapeutic catch-all phrase to deal with the inner person, thus sidelining the Bible's perspective on care for your inner person. And are we the better for it? With one out of six people being diagnosed with a mental illness, obviously not.

What if mental health theory has actually encroached on spiritual territory reserved for salvation and sanctification? If you have unrepentant sin, how will you "practice good self-care"? Or, if you are failing to trust the Lord with a fear that you have, and it is leading to anxiety, the solution is not to just "focus on your mental health" and self-care (though this is not to say that all inner-person issues are a sin!). And if you don't fundamentally understand that salvation capacitates the mind and sanctification makes it more like Christ's, what good will developing coping strategies do?

We, as Christians, need to wake up to the reality that secular mental health professionals have changed the conversation from a spiritual, God-focused orientation toward a medicalized one. Instead of viewing ourselves through the lens of the Bible, we have adopted the medical terminology and allowed those who reject Christ, reject a biblical understanding of the mind, reject salvation in Christ, and reject sanctification to be the ones to help us with our minds.

Mental health refers to the immaterial component of who we are. The term is a red herring of sorts, distracting us from phrases that would convey a more accurate understanding of people. It takes discernment to translate what the culture means by mental health through the lens of the Bible. Otherwise we create a category of "mental health" that seems to be different from mind renewal.

Even some Christians don't know the difference between mental health and mind renewal, and thus consider mental health treatments to be an important part of overall spiritual wellness. Seminary professor and counselor David Murray says, "Christians can have mental illness simply because they are human. Christians can have mental illness because they are sinners. Christians can have mental illness because they simply are Christians."[6]

Murray continues: "All depression, anxiety, bipolar disorder, schizophrenia, PTSD, personality disorders, and so forth, can be traced to this terrible turning point in world history [referring to the Fall in Genesis 3]. . . . When sin invaded the world, mental illness invaded our minds."[7]

While in a way I agree with much of his second point, is mental illness even a category we should accept? In a later chapter, I'll answer the questions about mental health diagnoses, but first, in this chapter, I'm going to show how "mental health" should more accurately be called "mental transformation," or even better, "mind renewal."

Is "Mental Health" in the Bible?

Remember, we are talking about the spiritual, *immaterial* components of who we are, as revealed in the Bible.[8] Semantically, it is confusing to talk about our immaterial components with medical terminology. For instance, if I were to say, "I have a mental abrasion," that would mean that I have a small cut on my mind, which is not possible. Again, if I said, "I have a mental contusion," most of you would begin to wonder, "How does your mind get a bruise?"

Yet we use the term *health* to describe the state of our mind. This is confusing, because it's the same medical term that generally refers to entities that can be physically well or unwell. Bone health. Back health. Gut health. Even brain health. But mind health?

While *health* most often means "freedom from physical disease or pain," sometimes it has metaphorical meanings that aren't medical (such as "financial health").[9] However, because the brain and mind are connected, and often conflated by secular therapists, and since some believe that you can have a physical problem with the mind, it is especially confusing to use *health* when we're talking about our mind.

In Scripture there are a few instances where we see *health* associated with the inner person. One of the clearest is 3 John 2, where Gaius is wished well by John, but read carefully the words of John here: "Beloved, I pray that all may go well with you and that you may be in good health, as it goes well with your soul." John actually wishes that Gaius would be able to thrive in his outer person much like he is thriving in his inner person. The NIV translates "as it goes well" as "getting along well," and the LSB translates it "as your soul prospers." John uses a term that can be translated as "prosper" (εὐοδοῦταί). It means to "have things turn out well."[10] Paul uses the same term to say that perhaps he will "prosper" in coming to the Romans (Rom. 1:10) or that the cheerful giver in 1 Corinthians 16:2 gives "as he may prosper." The ESV uses the phrase "be in good health," but that is *not* a reference to Gaius's soul; rather it is to his body. John does not confuse the "health" of the inner person.

Two other notable instances are in 2 Peter, where the inner person is described in ways relatively close to "unhealthy." Specifically, it is a lack of steadiness or soundness. The false teachers addressed in the book were twisting the Scripture (2 Pet. 3:16). They were insatiably desirous of sin (2 Pet. 2:14) and the result was that the false teachers were "unsteady" or "unstable." This term refers to an instability or weakness like that of a person who is struggling to walk.[11] The false teacher is unstable and weak. They are not healthy, but only in the metaphorical sense of them being unsteady.

Other than these verses, it's difficult to connect the word *health* to our inner person in Scripture. However, *sickness* is a bit more common description for the inner man. Consider some of the following passages that speak to the soul or inner person being sick:

- "The heart is deceitful above all things, and desperately sick; who can understand it?" (Jer. 17:9)
- "Hope deferred makes the heart sick, but a desire fulfilled is a tree of life" (Prov. 13:12).
- "And the king said to me, 'Why is your face sad, seeing you are not sick? This is nothing but sadness of the heart.' Then I was very much afraid" (Neh. 2:2).
- "My joy is gone; grief is upon me; my heart is sick within me" (Jer. 8:18).
- "How sick is your heart, declares the Lord God, because you did all these things, the deeds of a brazen prostitute" (Ezek. 16:30).

As you survey the Scriptures, you will see that, when not describing an ailment of the physical body, sickness primarily refers to discouragement, love, or to sin.[12] Yes, according to Song of Solomon 2:5, it is possible to be "love sick"! (All of you romantics reading this can smile now! *Awwww.*)

When the Bible uses the term *sick* when speaking of the mind or immaterial heart, it is saying the mind is sick through discouragement or sin, not a so-called mental illness or pathology. Again, this is not to say every mental battle is sin, but if you use *sick* the way the Bible uses it, then you are usually speaking of sin or sadness.

Conversely, what makes a mind truly healthy? Again, if we are letting the Bible inform our understanding of what mental wellness looks like, then we need to clarify a few terms.

As stated above, unless used metaphorically, *health* means a state of freedom from physical illness or injury. And, as we saw at the beginning of this chapter, *health* has a connotation that carries a lot of the cultural baggage of secular therapy.

So it would be clearer to say that a truly "healthy" mind comports more to what the Bible would call the "renewed" mind (cf. Rom. 12:2). Ephesians 4:17 makes it clear that an unbeliever has a futile mind, which means without use or value.[13] Romans 1:28 specifies that those who suppress the truth have been handed over to "debased minds," which means "base or worthless."[14] The mind that is sick, according to Scripture, often refers to a mind that is plagued by sin. Thus it needs "renewal."

Renewal is the restoration to an original, untainted condition. Paul uses the word twice in the Bible. The first time is Romans 12:2 and the second refers to the work of the Holy Spirit in regeneration in Titus 3:5.

As discussed in the previous chapter, the Holy Spirit renews your mind at the moment of conversion. In the biblical use of wellness, or health, or wholeness, the truly "healthy" mind is one that has been renewed. A person can have a functioning mind that is futile (Eph. 4:17), does not understand the things of the Spirit (1 Cor. 2:15–16), is spiritually blind (2 Cor. 4:4), or is debased (Rom. 1:28). Remember, the mind is still functioning; it is simply void in its function. But the mind that is well is renewed (Rom. 12:2) and is growing in that renewal (Eph. 4:23).

In this way, what makes a mind well is regeneration by the Holy Spirit. This is different from physical wellness of the outer man, such as the brain, which wellness is only temporary (2 Cor. 4:16–18). Although Christians are not zapped into instant holiness, the mind has been made new at salvation. The renewal of the mind is also progressive and eternal, which brings with it eternal benefits (2 Cor. 4:18).

While we are still on earth, we will still struggle with sinful thoughts and desires, but if the Holy Spirit has renewed your mind, then you will never again have a mind that is debased!

So should Christians jettison the term *mental health* in this case? I think so. Let me explain.

The Problem with *Mental Health*

I have been thinking on this for some time. Originally, I thought the term *mental health* was actually another way of saying "soul health." To my own chagrin, I have taught it as such at conferences.[15] While I don't believe this to be a gross error, the reality is that the term *health* is quite ambiguous. Then, during one writing project, my university's president, Dr. Abner Chou, asked me, *How are you defining "health"?*[16]

To use medical and hygienic terminology for the immaterial mind will always cause confusion. The term *mental health* suggests a lack of clarity regarding the immaterial nature of the mind. For instance, if I were to say to you, "That person really seems to have some mental health struggles," that should raise a couple of questions: Are those "struggles" issues of the mind, or medical issues with their brain? Is the person battling anxious thoughts rooted in a low view of God, or are they detached from reality and have been diagnosed with schizophrenia?

If someone does use this phrase, I don't recommend being theologically nitpicky. Many times in class I will joke with my theology students that we can become Mr. or Mrs. Exact and thus annoy everyone one around us. (Insert throat-clearing sound.) "Excuse me, but the church is not the building, it's the people . . . Excuse me, but the translation of Scripture is a *copy of the Bible*, not the original manuscripts. Excuse me, the mind is immaterial, not material." Have your own theological clarity, but don't become Mr. or Mrs. Exact who requires others to phrase things with precision for the sake of absolute theological clarity. We don't want to be unnecessarily abrasive by always feeling compelled to critique someone else's choice of words.

Yet, when you speak about the idea of a person's mind being well, I would encourage you to try to find the most accurate biblical terminology for their specific struggle. It will help clarify what we are *truly* talking about. *Mental health* is too loaded with ideological baggage and imprecision.

For a Christian, using the term mental health *is unhelpful at best.*

So instead, simply say "mind renewal," or even just bring up the idea of sanctification. And when someone else uses the term *mental health*, here are some things to keep in mind:

- Clarify what they mean by *mental health* if it seems they are legitimizing sinful actions. For instance, "I'm sorry for yelling at you . . . I haven't been taking care of my mental health."
- Clarify what they mean by *mental health* when mental health is actually taking the place of sanctification, or the means of sanctification (also referred to as the "means of grace"). If a person says, "I need some time away to really focus on my mental health," then you should seek to guide them back to the Bible and their need for renewing their mind and drawing near to God (Mark 1:35; Luke 6:12; James 4:1–10).
- Clarify if they are offering "unstable mental health" as a reason for poor performance. "I'm not in a healthy place mentally" warrants clarification for the Christian. Does that mean that they are feeling overwhelmed? Grieving a death? Wrestling with a besetting sin that has them discouraged? Or are they saying they have a physiological issue (such as a diagnosed hormonal or brain issue) that makes it more difficult to "feel normal" or put on the mind of Christ?

Here is the principle before we become too nitpicky: *if the phrase is justifying perpetual unfaithfulness, we are going to critique it*. But other than that, we should not be overly critical of others' terminology. We want to err on the side of believing the best (1 Cor. 13:7) and also be people who have understanding (Prov. 14:29). However, we don't want to be complicit in perpetuating error. I personally will not use the term *mental health* but rather say "so-called mental health."

In one counseling session with a married couple, the wife was obviously in a very bad place. She was losing hair, not eating, and an insomniac. She would zone out during conversations, and never completed the homework I assigned her.

We met for a few sessions via Zoom, but I told her husband that she wasn't doing the things I asked, and that he should try to find another biblical counselor who was local, a counselor who could work as part of a team to help this poor woman. She needed to rest and sleep well. To eat something of substance.

If we are going to meet, then sleeping, eating, and regulating your schedule are essential. She had antidepressants prescribed, and I encouraged her to use those until she could get out of this black hole of insomnia, being zoned out, and losing weight. I told the husband that she wasn't "counselable" until she started to steward the rest of her outer man. It is almost impossible to counsel someone who is an insomniac, on drugs, spaced-out, fatigued, and/or emaciated. She needed a local counselor, a female preferably, who could meet with her in person to encourage her to work on these things. She needed a local church to come around her. I couldn't be a great help in a long-distance Zoom counseling. A person needs to learn how to be a good steward of their outer person, ensuring that their outer person is being cared for to the best of their ability.

So-called mental health strategies often take commonsense aspects of stewardship of the outer person and call them "self-care." According to the National Institute of Mental Health, "Self-care can play a role in maintaining your mental health and help support your treatment and recovery if you have a mental illness."[17] Another federal agency says, "Practice good self-care. Reach out to family and friends. Develop coping skills. Get enough sleep."[18]

Here are the top recommendations for self-care from the NIMH:

- Get regular exercise.
- Eat healthy, regular meals and stay hydrated.
- Make sleep a priority.
- Try a relaxing activity.
- Set goals and priorities.
- Practice gratitude.
- Focus on positivity.
- Stay connected.[19]

Half of these recommendations are about the outer person and are directly oriented to your body. The other half are inner-person recommendations that will affect your mind. Outer-person stewardship is important but obviously won't change your mind.

The Christian is to use his body to glorify God (Rom. 12:1; 1 Cor. 6:19–20). That is the first aim of the physical body, not necessarily making your body last as long as it can. When you eat or drink, you do so to the glory of God (1 Cor. 10:31). Whatever sleep you receive, you receive as a gift from the Lord (Ps. 127:2). You learn how to work hard (Col. 3:23) but to also take a rest (Exod. 20:8). All of these are basic concepts on the stewardship of the outer person, and each should be guided through the lens of Scripture. The Bible doesn't mandate a certain hour amount for sleep but it does give you principles for rest (cf. Prov. 6:9–11).

Secular mental health culture has hijacked basic concepts for stewardship of the body and incorporated them into the idea of self-care. In reality, these are basic concepts for caring for one's outer man. Good stewardship of the outer man does not equate to being mentally well—a healthy body may be home to a mind that is hardened in its own corruption and needs renewal. You can be a superfit immoral person.

If someone goes on a vacation as part of self-care, to grow only in selfishness and materialism, their self-care isn't truly helping mind renewal. They might have practiced self-care in giving their body rest, but they likely didn't address the issues that have been plaguing their "mental health." Thus their mind is even further corrupted.

So yes, get help from the nutritionist, the sleep aid specialist, the general practitioner, but don't confuse that with what really comprises mental transformation. You cannot "self-care" your way into a renewed mind. You cannot sleep enough to finally renew your mind. Get help from your medical doctor with issues of the brain/body. But get help from your pastor/biblical counselor for your mind. Sure, there is a place for outer-man stewardship, but that has no renewal effect on the mind. The mind cannot be made new through a salad or a vacation or a nap—and I really enjoy two of those.[20]

How to Renew Your Mind: Put Off and Put On

"How do I practically renew my mind?" That's a common question I receive when teaching at The Master's University. Students will see the biblical need to renew their minds but lack the know-how it takes to do so—and I don't blame them. These are things that I learned throughout my education, and it takes effort to practice them.

The Bible provides practical steps for renewing your mind and "thinking like Jesus" (Phil. 2:5). One key principle, the *put off/put on* dynamic, is found in a few passages, the clearest of which is Ephesians 4:22–24:

> *To* put off *your old self, which belongs to your former*
> *manner of life and is corrupt through deceitful desires,*
> *and to* be renewed *in the spirit of your minds, and to*
> *put on the new self, created after the likeness of God in*
> *true righteousness and holiness. (Emphasis added)*

The first step to biblical change is to put off your old nature—the desires and thoughts that defined who you were before you were saved (Gal. 2:20). That "old you" died at the moment of salvation and no longer defines you, now that you are a new creation (2 Cor. 5:17). Previously you were in Adam but now, as a Christian, you are in Christ (Rom. 5:19). Even so, we each still wrestle with our flesh, and though we have been raised to new life in Christ, we still need to learn to walk with Him.

Practically speaking, you put off sinful actions and attitudes. In Ephesians 4:25 and following you see examples of this. Put off:

- falsehood (v. 25)
- sinful anger (v. 26)
- stealing (v. 28)
- corrupting talk (v. 29)
- anger, wrath, and bitterness (v. 31)

The Lord calls us to turn from these things, to repent of thoughts that are dishonoring to Him. Sometimes you just need to pray, "Lord, please forgive me of thinking this sinful thought." That's what it means to put it off.

But renewing your mind isn't just putting off. It requires putting on (Eph. 4:24). Start doing something else. In other words, "so now present your members as slaves to righteousness leading to sanctification" (Rom. 6:19). This is important to remember. If you are just saying "don't" without saying "do this instead," you will not repent or change.

With that in mind, the way to practically "put on" is illustrated in Ephesians 4. Above I said put off stealing, corrupt communication, and so forth. Consider the put-ons that correspond to the put-offs in Ephesians 4:

- speaking the truth (v. 25)
- righteous anger (v. 26)

- working hard (v. 28)
- edifying speech (v. 29)
- kindness (v. 32)
- tenderheartedness (v. 32)
- forgiveness (v. 32).

If you need to put off lying, what do you need to put on? Speaking the truth. After all, a person can become mute, and therefore unable to speak lies, but he still might be a liar at heart, dishonest in his motives.[21]

Take this a step further regarding renewal of your mind. What thought do you need to put off? According to the Bible it is those thoughts that don't honor Christ (2 Cor. 10:5) and aren't pure, lovely, truthful, honorable, just, praiseworthy, or excellent (Phil. 4:8). In fact, I list the qualities of Philippians 4:8 as a thought filter in my book on PTSD.[22] If you are thinking thoughts that are not true, put off those thoughts and put on thoughts that are true.

Here is an example of what this looks like in our thoughts:

Put Off	Put On
"I'm not good enough."	"My boast is in the righteousness of Christ, not my own.
"That person annoys me!"	"Lord, thank you for that person and allowing me to be in their life."
"If I took my life, would anyone miss me?"	"Lord, my life is yours and I trust you have a purpose for me."
"Do they think that I'm a failure?"	"Lord, I cannot control how people view me, I can only be faithful."
"Wow, they sure are good-looking."	"Lord, help me to have pure thoughts about so-and-so. Please bless them and help them to seek you."

It is of paramount importance to learn to put off and to put on—especially in your thoughts. Only you and the Lord know your thought life. However, notice one more aspect of Ephesians 4:22–24: Paul says *"be renewed* in the spirit of your minds." That "be renewed" is in the passive voice. We are acted upon as we put off sin and put on faithful, God-honoring actions. Who acts upon us to renew us? God. Technically, we do not renew our minds, it is God who renews our minds. We have a responsibility to "work out our salvation" (Phil. 2:12) and each of us is commanded to "train yourself for godliness" (1 Tim. 4:7). However, the work of renewal is really God's work. And how does He do that? He does that as we put off thoughts that are dishonoring to Him and put on thoughts that are honoring to Him.

Over time, our minds are renewed as we practice putting off and putting on. And the wonderful part is that you start to think the thoughts God would have you think. This is truly the mind of Christ: when you think, you see yourself and this world the way God does. Doesn't that sound like such a wonderful thing? It truly is. And secular therapy has no remedy even close to the renewed mind.

So, what do we do with mental health holidays? What of colleagues and friends who take R&R to work on their mental health? Some of us are in environments where others might question our hesitation to focus on so-called mental health. They might even say it's a sign of poor mental health!

I would say that if you are given "mental health" holidays, then take advantage of them, and see them as opportunities to serve the Lord, spend time with Him, and work on being renewed in the spirit of your mind (Eph. 4:23). Take a "mental health holiday" from your employer to go to the men's or women's retreat at your church. Understanding that what secular therapy calls mental health is really what the Bible calls "renewing of the mind," work toward the goal of the Holy Spirit renewing your mind through the application of the Bible. You already have the mind of Christ, as a Christian (1 Cor. 2:16), but you also still need to grow in thinking like Christ (Phil. 2:5). Use your "mental health" holidays to do that. Don't be distracted by "mental health" ideology.

Finally, consider this: that ideology is often providing methods of change without looking to the God who made us, or to His Word. It tries to change our lives and address the afflictions of our souls without any help from the only one who can truly transform and comfort us—the Holy Spirit (Tit. 3:5). No matter how much you practice "good mental health" to bring healing to your inner person, you will always fall short if you lack the renewed mind. And for your mind to be renewed, you need the Gospel's saving power, the deep soul work of sanctification, and the transforming work of Christ through the Holy Spirit.

Jesus *is* the answer to a mind that is darkened, calloused, fleshly, futile, or without understanding. He alone can provide the truest form of mental wellness: transformation into His own likeness. That transformation comes through faith and trust in Jesus Christ and renewal of the mind through the Holy Spirit. Said another way, mental health awareness month is a counterfeit to the superiority of the gospel. Mental Health Awareness Month may provide symptomatic relief from certain aspects of an inner-person struggle, but it does not deal with the real issue. The mind needs renewal and transformation—not self-care.

Mental health ideology is misinformed or incomplete at best or an empty counterfeit to Christianity at worst, depending on the context. When we as Christians imbibe mental health culture and seek help from secular therapy, with its methods based on medicalized ideology, we will (and do) find that we are lacking any genuine change, just like the millions of unbelievers currently seeking mental health treatment, only to be disappointed. Medicalized understandings and diagnoses of the inner person cannot compare to the work of Jesus Christ in a person's life. Would it not make sense to go to the One who created the mind for the restoration of the mind? It would indeed. As biblical counselor David Powlison wrote:

> The good news of Jesus refuses to be relegated to a religious
> sector of life. It is the explicit need of the psychologically

honest and the clear seeing. All other psychologies—
whether formulated into personality theories or merely lived
out in the workings of individual idiosyncrasy—traffic in
myth, lie, false consciousness, and perverse speculation.[23]

It's time for Christians to jettison mental
health ideology and embrace what
the Bible says about the mind.

PART III

Christian Living in a Therapeutic Culture

CHAPTER 8

Medications Cannot
Treat the Mind

> For the sake not just of the science but of all the suffering
> people whom the science should be serving, it is time for
> us all to learn and to tell better, more honest stories.
> —ANNE HARRINGTON, *MIND FIXERS*[1]

> I feel like I'm taking crazy pills.
> —JACOBIM MUGATU, *ZOOLANDER*[2]

Tens of millions of Americans are taking antidepressants and antianx-iety medications.[3] The Citizens Commission on Human Rights International has estimated that as of 2020, 76 million people in the United States are taking psychotropics.[4] That is roughly one in four people, if you base those numbers on the 2020 Census.[5] The estimates published by the insurance journal have only gone up over the years.[6] Some even have children who have been prescribed psychotropic meds. I can think of multiple people in my life, dear friends, who have used or are currently on antidepressants. Perhaps your own family is affected by this.

Christians often disagree about the use of psychotropics. Some believe such medications are a sign of spiritual failure, or compromise. It's as if taking an antidepressant is a sign of giving up and allowing the secular culture to win. You might be surprised by how many Christians feel guilty about taking a legally prescribed psychotropic medication. It's no wonder, then, that I usually receive questions like: Is it okay to take psychotropic medications as a Christian? Is it a sin to take antidepressants? Do I recommend allowing minors to take ADHD medications?

One couple I counseled were missionaries overseas. The wife had been prescribed medication for depression, but she didn't take the medicine. However, she was anxious, losing weight, lacked appetite, and struggled with panic attacks. It consumed her. She would step into the next room when a panic attack happened, curl up into a ball, turn the lights out, and just cry.

Her children, whom she homeschooled, didn't know how to respond. Her husband was at a loss for how to help. And as I sought to unpack what was going on, I found that she didn't want to take the antidepressants because she was concerned they might make matters worse—and thus there was no change.

These were missionaries. They had been through a thorough biblical education and had extraordinary life experience. Some people genuinely feel a great concern about taking psychotropics.

We'll come back to this couple later, but for now understand that this is one of the many perspectives that sincere Christians can have on psychotropics. Another potential position is an undiscerning dependence on psychotropics. This view doesn't differentiate between psychotropics and other types of prescribed medications. Rather, it holds that since medications are generally helpful, using any kind of medication, including psychotropics, is perfectly acceptable.

David Murray, a Christian counselor, writes,

> If assessing your feelings and thoughts (steps 2 and 3) does not work or you can't even get started, then I would suggest that you seek out trained medical personnel for diagnosis and possibly prescription of appropriate medication. And please do not wait until things have gotten so bad that you "crash" to a halt. The farther you fall, the longer it will take

to return. Even a low dose of anti-depressant is sometimes enough just to begin to restore depleted brain chemicals and pick up your mood sufficiently to enable you to begin to take the steps necessary to correct your lifestyle and thoughts. However, more serious depressions sometimes require medication for two to five years in order to permanently restore the brain's chemistry and processes.[7]

This position is sometimes mistaken, because it can fall into the secular confusion of trying to address the *mind* by fixing the *brain*. If you are a Christian in this camp, like David Murray, I would encourage you to consider what psychotropics are *actually* doing, as we'll explore shortly.

Regardless of your convictions on psychotropics, we need to think through the role of medication in light of what the Bible says about the mind.

In sum, psychotropic medications cannot treat the mind, only the brain.

In her 2019 book, *Mind Fixers*, Harvard professor Anne Harrington, who is not a Christian, takes "a deep dive into our long effort to understand the biological basis of mental illness and above all why it has been so troubled."[8] In other words, it is a history of the different theories that leading therapists and researchers have used to try to understand what we today call mental illness.

Harrington's assessment is that Freudian psychoanalysis morphed into "biological psychiatry." Psychoanalysis was an early approach to therapy, but it would eventually be replaced by empirical science and "research psychiatrists."[9] In other words, the field of psychiatry was advanced under the banner of empirical research and science, specifically neuroscience. Psychiatrists were the new up-and-comers who would bring psychoanalysis out of the dark ages and find the significant medical support for the biological reasons behind mental illness (inevitably, this sounds like a broken promise).

She also writes that the 1980s in North America were a turning point in therapy moving toward biological psychiatry, because there was supposedly "irrefutable evidence that mental disorders were brain diseases," which in turn emboldened new psychiatrists to bring back the brain as the "primary object" of research.[10]

The only problem, as Harrington states it, is that the research was "wrong—not just slightly wrong but wrong in every particular."[11]

Freud had taught that there were inner psyche problems with a person, and this was the primary motivational component behind why we do what we do. But by the 1980s, a shift began to place an emphasis on the body and the brain, and this influences how we understand mental health today. In 2013, Dr. Thomas Insel, then director of the National Institute of Mental Health, said:

> What I've been talking to you about so far is mental disorders, diseases of the mind. That's actually becoming a rather unpopular term these days, and people feel that, for whatever reason, it's politically better to use the term "behavioral disorders" and to talk about these as disorders of behavior. Fair enough. They are disorders of behavior, and they are disorders of the mind. But what I want to suggest to you is that both of those terms, which have been in play for a century or more, are actually now impediments to progress, that what we need conceptually to make progress here is to *rethink these disorders as brain disorders.*[12] (Emphasis added)

As Insel demonstrates, there has no doubt been a renewed emphasis on the biological triggers for so-called mental illnesses. But to Harrington's point none have been found.

Yet the biological emphasis remains.

Since the brain became the primary focus for understanding so-called mental illnesses, fixing the brain became the primary goal of psychiatrists. As Dr. Daniel Amen has said, "Once people understand that the brain controls everything they do and everything they are, they want a better brain so they can have a better life."[13]

So, psychiatry has searched for biological reasons for so-called mental illness. And what has become the standard way of fixing the brain for psychiatrists? Psychotropics.

The most common psychotropic medications are antidepressants, mood stabilizers, antianxieties, antipsychotics, and stimulants. Do you want to guess why they are prescribed? Depression, ADD/ADHD, and anxiety are the top reasons for receiving a psychotropic.[14]

It really has been quite the evolution, from the immaterial psycho-dynamic to the biological determinism of our era. Not to mention the billion dollars a year that these medications are bringing in for their manufacturers.

Follow the logic here: You meet with a psychiatrist who asks you questions, maybe gives you some screening questionnaires before meeting with you. After asking questions, the psychiatrist then offers a medication—or combination of medications. In most instances, the psychiatrist never takes your blood, never takes a CT scan of your brain, and never tests you for vitamin deficiencies. The psychiatrist has no clue how your thyroid is doing. Rather, they verbally assess you based on arbitrary symptoms and then offer a medication recommendation for you. I'm not exaggerating when I say this is exactly what you can expect. How did we get here? Let me explain.

Medicalizing the Mind

Although they are considered medical doctors, psychiatrists are often seen by other medical doctors as practicing something more along the lines of pseudoscience. After speaking at a conference, an ER doctor came up to me and said, "Dr. Gifford, I've been saying these things for years." Even Daniel Amen said, "All other medical professionals look directly at the organs they treat, but psychiatrists are taught to assume what the underlying biological mechanisms are for illnesses—such as depression, ADD/ADHD, bipolar disorder, and addiction—without ever looking at the brain."[15] This is quite the assumption, isn't it?

In 2019, three researchers in the United Kingdom published an article in *Psychiatry Research* that said the current system for diagnosing and labeling mental illnesses is "a disingenuous categorical system."[16]

In a University of Liverpool press release about the study, Dr. Kate Allsopp, who led the research team, said, "Although diagnostic labels create the illusion of an explanation they are scientifically meaningless and can create stigma and prejudice."[17] One of the other authors of the study, Dr. John Read of the University of East London, said, "Perhaps it is time we stopped pretending that medical-sounding labels contribute anything to our understanding of the complex causes of human distress or of what kind of help we need when distressed."[18]

Psychiatrists, who by definition are focused on mental, emotional, and behavioral disorders and have legal authority to prescribe medication,[19] have used medical terminology for describing and attempting to treat the immaterial. To nobody's surprise, it has not worked.

It would be more accurate to say that what the psychiatrist is doing is seeing the effects of the mind on emotions and behavior and then seeking to prescribe medications to address those downstream effects. It's much like treating a headache. Why do you have a headache? Not sure, but here is some Tylenol.

For instance, if a person is entertaining dark thoughts about death, that is a mind issue. And if they are prescribed antidepressants, it might affect their brain, but the brain is not *why* they were thinking dark thoughts that lead to depression. No, the depression is a symptom. The dark thoughts of the mind are the true cause.

To be candid, thinking about really sad, dark things could incline almost all of us to be depressed. So, if a psychiatrist prescribes antidepressants because of those dark thoughts, they are treating the symptom, not the cause, of the problem. That will *always* be true because the mind is the source of cognition, not the brain. (If you missed this in early chapters, be sure to go back to review.)

We must remember that the brain does not cause disordered desires. Yet, as already discussed, the brain can be affected by the mind. If the mind is truly the source of these operations, then we must acknowledge that medications will not change the mind, only the way the mind expresses itself. Can a person take medication that seems to slow their thoughts down, as in the case of ADHD and taking a stimulant? Yes, because the medication is affecting the brain, not the mind. Can a person take an antidepressant to help with mood regulation? Yes, because the medication is affecting the brain, not the mind.

This brings us to the role of the psychotropic medication.

One medical textbook defines psychotropics as "medications that affect the mind, emotions, and behavior."[20] The word is really an umbrella term for various types of drugs, as demonstrated in this definition: "A psychotropic describes any drug that affects behavior, mood, thoughts, or perception. This can include medications for anxiety and depression as well as antipsychotics, among others."[21]

Psychotropics are the most common way to refer to the medications that are prescribed for so-called mental illnesses. The basic thought behind them is that they affect the neurotransmitters of a person's brain. You've heard of dopamine, norepinephrine, and serotonin, all of which are neurotransmitters. Psychotropic medications are thought to affect these chemicals and thus affect so-called mental illnesses. Healthline says that psychotropics "work by adjusting levels of brain chemicals."[22]

Well, it should be made clear that psychotropics *supposedly* work by adjusting levels of brain chemicals, but one problem is that when a psychiatrist assigns them, they have typically done no work to measure the chemicals of a patient's brain.[23] It is believed that psychotropics are treating a known medical issue, but that claim is hotly debated. Even secular researchers cannot agree on what a psychotropic is treating.

Robert Whitaker, author of the 2010 book *Anatomy of an Epidemic*, is one such researcher. He says that "the hypothesis—that the drugs balanced abnormal brain chemistry—never panned out. Although the public may still be told that the drugs normalize brain chemistry, the truth is that researchers did not find that people with schizophrenia had overactive dopamine systems (prior to being medicated), or that those diagnosed with depression suffered from abnormally low levels of serotonin or norepinephrine."[24] In 2022, Dr. Jonathan Raskin of the State University of New York told the *Daily Mail*, "many medics continued to prescribe the medication [antidepressants], even while they were unsure if they were effective, because it was 'easier' than offering more time-intensive care."[25]

Psychotropics are assigned based on symptoms, not empirically verifiable criteria. The logic goes something like this:

1. So-called mental illnesses are medical issues that are related to chemicals in the brain.
2. The psychotropic medication affects the chemicals of the brain.
3. Therefore, the psychotropic is treating so-called mental illnesses.

Yet, by this point, you should already be skeptical about the first two assumptions. If the mind is immaterial, we know the psychotropic isn't treating the mind. Strike one. The psychotropic may affect the chemicals of the brain, but those are not what is causing so-called mental illnesses in the first place. Strike two.

In this way, the psychotropic is not actually treating the root of the issue in so-called mental illness. Rather, the psychotropic is treating chemicals in the brain. *Three strikes; you're out!*

Simply put, psychotropic medications are for symptom relief. So, for example, the psychotropic does not remove anxiety, if we are talking about anxiety in the biblical understanding of the word (cf. Matt. 6:25). Rather, the psychotropic alleviates the symptoms of (or the *feelings* of) anxiety. You cannot take a pill that will convince you to entrust your circumstances to God. That is a matter of your faith (Matt. 6:30). Symptoms of anxiety might include, however, increased heart rate, racing thoughts, hyperventilation, sweating, feeling nervous or restless, or some combination of these. When you take a psychotropic, you may be able to alleviate these symptoms, but you are not taking it to actually change your thought processes, which is what anxiety is. To put it another way:

Psychotropics cannot renew your mind.

Symptom relief is not inherently bad, to be sure. It would be odd if we wanted *worsening* symptoms, right? "C'mon, Doctor, bring the pain . . . let me have it until my heart rate is 190!" But there are two principles that can help guide you through the use of psychotropics.

1. Obtain Psychotropics Legally
It should go without saying that if you're obtaining psychotropics through some illegal source, you are breaking broader laws and therefore violating Romans 13:1–2. If you were not prescribed the medication, then you should not use it. In some states, taking prescriptions are illegal if they are not yours. Even if you have really poor health coverage, or no health coverage, I would encourage you to draw a line in the sand of not taking meds that were not prescribed to you. This

eliminates all of the black-market forms of psychotropics that are circulating, because as Christians we should want to submit to governing authorities (1 Pet. 2:13–15).

2. Maintain God-Honoring Motivations While Taking Them

One of the pitfalls of secular therapy is that it often prizes self-esteem, happiness, and *feeling* better as a key standard of success, rather than obedience to Scripture.[26] One of the theories underlying much of modern psychology is Abraham Maslow's hierarchy of needs.[27] This theory ranks various needs that Maslow believed we all must fulfill, and at the top of that list are self-esteem and self-actualization. According to this framework, the highest level we should reach for is not to glorify God, keep His commandments, and enjoy Him forever, but rather to reach our "full potential" and have a strong sense of self-worth.[28]

But even without a psychologized mindset, it's easy for us to believe that the goal of life is to be happy and as comfortable as possible. And while feeling good is not something the Bible says is inherently bad—we're not commanded to be self-flagellating or to pursue discomfort for the sake of discomfort—it's not our ultimate goal as Christians.

So when it comes to taking psychotropics, it is possible to make symptom relief the ultimate goal, and this would be idolatrous. If you place your hope in a pill as the only means of making it possible for you to continue to live and function, your hope and faith is in something other than God. However, when we trust in anything other than God as our ultimate hope—to include medication—that thing has become our true god (Isa. 44:6). In this way, our motivation to use the medication can be sinful if we let the medication be our ultimate hope.

Next, if we make excuses for sinful behavior because we are taking (or not taking) medication, then we have set the medication up on the pedestal of idolatry, ascribing to it power over us that it does not have. If we legitimize anger, anxiety, self-harm, or the thoughts associated with such things, and then say that it is a medication issue, we are shifting responsibility away from ourselves. "I'm sorry, I didn't take my meds" is a mentality that excuses sinful behavior and disbelieves the Bible's promise that Christians are not slaves to sin (Rom. 6:6).

Yes, while not on medications you might have an inclination to anger, but at the moment you give in to that unrighteous anger, you are sinning (Eph. 4:26, 31). And you don't have to sin, as a Christian. You are no longer a slave to sin, and our body cannot make you sin. What a dangerous mentality to have when we think we cannot help but to sin because of our body! The Bible says the opposite: yes, your body can encourage sinful responses from your mind, but you never *have to* give in to sin (1 Cor. 10:13; 2 Pet. 2:9).

What does it look like to maintain God-honoring motivations while taking psychotropics? It means remembering that psychotropics are not our savior. Jesus is our Savior. I can respond in a way that honors Christ without my meds because God, the Holy Spirit, indwells me as a Christian (1 Cor. 6:19). Because of His indwelling power, I can be Spirit-filled and not gratify the desires of the flesh (Gal. 5:16). While the medications might help me be obedient to Christ, in the same way that consistently good sleep can, the medication does not cause me to obey or disobey.

The operative word in the above principle is *can*, meaning it is possible that psychotropics have benefits, but that does not necessarily mean I should take them. *Should* implies necessity. *Should* implies that without the medication, I am at a deficit or am handicapped in some way. The reality is that when a Christian has Christ, Christ is enough. "Not that we are sufficient in ourselves to claim anything as coming from us, but our sufficiency is from God" (2 Cor. 3:5). This is the point, and the concern of many: if we say that we need medications to be able to respond in a way that honors God, then what of the promises of our sufficiency in Jesus? Or what of the sufficiency of the Scripture? This is why we must use the word *can*: because we don't ultimately *need* psychotropic medications to honor the Lord, or function in daily life.

I am often asked in counseling whether I support the use of psychotropic medications. You might be able to guess the answer, but let me say it plainly: *No psychotropic will ever cure the issues of your immaterial mind.*

As an analogy, imagine that you had severe dental pain. Your jaw was throbbing to the point of headaches. Even breathing brought severe pain. If you were in this situation, Tylenol would not be *the* answer, or *the* cure to your problem. But Tylenol would help you get to a point where you could deal with your problem, which is most likely some infection in your tooth (I'm speaking from my own dental woes).

Similarly, a psychotropic is not going to fix a problem in your mind. It simply won't. However, the psychotropic will potentially alleviate symptoms so that you can focus on the deeper issues of your mind. So, it is possible to use the psychotropic to help focus on the true problem, which is the mind, then wean off the psychotropic medication (assuming you are not taking them for true brain or neurological conditions).

Consider one example in the Bible where we see the recommendation of medication for physical issues. For one, Paul told Timothy to "use a little wine for the sake of your stomach and your frequent ailments" (1 Tim. 5:23). Due to the potability of the water and whatever gastrointestinal issue Timothy was facing, Paul recommended a little wine. The toxicity of this wine would be very different from modern wine, but Paul nevertheless encouraged Timothy to use wine for medicinal purposes.[29]

It bears emphasis: I said *physical* issues. While false teachers, especially from the prosperity gospel movement, often teach that Christians who seek medical treatment don't have enough faith, that idea is nowhere found in the Bible. Christians should support good medicine, and historically they have been among the greatest contributors to its development. When we actually have a physiological problem, we should feel completely fine receiving medical treatment for those problems of the body.

Here is biblically where you need to be discerning: psychotropics can affect the chemicals in the brain, but chemicals in the brain are often not the issue. *Psychiatric Times* admits that "[s]cientifically speaking, there never was a network of validated hypotheses capable of sustaining a full-blown, global chemical imbalance theory of mental illness."[30]

So, it is not a sin to take psychotropics, but psychotropics are not treating the real issue. They are like Tylenol, a symptom relief that sometimes can even mask the real issue. That leads me to one more biblical consideration for Christians who are considering using psychotropics.

If you were to meet with a man who was considering using antidepressants because he had lost interest in daily activities and was losing weight, not sleeping, and struggling with motivation, antidepressants would seem like a pretty normal treatment. But as you spoke with him, you found out he was secretly engaging in sexual sin: pornography. He feels hypocritical, fake, and condemned. He believes he's unable to approach God, but he also isn't finding any other balm for his guilty, fearful conscience.

Proverbs 28:13 says, "Whoever conceals his transgressions will not prosper." Well, you cannot expect a person to feel well while hiding personal sin. Insomnia, depressed mood, loss of interest in daily activities, and weight loss can all result from harboring secret sin in your life. David said, "For when I kept silent, my bones wasted away through my groaning all day long. For day and night your hand was heavy upon me; my strength was dried up as by the heat of summer" (Ps. 32:3–4).

What would antidepressants do for such a man? They would mask the symptoms of the real problem of unrepentant sin.

Am I saying all depression comes from sin? No. *Some* depression comes from personal sin, and that means that in such instances, taking antidepressants doesn't treat the real issue.

One such case in my own counseling was a man who was being unfaithful to his wife. Neither his wife nor I knew it at the time, but they came to me for counseling because their marriage wasn't doing well. He said that he was depressed and had actually been prescribed antidepressants. She was willing to work on the marriage but he just kept saying, "I'm not in love with you anymore."

Even after months of counseling, and using his antidepressants, there was no change—that is, until we found out he was still cheating on his wife. A friend of the wife caught him visiting his mistress and told the wife about it.

Why did his feelings of depression not go away? Hmm. Let me guess. After this he repented of this sinful relationship and saw God begin to restore his marriage in beautiful ways. His wife was a trouper during this season of their relationship but it underscores how the medications weren't going to address the real issues.

By the way, in this situation, they wouldn't have helped the wife either. Hearing your husband say "I'm not in love with you anymore" would definitely cause you to feel depressed, but taking an antidepressant to feel better wouldn't help you with the source of that depression.

In this context, antidepressants are like Tylenol, masking the symptoms when a person needs deeper help with their mind. They need help with repentance, which is a change of mind.

What if the person is an unbeliever? This is important because an unbeliever is starting from a very different worldview. Should we just give medications to those who are, as Paul says, "natural people" (1 Cor. 2:14)?

The front lines of medicine do not often differentiate care for their patients based on whether they are Christians or non-Christians. But even though it is not necessarily a real-world situation, the question still warrants an answer. If you were a Christian medical doctor and told a person who was not a Christian that their problems were not physical but spiritual, that person would most likely still want the medications. If your worldview has no place for the immaterial mind, then you would more likely want a pill to fix your problem, or the symptom of the problem. That's the reality.

So, if someone does not want to focus on their mind and simply wants symptom relief, I'm not sure there is a choice except to graciously remind them that the psychotropic medications are not addressing the root of the issue, and then to give them the medication. Real change for the unbeliever starts at repentance from their sin and faith and trust in Jesus Christ to reconcile them to God and transform their mind (1 John 1:8–9). No psychotropic will renew their debased mind (Rom. 1:28). It will only affect chemicals in the brain, which are not the real issue.

Using Psychotropics for Apparent Nonsanctification Issues

While I was writing this book, I released an episode of the *Transformed* podcast titled "ADHD or Just Misunderstood?" Honestly, there were many good conversations that occurred through listeners writing in or listeners engaging me through social media. A few people wrote in with concerns, but none of them were biblically compelling. But one question that I received—and I've been asked this in the past when counseling—was "should a parent help their child get medication for ADHD?"

Now, to have a busy mind is not necessarily a sin. Neither is struggling to focus, or to find certain tasks more interesting than others. The question is more along the lines of "We know that Adderall isn't treating the root issue, but it does seem to help with focus. Should we let our kids take it?"

The first theological answer—not to be nitpicky—is that all issues are a matter of sanctification, even ones that are seemingly benign, like that of focus and sitting still. If we are to exercise self-control and do all things to the glory of God (1 Cor. 10:31), then focusing and sitting in a chair are "from him, through him, and to him" (Rom. 11:36). In this way, being distracted is not a sin, but why should a student want to sit in their chair and focus on their schoolwork *ultimately*? Not ultimately for a good grade, but because they want to glorify God.

Most of the time, Adderall and Ritalin are prescribed on an as-needed basis. So, if the medication is seemingly helping a student focus, then there are no biblical prohibitions preventing them from using it for a season, and that means that we have Christian liberty to use it if it is helping.

But remember, Adderall is affecting your body in some way that seems to be *helping* your focus. It's making it *easier*, not ultimately empowering you to obey God, or preventing you from doing so. So, you don't *need* Adderall to focus; it helps you to focus *more easily*. Adderall is seemingly helpful. If your child can use it without becoming dependent on it, then I would say that it is permissible for a time. Treat it like many people treat coffee at work. It helps them focus and allows them to get their work done, but unless they were up all night, they should not *need* coffee to be a good worker.

However, if your child has an attitude of "I need my meds to do my schoolwork," then I would say that the better part of wisdom is to rely more on all the other ways that you can set up your child for success, like tutors, different study strategies and habits, or accommodations at school. Don't feed the mentality that you "need" your meds when in fact there is no proof that you do need them, because that idea is insidious. Dr. Gary Wenk wrote in *Psychology Today*, "Psychiatric drug development programs have demoralizingly low success rates," and that placebos seem to be just as effective.[31] If a student begins to think of themselves as "needing" medications in order to do certain things, they are thinking about these medications wrong. They may do better in one environment or circumstance over another, but that does not mean that they "need" it.

When It's Time to Wean off Psychotropics

What is a helpful metric for knowing when a person has become overly dependent on psychotropics or should do their best to wean off with medical supervision? Well, we know that a person is too keen on psychotropics when they are being unfaithful to what God has entrusted to them in other areas of life. Easy examples of this are work. If a person is incapacitated from working because they have been zombified by their antidepressant, then they know that their antidepressant is discouraging faithfulness. Every person is called to work with their own hands and provide for themselves (2 Thess. 3:12). If your psychotropics are encouraging you to be unfaithful to your responsibilities as a mom, dad, worker, church member, boss, husband, wife, or some other responsibility, then you should consider weaning off of them under medical supervision. This could be because you feel "out of it" or neither high nor low, just a shell of who you were. People have told me they hate the way their antidepressant makes them feel tired all the time and clouds their thinking. Sometimes we lose a loved one to psychotropics, as they become sleepy versions of themselves.

Another consideration would be age. All of us should be highly cautious about having our children (under eighteen) take psychotropics for a long, ongoing time. We want our children to learn to depend on the Bible, the work of the Holy Spirit, and the church to grow in difficult seasons, not their medication. If your kids have a medication, they must see that Jesus is their Savior and the One on whom they should depend. They cannot slip into functional naturalism, where they see their anxiety as a medication problem only. If your teenage daughter uses antianxiety medications for a time, help her to work on renewing her mind while doing so. Otherwise her anxieties will not be removed by the meds. This way she is focusing on her mind and the meds are helping alleviate symptoms of her anxiety. That's the right way to think about psychotropics. When a child who was active and bright now has lost interest in what they formerly loved, their food intake has changed greatly, they are sleeping 24/7, or not sleeping like they should, these are often a sign of the medication hurting, not helping.

Furthermore, we don't want our children to become accustomed to the way that the psychotropic is affecting their brain, especially when there is little emphasis on helping them with their mind. And those who have been diagnosed with anxiety or depression need to use the medications under medical supervision, with the goal of weaning off of them when their mind has been renewed. We don't want our teenagers becoming dependent on antidepressants or antianxiety medications. In many counseling cases, I find that once you address the underlying issue you no longer feel compelled to take the meds. Won't that bless them going forward?

One last principle for knowing when psychotropics are being unhelpful is when a person only takes their psychotropic medications but is unwilling to focus on the mind. This is true in many instances where the antidepressant is *the* hope and *the* only practical steps a person is taking toward change. In these cases, a person is not using the psychotropic for what it is biblically intended. Instead, this type of person should recognize that their psychotropic isn't doing what they thought it would. So they spend the money for the medication month after month when they should be spending that same time meeting with a godly pastor or certified biblical counselor to focus on their mind. If you only take the medication and don't work on your mind, it is time to reevaluate your use of the medication.

One last disclaimer: *going off psychotropics cold turkey is an absolutely dangerous and horrible idea*. Out of guilt, some feel a compulsion to work through their problems without any help of a psychotropic. Other times, people are taking their antidepressant, feel fine, and then quit without easing off or seeking advice from a doctor because they don't think they need these anymore. In either case, you can really hurt yourself and send yourself into a tailspin for weeks. If you are thinking that it is time to wean off, then do so under the proper oversight of your general practitioner. Don't let the confidence that you are ready to wean off cause you to do so in a way that will create more problems!

Hope for the Missionary Couple

The missionary couple whom I mentioned at the beginning of the chapter did not end up taking the antidepressants, to my knowledge. The wife worked through what was happening in her inner person, lessening some of the expectations of herself, and reorienting a vision of what God expects of her during counseling together, and being refreshed in the Word. God did bring about mind change through the power of His Word.

I've seen this happen over and over again in counseling. Often a person starts by being prescribed medication, yet there is no evidence of a medical issue, and then they address the issues of the mind. After that step there is less of a desire for psychotropics because the symptoms (anxiety, depression, etc.) are much less.

Does this mean I am a healer? Absolutely not. The point is that when there is no known medical issue, which your general practitioner can *and should* confirm, then you should focus on what's happening in your mind. In fact, I never told the missionary wife to take antidepressants or to not take them. I try to help my counselees think biblically about the role of medication, as we've done in this chapter, and encourage them to make a biblically informed decision.

You will find that when you've received a clean bill of health from a medical doctor, your focus should be on unpacking what's happening in your mind. And if you address what's happening in your mind, then the seeming need for psychotropics often goes away. You will find that the Bible has better answers for issues of the mind than secular therapy ever has or ever will.

CHAPTER 9

There's No Better Treatment Than the Truth

Anxiety in a man's heart weighs him down,
but a good word makes him glad.

—PROVERBS 12:25

I have this annoying lemon tree in my backyard. No matter what I've done, I cannot seem to get it to actually produce lemons. I've researched, fertilized, trimmed, and watered it; prayed over it and used bug repellant; and tried just about every remedy on earth for the past three years. *Yet it doesn't produce lemons*. Even my friends in Bible study poke fun at my lemonless tree. It truly is sad.

Not everyone's a tree expert, but anyone can tell that there is a problem. Maybe it's a lack of nutrients in the dirt, the amount of water the tree is getting, the sunlight ratio, or something else. So, imagine how silly it would be if I went to the local grocery store, bought twenty new lemons, and attached them to my tree. This would obviously be effective for a few days, but the fruit would still go bad.[1]

This is fruit-swapping. It's avoiding the root issue.

It is common for therapists today to recommend nonphysical treatments for helping the mind. Things like CBT, yoga, mindfulness, new friendships, vacations, and self-care are all enveloped in this vortex of care for the mind. But pause and ask yourself this: When a person's mind is depraved, darkened, futile, and corrupt, what will yoga do for it? Yoga and CBT may seem innocuous, but they are not grounded in the truth of the Bible. You can recommend breathing techniques, for sure, but that doesn't address the mind's need to be made alive. Sure, you can articulate "achievable goals" with a cognitive behavioral therapist, but you cannot plan your way to greater sanctification.

Divorced from the truth of the Bible, secular therapeutic treatments for the mind will never be enough because they cannot transform a corrupt mind or provide renewal for a saved mind.

In this chapter, I want to show you why some of the nonpsychotropic treatments and strategies for mental health are counterfeits, sometimes even completely contradictory to biblical care for the mind. The secular therapist is perhaps a well-meaning fruit swapper, but a fruit swapper nevertheless.

Cognitive Behavioral Therapy: What It Is and Who Recommends It

I met with a psychiatrist when researching for this book. At the end of our meeting, she diagnosed me with mild depression and offered psychotropics or cognitive behavioral therapy (CBT). The choice was mine.

I wanted to know more about CBT, so I asked her what the goal of CBT was. She replied that the therapist would help me set *achievable* goals.

"*If* I wanted to become a murderer, does the therapist help me reach that goal or would they say that is wrong?" I asked.

The psychiatrist smiled and said that the therapist doesn't dictate what is right and wrong, but helps you focus on what is achievable.

Technically, though, becoming a murderer is achievable. (Please note, I *don't* want to become a murderer. Don't call the cops!)

But that one question showed that this therapy has no objective moral standard. The CBT therapist will simply recommend and help you define your goals based on his or her subjective and, most likely, secular standards, which, needless to say, have changed dramatically in the past ten years.

CBT is considered the gold standard of counseling and therapy and is recommended by secular therapists in America today.[2] According to *Psychiatric Times*, CBT "is the most extensively researched and widely practiced form of psychotherapy in the world."[3] If you have never experienced it, CBT is what you most likely think of when you think of therapy or counseling: a person in an office, meeting with a professional therapist or counselor for an hour. Here's the American Psychological Association's definition of cognitive behavioral therapy:

> Treatment [that] usually involves efforts to change thinking patterns. These strategies might include:
>
> - Learning to recognize one's distortions in thinking that are creating problems, and then to reevaluate them in light of reality
> - Gaining a better understanding of the behavior and motivation of others
> - Using problem-solving skills to cope with difficult situations
> - Learning to develop a greater sense of confidence in one's own abilities[4]

The American Psychological Association goes on to say:

> CBT treatment also usually involves efforts to change behavioral patterns. These strategies might include:

- Facing one's fears instead of avoiding them
- Using role playing to prepare for potentially problematic inter-actions with others
- Learning to calm one's mind and relax one's body[5]

Essentially, CBT is talk therapy. The therapist will ask questions, guide you with teaching about life skills, and even give you practical things to do between counseling sessions as homework.

One of the blessings of my life is the opportunity I had to work at a biblical counseling center in Charleston, South Carolina, where I met with people for counseling as my full-time job. I enjoyed it greatly. When I was there, people would call and ask, "What type of counseling do you guys do?" I would respond, "We believe the Bible is God's Word and use it to counsel from." More times than I can remember, people would then say, "Oh, so like cognitive behavioral therapy."

The goal for CBT therapists is to "recognize and change false and distressing beliefs."[6] The issue with that is, Who gets to define what beliefs are false, or distressing? CBT therapists are always working under a worldview. For instance, if you are meeting with someone trained in humanistic psychology, the therapist will not tell you what is right and wrong, but rather will guide you to a conclusion that makes sense to them and corresponds to the latest theories in psychology.[7] If you are looking for moral judgments and direction, or absolute truth, you will be disappointed with many of these therapists.

Other therapists, meanwhile, will inevitably offer moral judgments, with their own definitions of what is "false" and/or "distressing," but if their judgments and counsel are not grounded in the Bible, then is it really helpful in the first place?

In this way, the CBT therapist is a secular pastor. Without an authoritative source of truth, each therapist is subject to counsel by their own schooling and by their own personal worldview. What do you think a CBT therapist is going to share with you? Truths from the Bible? Most likely not. As a Christian, you are going to a secular pastor to get help with your mind when the secular pastor is offering advice based on not only a different, but an opposing worldview! Why would a Christian go to an unbelieving therapist for help with worldview issues when the therapist also has his or her own?

The next issue with CBT is the way it sets goals. I have a friend who used to work in Los Angeles as a clinical psychologist. She is a Christian who learned about biblical counseling after she was already in her practice. She told me that she had to practice CBT with her clients but was only allowed to introduce "faith-based" counseling if that is what the client wanted.

I'll never forget a story she told about a non-Christian man she helped be free of symptoms of extreme anxiety. However, when his anxiety declined, he abandoned his wife and four-year-old son.

This man's anxiety had kept him dependent on his family, but once the anxiety was gone, he left them. His goal was to get rid of the symptoms of anxiety, and in a client-centered model like CBT the client's goals also become *the* goals of therapy. The CBT therapist cannot tell you they are unworthy goals. If a person sets awful goals in CBT, the therapist cannot rebuke them. "Don't leave your wife!" won't often come from the lips of a secular CBT therapist. Although it wasn't my friend's desire, or counsel, for this man to abandon his family, he did. Without absolute biblical moral clarity, CBT can help people achieve sinful goals. Having client-centered goals might sound noble, but it is awkwardly incongruent with the Bible. Focusing on the client's goals is not the same thing as a biblical goal.

Does God want you to be free from anxiety if you abandon your family? Does changing one sinful thought to another one really help? Does it really help to begin to have more positive thoughts about yourself when you are in a state of enmity with God?

Paul says in Romans 8:7, "For the mind that is set on the flesh is hostile to God, for it does not submit to God's law; indeed, it cannot."

It cannot. CBT cannot help the unsaved or unsanctified mind with its deepest needs. It will only perpetuate faulty thinking. There is undoubtedly an issue with thinking awful thoughts about yourself all day, but the answer is not to think more positively about yourself—especially if you are not reconciled and restored to God through Jesus Christ. Rather, you want to think about yourself the way God thinks about you (Rom. 12:3). If you think you're ugly, the solution is not to think you're pretty. Maybe you do genuinely lack the beauty that the Bible speaks of in 1 Peter 3:4: "but let your adorning be the hidden person of the heart with the imperishable beauty of a gentle and quiet spirit, which in God's sight is very precious." The answer is to put on God's thoughts about yourself.

"Wait!" you might object. "Isn't what you're recommending just the same thing as CBT, but with the Bible?" Well, CBT does correctly understand that our thinking affects our behavior, but it fails to point to the right object of meditation and thinking. Yes, CBT does address the inner person and the mind, but it doesn't truly understand the mind, or what a person should renew their mind with. So the only similarities between CBT and biblical counseling are superficial. They both involve talking, but the standards, goals, methods, and source of truth are all different.

"Yes, but CBT *does* help some people," you might say, to which I would agree. In fact, I didn't say it never helps. I said that, without a biblical worldview, CBT deals only with the symptoms. It's like a spiritual Band-Aid. A CBT therapist can make commonsense observations about why you should not stay up all night, but the secular CBT therapist cannot tell you the purpose of sleep in the first place. CBT therapists cannot tell you why you are anxious and the *true* remedy for anxiety. So, yes, a CBT therapist can provide fruit-swapping symptom relief, yet they will always (and I am cautious when I say "always") fall short of the Bible's superior remedies for our inner-man issues.

Yoga: Self-Care and Stretchy Pants

Remember Bessel van der Kolk? His book *The Body Keeps the Score* has a chapter on "Learning to Inhabit Your Body: Yoga," in which he writes, "Only making it safe for trauma victims to inhabit their bodies, and to tolerate feeling what they feel, and knowing what they know, can lead to lasting healing. This may involve a range of therapeutic interventions (one size never fits all), including various forms of trauma processing, neurofeedback, theater, meditation, play, and yoga."[8]

Secular therapy has increasingly seen yoga as a meaningful option for helping improve mental health. In 2021, Harvard Health published an article stating, "With its emphasis on breathing practices and meditation—both of which help calm and center the mind—it's hardly surprising that yoga also brings mental benefits, such as reduced anxiety and depression. What may be more surprising is that it actually makes your brain work better."[9]

Stretching and breathing are good for the mind? For a believer, they are stewardship of the outer person. I have no doubt that breathing in more oxygen is beneficial to the brain. However, stewardship of the outer person does not change the mind. What can a corrupt, defiled, darkened, or calloused mind stretch its way into? More corruption, darkness, or callousness.

If you grew up in the church, you're probably familiar with concerns that yoga is grounded in Eastern mysticism and thus has a level of spiritual danger. As Christians, we worship the living God and are not to participate in the practices of other religions. However, I know this isn't the case for every person who practices yoga. Regrettably, I experienced torture-by-yoga when I was in the Army. One morning while I was in Officer Candidate School a fellow classmate led us through about forty-five minutes of that suffering he called yoga. (It doesn't help that I am the least-stretchable person on the planet.)

When we did yoga that morning, I was stretching and trying to breathe in between holding very difficult positions. I wasn't engaged in Eastern mysticism. There was no grounding or chanting. I was simply stretching, breathing, trying to hold the positions, and dying slowly of pain. It does seem like some Christians approach yoga this way, simply as exercise (just as you might stretch to warm up or cool down at the gym).

Physical activity is helpful for the brain and body. No doubt learning to control breathing or becoming more flexible is a blessing. The older we get, the more we value staying mobile and as limber as is possible. But let's also be clear: Having a strong, healthy body will not promote renewal of the mind. You can help the body and not have a renewed mind. Many people are attending yoga classes all over the world today but have darkened minds.

Yoga for so-called mental health is more like exercise for your body that helps your body be healthier and less of a trial on your soul. The Bible talks about stewarding your body in things like physical exercise (1 Tim. 4:7), food (1 Cor. 10:31), sexual purity (1 Cor. 6:19), or sleep (Ps. 127:2–3). You should steward your outer man while recognizing that your mind is only influenced by your outer man, not determined. So, yes, be physically active, but recognize that no amount of exercise will bring mind transformation. Yoga can distract you from true mind renewal that comes through God's Word. Don't settle for less, and don't practice Eastern religion.

Eye Movement Desensitization and Reprocessing

Secular therapy also offers eye movement desensitization and reprocessing (EMDR) as a means of improving mental health. Van der Kolk again advocates for this in *The Body Keeps the Score* as a way of working through your past.[10] EMDR is a "structured therapy that encourages the patient to briefly focus on the trauma memory while simultaneously experiencing bilateral stimulation (typically eye movements), which is associated with a reduction in the vividness and emotion associated with the trauma memories."[11]

In other words, you talk about the traumatic event while a therapist has you stare at their moving fingers, experience some form of bilateral tapping, or look at bilateral lights. The thought is that EMDR helps because the "bilateral stimulation" of your eyes will help you experience traumatic memory less emotionally. It is regularly prescribed for those with PTSD, since trauma is obviously the trigger for PTSD. According to the EMDR Institute, "EMDR therapy shows that the mind can in fact heal from psychological trauma much as the body recovers from physical trauma."[12] Researchers theorize that the movement of your eyes can retrain your emotions and promote so-called psychological healing. You should google a session of EMDR, because it is quite fascinating.

Despite its speculative assumptions and effectiveness, EMDR fails to differentiate between the mind and the brain. (I know, you're probably shocked!)

The EMDR Institute says, "EMDR therapy demonstrates that a similar sequence of events occurs with *mental* processes. The *brain's* information processing system naturally moves toward mental health" (emphasis added).[13] Biblically, how do you renew your mind? Not through moving your eyes around or other physical movements, but through the truth of God's Word (Eph. 4:23). EMDR wants to lessen the "vividness and emotion associated with the trauma."[14] Again, as Christians, our goal is not to lessen the emotion per se, but to respond to the trauma in a God-honoring way. If I am suppressing the truth in unrighteousness, while lessening the negative emotions of trauma, is that desirable? What if God is using this traumatic event to draw me closer to Himself (cf. 1 Pet. 1:6)? Remember, the goal of the Christian is sanctification and greater Christlikeness (Rom. 8:29). In fact, God may be using these negative emotions to help me trust Him more, which is actually a success.

EMDR is also very deterministic. People are not robots where x + y = diminished vividness of traumatic memories. Don't you wish it were that easy! Behaviorism, as a school of psychological thought, believes that you can correct bad behavior through new behavior.[15] Your mind and brain are absolutely connected, but if you could retrain your mind through eye movements, why not rid yourself of impure thoughts? Or anxious thoughts? EMDR is reductionist in this way, as if you could program the immaterial mind.

EMDR won't promote the actual renewal of your mind. Recall that sanctification happens when the Holy Spirit sets you apart to greater holiness (Tit. 3:5). You may desensitize yourself to a traumatic memory, but that is not genuine mind renewal. You may lessen the negative emotions associated with the traumatic memory, but that doesn't mean you've learned to interpret what happened through the lens of Scripture. I find it odd to say that we are truly helping the mind if we are *only* alleviating negative emotions. Desensitizing your negative emotions may or may not actually address what is happening in your mind. Have you paused to ask if those negative emotions are right because of something we did wrong in our past? To say it another way: God wants us to feel poorly when we disobey Him (Ps. 32:4). If you want to rid yourself of negative emotions of conviction due to sin (and not all negative emotions stem from sin), then you are really masking the root problem. Like other therapeutic practices, EMDR is reductionistic fruit-swapping.

Mindfulness/Eastern Meditation

One last secular mental health strategy that's popular today is practicing mindfulness. Yes, mindfulness. It started from Eastern mysticism, including Buddhist practice, to help a person grow in awareness in their present circumstances.[16] Now mindfulness is its own version of talk therapy, known as mindfulness-based cognitive therapy (MBCT).[17]

MBCT is "a modified form of cognitive therapy that incorporates practices such as present moment awareness, meditation, and breathing exercises."[18] Essentially, you are attempting to use your senses to reach a heightened awareness of the present.

Normally MBCT is going to focus on breathing and meditation techniques, and how to incorporate those into daily life. So a MBCT therapist will work with you to evaluate what is happening in your thoughts and emotions while interacting with the world (that is, how do you respond when you hear a car horn or screeching brakes). One MBCT therapist said that when you grow in mindfulness, it generally helps the negative emotions go away.[19]

Mindfulness is similar to meditation, specifically meditation on what is happening in your life at that moment—and how to respond. It could be just becoming more aware of your circumstances. One study suggested that "[m]indfulness has become an increasingly popular part of our repertoire for enhancing brain health."[20]

Another tool for the . . . brain? Wait a minute. Are we sending electrical signals to the brain? Nope. Are we taking medication to address faulty neurotransmitters? Also no. MBCT believes that you are thinking your way to a healthier brain. But as a Christian, you have to ask how a person with a corrupt mind (Tit. 1:15) can think their way into better so-called mental health. How does that happen? Whether someone uses meditation or not, to seek to understand life apart from God is the epitome of foolishness and of possessing an earthly knowledge (cf. Ps. 14:1 and 1 Cor. 2:14). An unbeliever cannot understand the world accurately apart from the work of God in their life, having a renewed mind.

Even as a Christian, if I am seeking to understand the world in a way that is not consistent with God's Word—the Bible—then I am not truly understanding the world either. My perception is not authoritative; rather, God's Word is authoritative. There are times when I need to remember that my perceptions are straight-up wrong and remind myself that the Bible is right (cf. 2 Pet. 1:16). To meditate or attempt to be mindful apart from the Bible is never helpful. In fact, it is damning. Over and over again, the Bible warns us against human wisdom and calls us to embrace the wisdom of God (1 Cor. 1:20, 25).

The Bible is not one additional form of knowledge to add to an otherwise accurate world. Rather, the Bible is *the authoritative source of knowledge* that directs how we understand the world (John 17:17). Thus to practice MBCT is like groping in the dark—you can feel things, undoubtedly, but you cannot understand what you are feeling apart from the Bible.

Can These Therapies Benefit? Yes, for Symptom Relief. No, for the Real Issue

Inevitably you may be thinking, "Yes, but can't there still be a benefit for meeting with a secular therapist and using these methods?"

That's a fair question.

First, let's define *benefit*. If you suggest that *benefit* means something like "produces good or helpful results or effects or that promotes well-being,"[21] then you have to ask, "Do secular therapies promote well-being?"

Is it helpful to take Tylenol when you have a toothache? In one sense, yes, Tylenol is helpful with the *symptoms* that come with having a tooth infection. But what if you only took Tylenol and didn't address the reason why your tooth was hurting in the first place? Then we would say no, Tylenol is not helping you. It is only masking the symptoms of your true problem.

Likewise for these therapies: If you are not dealing with the true problem, then you are simply attempting to mask the symptoms of it. If you are doing breathing exercises for stress or seeing a secular CBT therapist for depression, you may experience Tylenol-like symptom relief—you may *feel* better.

But for a Christian, the goal should be more than just to feel better.

We are called to sanctification, so we should want to address what is happening in our minds. If you're depressed, wouldn't you want to know what's happening in your mind that might encourage depression? If you are anxious, wouldn't you want to know what's happening in your mind to encourage anxiety? Don't accept the Tylenol without addressing the root cause. Just because you feel better, that doesn't mean you are doing what honors the Lord.

In counseling, primarily through my local church, my advice to people who go to see a secular therapist is Plan C, not even Plan B.

Plan A is to find someone in your local church who is skilled in the Bible, has a level of experience in what you're facing, and is willing to help. I'd encourage you to go through thorough medical checkups with your general practitioner at this phase. Some churches have counseling pastors or even entire biblical counseling ministries, and that is an ideal situation. However, not every local church can support this type of ministry for varying reasons, so a good Plan B is to find another Christian who is outside your church but skilled in the Bible and also has experience with what you're facing. (See the appendix on "How to Find a Biblical Counselor.")

If neither of those is an option, *then* Plan C is to accept the potential help of a secular therapist. The times when this is most likely the only option are when you're engaging with an unsaved teenage child, you are in a location where you cannot find a biblical counselor (as in the military), or you are married to an unbeliever who won't see a Christian but will see a secular therapist. In cases like these, do what you can to move toward meeting with a biblical counselor, but even if that doesn't work out, the secular therapist may help with reducing a symptom. (Unfortunately, sometimes they make matters worse.)

There is no guarantee that a secular therapist will indeed help. In fact, I've had multiple marital counseling cases where a secular marriage family therapist actually provided *unbiblical* counsel, which was to pursue divorce and move on with life. The Bible does provide parameters for divorce (Matt. 5:31–32; 1 Cor. 7:15), but these individuals didn't meet those parameters. In one counseling situation I had, my counsel, based on the Bible, was to work on the marriage, but the marriage and family therapist (MFT) counseled to abandon it. Thus the secular therapist legitimized sinfulness. So there are situations in which the secular therapist may do a great deal of harm when it comes to lasting benefits that come only through honoring the Lord.

In short, if you believe that meeting with a secular therapist is better than nothing, you might be wrong. Sometimes they actually bring harm. So if that is your only option, be extra careful.

Muddy Water

In *The Weight of Glory,* author C. S. Lewis describes a desire for the world and sin over the promises of God made in the Gospels. "We are half-hearted creatures, fooling about with drink and sex and ambition when infinite joy is offered us, like an ignorant child who wants to go on making mud pies in a slum because he cannot imagine what is meant by the offer of a holiday at the sea. We are far too easily pleased."[22]

Christians, when we depend on secular therapy's solutions for our struggles, we are settling. Like an ignorant child who wants to play in the mud rather than enjoy a holiday at sea, a Christian going to the secular therapist seeking help for their mind is accepting muddy water. It's gross, contaminated, and even potentially dangerous. It might make you sick, or make your kids sick.

Yet in the Bible, God describes Himself as the "fountain of living waters" (Jer. 2:13) in comparison with Israel's preference for broken cisterns. Jesus says that when you drink the water He provides, you will never thirst again (John 4:14). When you fully depend on the help of secular therapists, you are missing the superior answers found in the Bible. You are drinking the muddy water over the fresh, mountain spring water. Modern therapy paints itself as sophisticated, developed, research-based, and a myriad of other terms that seek to gain your trust. But it is bankrupt.

Consider the words of Psalm 19:

The law of the Lord is perfect,
reviving the soul;

the testimony of the Lord is sure,
making wise the simple;

the precepts of the Lord are right,
rejoicing the heart;

the commandment of the Lord is pure,
enlightening the eyes;

the fear of the Lord is clean,
enduring forever;

the rules of the Lord are true,
and righteous altogether (vv. 7–9).

The Bible is *the* source of true sophistication from which all true wisdom and knowledge is derived. The Bible isn't for simplistic people who refuse to acknowledge the medical sciences. The Bible is for those who want to understand themselves and the world as it truly is, as God has made them. We are experiencing a mental health epidemic, and the secular therapeutic foot soldiers continue to promote Band-Aids at best and erroneous teachings at worst.

We have the sufficient, capable, dynamic Word of God that allows us to address not only the symptom but also the cause. We don't have to settle for shallow fruit-swapping with those who truly don't understand the mind—or worse, whose own mind is still darkened (that is, the secular therapist). As Christians, we should want the Bible to guide us through our own struggles because it is the very word of God, and it is.

The answers in God's Word are not mediocre. The Bible is *the* superior wisdom for the most complex problems in life. If you see the Bible as anything other than the expression of the wisdom of God, then you do not see it for what it is. Turn to its pure waters. Join the Psalmist in saying:

> *"Your testimonies are my delight;*
> *they are my counselors."*
> —PSALM 119:24

CHAPTER 10

What Then of Mental Illness?

My claim that mental illnesses are fictitious illnesses is also not based on scientific research; it rests on the materialist-scientific definition of illness as a pathological alteration of cells, tissues, and organs. If we accept this scientific definition of disease, then it follows that mental illness is a metaphor. . . .

—THOMAS SZASZ, *THE MYTH OF MENTAL ILLNESS*[1]

Societies have categories for thinking about people and identity, and a real problem occurs when those categories are simply not adequate or appropriate.

—CARL TRUEMAN, *THE RISE AND TRIUMPH OF THE MODERN SELF*[2]

In Frances Hodgson Burnett's 1911 book, *The Secret Garden,* a young girl named Mary is orphaned and moved to her uncle's house in England. As she explores the grounds of her uncle's house, she finds a forbidden, secret garden. Mary cannot hold back her excitement! It is a beautiful but neglected place, locked away because of her uncle's grief over his dead wife.

After discovering the garden, Mary hears cries reverberating through the house at night, and soon finds another secret: Her uncle has a son named Colin, who is also her age.

Colin is bedridden, only getting around by wheelchair. But one day (spoiler alert!) Colin, in his indignation, *stands* to rebuke someone calling him a cripple.[3] To his surprise, and that of Mary and her friends, Colin's legs are weak from disuse, not from a disease. He was told he was crippled, but indeed he was not.

Like Colin's apparent disability, mental illnesses are diagnosed without any evidence of pathological illness. In an effort to understand people rightly through a secular, materialist lens, researchers have created medical-sounding labels for spiritual problems of the immaterial mind: "generalized anxiety disorder," "oppositional defiant disorder," "sexual addiction."

Perhaps you've been told your whole life that you have a mental illness. Yet now you are beginning to wonder—rightfully—if there is even such a thing as mental illness. Your skepticism is justified. Why? Because the mind cannot get a biological illness. You may have been told your whole life that you have ADHD, but I'm telling you that ADHD is not a mental illness. You may be hyperactive, but you do not have a so-called mental illness. You may have experienced awful trauma and been diagnosed with PTSD. It can be real and yet not be a "mental disorder" or "mental illness." In this way you are affected by trauma but do not have a mental disorder—it's post-traumatic stress, but it's not a mental illness.

The purpose of this chapter is to help you think carefully through the very nature of so-called mental illness in the first place. You are not the disorder you have been told you are.

It's time to end the myth of mental illness. The struggles we call mental illnesses do exist, but they are not truly illnesses of the mind.

Secular Therapeutic Definitions of So-Called Mental Illness

The terms *illness* and *disorder* are often used interchangeably. The journal *BMC Psychiatry* published an article that said:

"Mental disorder," "mental illness," and "mental health problem" were effectively identical in meaning, but "psychological issue" was somewhat more inclusive, capturing a broader range of conditions.[4]

The American Psychiatric Association says mental illnesses are "health conditions involving changes in emotion, thinking or behavior (or a combination of these). Mental illnesses can be associated with distress and/or problems functioning in social, work or family activities."[5] Although the APA calls them "health conditions," they then mention all immaterial realities: emotion, thinking, or behavior.

The DSM states that a mental illness is "a syndrome characterized by clinically significant disturbance in an individual's cognition, emotional regulation, or behavior that reflects a dysfunction in the psychological, biological, or developmental processes underlying mental functioning."[6] This definition is more difficult, so let's dissect it a bit more.

First of all, mental illness is said to be a syndrome, or a collection of them. It is a "disturbance" in the cognition, behavior, or emotional regulation, according to the DSM. Pause to ask: Is cognition or emotional regulation immaterial or material? Does it come from your body? According to the Bible, it is immaterial because cognition happens in your mind. The term *disturbance* is ambiguous enough so that it doesn't have a strict medical or organic genesis, even though many take this "disturbance" as coming from a biological pathology.

The DSM states that mental disorders "reflect a dysfunction" in one of the areas that underlie "mental functioning." How does a person know what is dysfunctional? What is the proper function that we might deviate from? The ambiguity continues with the last part of this definition: a dysfunction in the "psychological, biological, or developmental processes underlying mental functioning." Remember that a biblical anthropology states that the body/brain does not determine mental functioning, it influences it. The DSM definition *assumes* there is a psychological problem, biological problem, or development problem but doesn't empirically say what the problem is or how to know when it is a problem in the first place.

With all this medicalized terminology, you will be hard-pressed to even specify what the medical issue is. So, take your meds. Go to the behavioral health unit at your hospital. Necessitate a medical doctorate for psychiatrists, but at the end of all of this, there is often no medically verifiable way to say that what you are experiencing is actually an illness at all! The issues we face are indeed real, but they are often not true illnesses. It is time to end the myth of mental illness, and to that end we must replace the terminology with a biblical view of our inner-man problems.

The Biblical Definitions of So-Called Mental Illnesses

I don't want to be the old curmudgeon who keeps yelling at the kids, "Get off my lawn!" Rather, I want to understand biblically what secular therapists label as "mental illness."

Recall that the mind is the center of cognition and your intellectual being. The commands of the mind are for the mind to be transformed (Rom. 12:2), renewed (Eph. 4:23), not quickly shaken (2 Thess. 2:2), and to have a mind of wisdom when understanding prophecy (Rev. 17:9). Clearly in the Bible, the mind is part of your immaterial self. Your brain, however, is a physical organ that is observable, tangible, and measurable. In fact, neuroscience has dedicated itself to understanding the complexities of this organ—which is praiseworthy and potentially helpful in counseling. Just like a lung, or your physical heart, the organ of the brain is your outer person; it is tangible (2 Cor. 4:16b).

Again, there is no medically verifiable way to diagnose a so-called mental illness—it is symptom-based diagnosing. This is the confession of leading organizations and so-called mental health experts (Insel and Allen, for example).[7]

So when someone has symptoms of a "mental illness," what is really happening? Let's look at a few "mental illnesses" and see how the Bible clarifies them.

Generalized Anxiety Disorder

According to the NIMH, generalized anxiety disorder (GAD) "usually involves a persistent feeling of anxiety or dread that interferes with how you live your life. It is not the same as occasionally worrying about things or experiencing anxiety due to stressful life events."[8] It is like anxiety, but on steroids. The Arnold Schwarzenegger of anxiety, if you will. It is diagnosed by its symptoms. The NIMH says a person with GAD might, among other things,

- Worry excessively about everyday things
- Startle easily
- Have trouble falling asleep or staying asleep
- Feel irritable or "on edge"
- Have to go to the bathroom frequently[9]

While there are outer-man symptoms (like going to the bathroom more frequently), none of these are actual medical problems. None. So, how should we understand anxiety biblically?

"Therefore I tell you, do not be anxious about your life, what you will eat or what you will drink, nor about your body, what you will put on. Is not life more than food, and the body more than clothing?" (Matt. 6:25). Anxiety is an issue of your mind, not a so-called mental illness. God actually commands us to not be anxious, with the Philippians commanded, "The Lord is at hand; do not be anxious about anything, but in everything by prayer and supplication with thanksgiving let your requests be made known to God" (Phil. 4:5b–6).

The Bible would say that anxiety is a sin, not a sickness. You cannot medicalize anxiety, but even if there were evidence of physiological influences, the Bible clearly condemns it. After all, there are physiological cravings for sex, yet lust simply is not an option for the believer. Is it possible that you are naturally a worrier? Yes, totally possible. We were born into sin, David says in Psalm 51:5. That's why you have to renew your mind (Eph. 4:23) and have to discipline your thoughts (Phil. 4:8). It's why we need to exercise trusting in God (Prov. 3:5–8; Luke 12:31). GAD is not a so-called mental illness; anxiety is rather a matter of having "little faith" (Matt. 6:30b). While some may bristle at this, it is not only biblical, but better than the alternative: If GAD is sin, then there is hope for real change, rather than only "coping" with anxiety. That God is, after all, working to save us from the power of sin.

Obsessive-Compulsive Disorder

"Obsessive-compulsive disorder (OCD) is a disorder in which people have recurring, unwanted thoughts, ideas or sensations (obsessions). To get rid of the thoughts, they feel driven to do something repetitively (compulsions). The repetitive behaviors, such as hand washing/cleaning, checking on things, and mental acts like (counting) or other activities, can significantly interfere with a person's daily activities and social interactions."[10] While it may seem odd, OCD is often personified in movies as a person who must lock the door, cannot step on a crack in the sidewalk, and is overly concerned about germs. Generally, these perceptions are true.

I have met with three or four gentlemen who have been diagnosed with OCD throughout my counseling career. It is a very unusual pattern of thinking and actions, but not a totally unique one. Just like the other so-called mental disorders, OCD is not diagnosed medically. It is diagnosed based on symptoms. The obsessions and compulsions are often coming from a mind that is unruly. The OCD mind needs renewal. It is alarmed, to use Paul's word in 2 Thessalonians 2:2.

The OCD mind *must check*, *must double-check*, and *must triple-check*. Ultimately, this person worships certainty and "needs" to be sure. Because the mind is alarmed, every little thing triggers a reason they might be guilty. Scrupulosity and a sensitive conscience might also be at the epicenter of OCD. Scrupulosity is a high view of justice, making everything an issue of right and wrong.

The secular therapeutic culture would like to make OCD a so-called mental disorder. Instead, the person wrestling with OCD should meet with a biblical counselor to examine what is happening in their mind. What are they thinking about? Are they seeing things the way God sees them in His Word? Most of the time, the OCD person believes deep down that they must atone for their "wrongdoings" with compulsions (such as washing hands), but they need to be trained to go back to God's Word and trust God to establish what is right, wrong, helpful, and unhelpful.

OCD is not a mental illness.

Narcissistic Personality Disorder (NPD)

You're going to love this one: narcissistic personality disorder (NPD). According to the Cleveland Clinic, NPD "is a mental health condition that affects how you view yourself and relate to others. Having NPD means you have an excessive need to impress others or feel important. That need can be strong enough to drive harmful behaviors, negatively affecting you and those around you."[11] It is total self-absorption, to the point of seeming as if you literally cannot understand other people or their perspectives. It's typically what abusers are diagnosed with because of their hardened high view of themselves.

I think we should call it "Nebuchadnezzar personality disorder." In Daniel 4, Nebuchadnezzar is walking on his rooftop and says, "Is not this great Babylon, which I have built by my mighty power as a royal residence and for the glory of my majesty?"

I'm awesome. You're welcome. That is the so-called narcissist. What does the Bible call Nebuchadnezzar? A man afflicted with a mental illness? Nope. He was proud. God abased him for a time, and then restored him back. At the end of that restoration, Nebuchadnezzar says, "those who walk in pride he is able to humble" (Dan. 4:37).

NPD is not a mental illness; it is a manifestation of pride. Self-absorption is not an issue of your brain, but of your mind. That's why a humble attitude is genuinely the "mind of Christ" (Phil. 2:5). If you imbibe the secular therapeutic, you treat a person rather than call them to repentance. But we would call them to put off pride, and put on a humble mind of Jesus.

Oppositional Defiant Disorder (ODD)

The DSM-V defines this as a "pattern of angry/irritable mood, argumentative/defiant behavior, or vindictiveness lasting at least 6 months as evidenced by at least four symptoms of the following categories, and exhibited during interaction with at least one individual who is not a sibling."[12] Those additional symptom categories are anger, defiance, and vindictiveness.

What is being called a mental illness is obviously an issue of rebellion, sinfulness, and an unruly heart. Ephesians 6:1–3 tells children to "obey your parents in the Lord, for this is right. 'Honor your father and mother' (this is the first commandment with a promise), 'that it may go well with you and that you may live long in the land.'"

Undoubtedly, there are children whose personalities are naturally more outwardly disobedient than others, but obedience to parents is an issue of sin, not sickness. If a child is vindictive, then this is a sin to repent of according to Romans 12:19. Again, vindictiveness is a sin, not a medical problem in the brain. If you tell children, who are largely the ones diagnosed with ODD, that they have the mental illness of ODD, then you are not helping them see their actions as sin to be repented of and freed from.

If you're the parent of a child who seemingly qualifies for ODD, don't lose heart. God has made your child unique and has equipped you with the resources to parent them (2 Pet. 1:3–4). Thus you are the person for the job! Like all of your children, you are learning about this particular child and how to graciously speak with them (Col. 4:6). God is using you. Consider reading a few resources like *Shepherding a Child's Heart* by Tedd Tripp or *The Heart of Anger* by Lou Priolo. Get equipped with the Bible to help your angry child, and don't accept a secular excuse for sinful behavior. Your child may struggle to obey, but the Holy Spirit is able to change the most hardened of hearts (Tit. 3:5).

Binge Eating Disorder (BED)

BED entails "eating, in a discrete period of time (e.g., within any 2-hour period), an amount of food that is definitely larger than most people would eat in a similar period of time under similar circumstances," and "a sense of lack of control overeating during the episode."[13] This so-called mental illness is diagnosed based on these symptoms, yet we are not talking about a medical problem only. Can binge eating create medical problems? Yes, of course. But *why* are you eating in the first place? Because of what is going on in your heart (Prov. 4:23).

When a person chooses to overeat, it may be connected to comfort (Phil. 3:19); it may be connected to covetousness (Col. 3:5); it may be connected to fear (Matt. 10:28) or some other internal motivation. But BED is not a mental illness; it is an issue of the inner person (the mind).

If you struggle with food-related disorders, you need to get to the root of the issue. What are you thinking about that leads you to eat too much? Do you think comfort is supreme? Do you see food as an escape? You must renew your mind with the fact that food is not your enemy, but is a good gift from God (1 Tim. 4:3–4). Therefore it can be eaten in a way that honors God (1 Cor. 10:31).

If you're wrestling with this issue, consider listening to my *Transformed* podcast and see the bookstore at Transformed.org. We have curated resources, primarily booklets, that are easy to read to help you in this area. One practical book is *Love to Eat, Hate to Eat* by Elyse Fitzpatrick.

Sexual Addiction or Compulsive Sexual Behavior Disorder (CSBD)

Much of the theory on this is speculative at best, and even many secular academics don't accept sexual addiction as a so-called mental illness.[14] But the World Health Organization (WHO) categorizes CSBD as an "impulse control disorder" in its International Classification of Diseases.[15]

Sexual sin, however, is just that—a sin (cf. 1 Cor. 6:12–19). If you were to view sexual addiction as a sickness, you would miss the heart of sexual misconduct (Matt. 5:27–28). Jesus says that adultery starts in the heart, not the brain or even the body. Can your body's hormones encourage sexual sin? Of course. But that doesn't make sexual sin a so-called mental illness. This is another example of how we are medicalizing inner-person realities without any medical evidence.

I would just add that sexual sin of any type should not be tolerated. Heath Lambert's *Finally Free* and *Passions of the Heart* by John Street are perhaps the two best books to show you what is happening with sexual sin. But in addition to those resources, you need to learn new habits and distance yourself from places and people that are not helping you. You don't have a mental illness—you are wrestling with severe sin. Sin that is putting a stranglehold on your life in unique ways. If your sin is prolonged, consider going to a biblical counseling center or actual home you can stay at in order to get control of it. If you leave this unchecked, it will destroy everything in your life that matters.

Note what I have not said, however. I have not said that GAD, NPD, ODD, BED, or CSBD does not exist. Rather, I've said they are not mental illnesses. They *cannot* be mental illnesses because it is not possible for the mind to get ill. We *may* be talking about issues of the mind, but we are not talking about the mind having a medical problem. You *can* be a binge eater, but you need help from the Bible, not secular therapy. You may also struggle with oppositional defiance, but you need help from God through His Word to become more humble and submissive. Secular therapeutic culture is calling things mental illnesses and distracting from the real issues of the mind.

Importantly, the same knife cuts both ways as well: secular mental health professionals have labeled as mental illness what appear to be biological problems.

The best example may be autism. As you may know, autism is considered to be a mental illness—autism spectrum disorder. The DSM-V would say autism spectrum disorder is characterized by "[p]ersistent deficits in social communication and social interaction . . . restricted, repetitive patterns of behavior . . . and the symptoms cause impairment."[16] Yet there is mounting evidence that this is not a mental disorder but rather a physiological/neurological problem.[17]

Calling autism a mental illness when it is really an issue of the brain is sloppy categorizing. Once again, the DSM doesn't seem to be helping anyone.

Can These Issues Exist and Not Be Mental Illness?

Absolutely. Remember how gender dysphoria and homosexuality were reclassified from mental illness to not mental illness? Homosexuality is a reality, but it is not a biological illness of the mind. It is a result of sin (Rom. 1:24–25). It is a moral issue of submitting to the superior plans of God for human sexuality (1 Cor. 7:1–5). But even though homosexuality is not and never was a mental illness, it obviously still exists.

Many people hear a criticism of "mental illness" and immediately jump to the conclusion that I don't believe in science, that I live in a basement, pack my own ammunition, wear aluminum foil hats, and probably believe in extraterrestrial life. I'm not denying reality though. Anxiety can be real, yet not be a mental illness. The same is true for PTSD and depression.

Secular therapy appears sophisticated and academic, and the Bible can *seem* simplistic by comparison. But the Bible helps you understand anxiety, depression, and PTSD better than the world's wisdom can. In fact, the Bible can help frame what is really going on *and* how to respond to these so-called mental illnesses. The Bible offers more than a description of the symptoms; in many cases there is also a clear articulation of what the source of the issue is—something the secular world cannot offer.

Clarifying that depression can exist and not be a mental illness allows you to more clearly and biblically help someone who is struggling with it. You need to ask what is going on. Do some data-gathering. Find out about any genuine health issues. Talk about disappointment. Is this person a follower of Christ? Where is their hope? Address issues of faithfulness. Find out about Bible reading, church involvement, and so forth. The Bible more exhaustively helps people. The Bible clearly articulates who you are, and what is happening in your life. It should not surprise you that the One who made us knows us best. And we know who we are in light of His description of us (Ps. 36:9).

While I was writing this book, there was a kerfuffle about this very topic. Dr. John MacArthur stated,

> Psychiatry and psychology is finally admitting the noble lies that they have been telling for the last hundred years, and the major noble lie is there is such a thing as mental illness.
>
> Now this isn't new. You have Thomas Szasz back in the 1950s writing a book—who was a psychiatrist—on the myth of mental illness. There's no such thing as PTSD.

There's no such thing as OCD. There's no such thing as
ADHD. Those are noble lies to basically give the excuse to,
at the end of the day, medicate people.[18]

MacArthur would later clarify what he meant, stating, "There's
no such thing as mental illness. That is not a new concept. . . . But
I'm not saying this: I'm not saying there's no brain disease; there
is. But that's different; that's pathological; that can be objectively
identified."[19] MacArthur has also stated that psychiatry is promot-
ing mental illness categories that narrow "the spectrum of normal
behavior."[20]

As you may imagine, many on the internet were agitated.

One response came from Gavin Ortlund, a pastor, author, and theologian. In a YouTube video titled "John MacArthur on Mental Illness:
This Is Bad Theology," Ortlund critiqued MacArthur's comments,
citing three primary reasons:[21]

(1) Mental health denial deeply damages people. (2) Mental
health denial is very common in conservative, evangelical
circles. And (3), Gen Z'ers (and older generations) are
experiencing mental health crises.[22]

Ortlund then begins to explain why he believes MacArthur's
views are destructive. The first reason he states is "it prevents people
from getting help when they need it."[23] What we need to understand,
according to Ortlund, is that "[t]he human brain is a physical organ,
and like every other physical organ in our body, in a fallen world, it
can be afflicted. It can get sick. And when that happens, medication
can often help."[24]

It appears Ortlund has, as we've seen over and over again, confused the mind and the brain. He then speaks of his brother-in-law's
experience and need for psychotropics, and further adds that deny-

ing mental illness shames people, as in telling someone with a broken leg, "Oh you're a wimp."[25]

You may watch this video, or videos like these, and think, "Yeah, let's not shame anyone. Let's support people and get them the help they need." And I agree that good counseling should strengthen and encourage weary souls. Yet in eighteen minutes and eight seconds of video Ortlund did not cite one—not one—verse from the Bible to critique MacArthur's position. He did cite two theologians and their definition of common grace, but provided no biblical critique. He didn't demonstrate from the Bible why MacArthur's position is wrong.

Ortlund argues that denying mental illness is destructive, but the same case could be made for diagnosing people with an arbitrary mental illness. He uses his brother-in-law as an example of the benefits of psychotropics, but you could make the same case for psychotropics and bad counsel from therapists harming countless families. As I hope to demonstrate with this book, the very mental health crisis he mentions might be caused by how badly therapy has gotten mental health wrong. Even Ortlund himself says toward the end of his video, "Sometimes medication and professional help doesn't work. That actually happens a lot. Or it's very limited, or there are side effects that are not good."[26] If this is bad theology, then please show me theologically—that is, in the Bible—where I have gotten it wrong.

But to clarify once again, I am not denying the struggles people truly have that are labeled mental illnesses. My argument is not "there is no such thing as ADHD, Anxiety, PTSD, or depression." Of course, those issues are real; they just are not truly illnesses of the mind, and removing medicalized, arbitrary language about what is happening with so-called mental illnesses brings hope and clarity. And if someone does have a real medical issue that is affecting their brain, then of course medication and other treatments make sense.

Hope and Clarity Come from Scripture

I remember meeting with one gentleman about ten years ago in counseling. On intake forms we always ask the counselee to describe the problem they are facing, and this gentleman wrote that he was a "sociopath." Honestly, that was a bit concerning, so I looked up the so-called mental illness for that to see how he was describing himself. The disorder that secular researchers say is behind being a sociopath is called antisocial personality disorder (APD). According to the Mayo Clinic, APD, "sometimes called sociopathy, is a mental health condition in which a person consistently shows no regard for right and wrong and ignores the rights and feelings of others."[27] If you were to receive this diagnosis, like the gentleman had self-assigned, then the recommended treatment would be talk therapy and medication.[28]

As the gentleman in counseling began to explain his life, he said that even though he was a part-time pastor he was very apathetic toward others. He almost never felt compassion. He was a husband and father, and one day this came to a head in his car when he raised his hand at his son, as if he were to strike him. Although he didn't do it, he didn't feel bad either. It was at this point that he knew he needed to get help and so reached out to me for counseling.

What was my counsel for this man? After wading through the mental health terminology, I told him that his lack of *compassion* was not a mental health issue, but in fact an issue of his relationship to the Lord. We looked at passages like Paul's commands to the Colossians: "Put on then, as God's chosen ones, holy and beloved, *compassionate* hearts, kindness, humility, meekness, and patience" (3:12; emphasis added). *Compassionate* literally means "display of concern over another's misfortune."[29] He didn't have "antisocial personality disorder," he had a heart that lacked compassion for others. His heart was myopic, self-focused, and hardened.

You know what is so good about removing medicalized terminology for so-called mental illnesses? There is hope to grow in compassion. The Mayo Clinic even discouragingly said, "Antisocial personality disorder is challenging to treat, but for some people, treatment and close follow-up over the long term may help."[30]

Maybe you have been told your whole life that you have a so-called mental illness. But because these are not pathological brain conditions, you in fact *can* change, to the glory of God. You are not stuck with this arbitrary diagnosis or the treatment plans that correspond to it. God is working in you to make you more like Jesus (Phil. 1:6). If you will interpret your problems through the lens of Scripture, not the secular terminology, then it brings great hope. I don't mean the hope of just *feeling* good, I mean biblical hope—confidence and joy in the Lord. Secular therapy gives us arbitrary labels and then medicates us, but God brings renewal and transformation of our minds. "So we do not lose heart. Though our outer self is wasting away, our inner self is being renewed day by day" (2 Cor. 4:16). Hope comes from understanding our mind as it is, rather than as secular therapeutics describes it to be.

When I told this counselee that he wasn't a sociopath but that he, through God's help, needed to cultivate compassion, it was as if I removed a burden from him. No, he wasn't instantly "healed" of his lack of compassion (I'm not Dr. Phil!) but there was freedom knowing that this wasn't genuinely an illness, but an area in which he could grow with God's help. We worked on considering others as more important than yourself (Phil. 2:3–5), growing in understanding how his actions were coming across (James 1:19), and dying to himself (Luke 9:23). When you understand the problem correctly, which is biblically, then you will have hope and clarity because hope and clarity come through God's Word (Rom. 15:4).

God's Word provides us with the only truly accurate view of who we are and the problems we are facing. The Bible helps capture what you are truly experiencing in your mind, so go to it. Go to the Bible and find hope and clarity.

What If I Need a Diagnosis to Get Resources?

Oh, that we lived in a world that was *always* neat and tidy. Breaking news: we don't. Many of us are in complicated scenarios, and sometimes we may need a formal so-called mental illness diagnosis in order to receive resources. If I had been diagnosed with PTSD, I would have received disability from the VA. In some instances, a mental illness diagnosis *is the only way* to receive services. What should we do then?

I recommend that you receive the additional support, aid, and resources that come with a formal diagnosis. But you should still interpret the so-called mental illness for what it is biblically. If you accept this diagnosis and begin to think, "I can't control my anger because I'm bipolar . . ." or "I can't stop being worrisome because I have OCD . . ." then you have gone too far. This so-called illness is becoming your identity, and who you are in Christ needs to be how you view yourself.

There is a great deal of benefit from receiving helpful resources, even though there is a wrong diagnosis of the problem. Personally, I did not have my son tested for a learning disability, but that meant I had to pay for a tutor—receiving the learning disability diagnosis would have paid for one at school. This would obviously need to be a conscience issue for you, but if you can in good conscience receive the resource without the imbibing secular therapeutic mindset, then I would support your decision (Rom. 14:23).

Danger of Accepting Mental Illness Diagnosis

The last danger of accepting a so-called mental illness diagnosis is that it becomes a person's identity. A student at The Master's University told me that her husband was medically disqualified from the military because of PTSD. This discharge brought with it not only a diagnosis, but a disability check from the military. She bemoaned that now all he does most days is play solitaire on his computer. From his perspective, he can't get a job because he has PTSD. According to her, he was distant and generally unhelpful around the house.

When your disorder becomes your identity, you fossilize in un-faithfulness. You stop striving for progress toward sanctification. A veteran might think they "cannot" work because of PTSD. It is the child who thinks they "cannot" sit still because they have ADHD. When these so-called illnesses inform how we view ourselves, it is insidious. So, instead of employing the secular therapeutic language, use the Bible to identify what you are experiencing. A good biblical counselor can help you do this. My suggestion is that when you are told you have a so-called mental illness, or hear of someone having one, you should reinterpret that diagnosis with the Bible.

We do this all the time with depression, as biblical counselors. If a person says, "I am depressed," our next question is to ask, "What does that look like for you?" For some people it means loss of inter-est in things they formerly enjoyed, while for others it means they are immobilized in bed and cannot eat or sleep. By pausing to ask what they mean, you can find out what is happening and compare that with the Bible. What does the Bible say about this? Take the symptoms being described with mental health terminology and then reinterpret them through the lens of Scripture.

There are certain written resources to help you do this. Marshall and Mary Asher have written *The Christian's Guide to Psychological Terms* (Focus Publishing). In it you will see the DSM diagnosis and a biblical breakdown of what *might* be happening. Resources like these will allow you to take what is being called a mental illness and then to begin to think through it with the lens of the Bible.

Of course, brain diseases are a reality, and there is much hope for learning more about them and treating them accordingly. Alzheimer's.

Dementia. Traumatic brain injury. Concussions. These all affect the organ of the brain. Employ brain disease terminology when referencing the outer man organ of the brain. Jettisoning mental health terminology does not mean that you are rejecting genuine brain diseases. Rather, you are being more precise with your language in describing the inner- and outer-man aspects of who we are.

If you dig into the mental health literature, you'll see that mental illnesses are nonverifiable descriptions of symptoms. Behind the curtain, secular therapy has no substantive help to offer the Christian. Rather, it has arbitrary so-called mental illnesses that change, often conveniently, to fit the politics or zeitgeist of the day. But the Word of God endures forever (Isa. 40:8). You can expect that at each new edition of the DSM, what is or is not a mental illness will keep changing. The secular therapeutic and zeitgeist of our age will continue to shape it—or rather, misshape—the DSM.

Contrary to what the scoffers say, the Bible isn't reductionistic or trite. It doesn't have "simplistic" solutions to complicated problems. It has intricate solutions to complicated problems. Depression, anxiety, or ADHD are not merely modern phenomena that the Bible makes no comment on. While I appreciate the well-meaning Christian who says, "We can ask God when we see Him," it is worthy to study the Bible to better understand the mind. The Bible talks about fear. It speaks to worry. It has much to say about wayward thoughts, or hurtful relationships. Intrusive thoughts and dark thoughts are addressed in the sufficient Scripture. If you see the Bible being about the flannelgraph stories of Jonah and the fish only but fail to see its relevance to your life now, then you are missing out. The Bible is not a storybook with a few moral principles; it is the lens through which we understand the world. Without the Bible, especially regarding things like the mind, we will create arbitrary categories of so-called illnesses and perpetuate error.

In sum, the Bible has better answers than the secular therapeutic enterprise regarding so-called mental illnesses.

It's time to end the myth of mental illness.
This is not to say that what are called mental
illnesses don't exist, but rather that they
are not truly illnesses of the mind. They are
struggles we have always had—struggles
the Bible still has the answers to.

CHAPTER 11

Insanity and the Mind

Paul, you are out of your mind; your great
learning is driving you out of your mind.

—ACTS 26:24

When Paul returned to Jerusalem, James encouraged him to take a Nazarite vow to demonstrate that Paul "lives in observance of the law" (Acts 21:24).

Well, that plan didn't work.

While worshipping in the temple, Paul was falsely accused and a bruhaha started. The Roman guards had to remove Paul from the crowd, after which he would preach and then be put on trial (Acts 21:37–23:10). Paul ultimately had to be snuck out of Jerusalem because of a plot to kill him, and he was escorted to the coastal town of Caesarea for both protection and trial.

It was there in Caesarea that Paul preached to Governor Festus and King Herod Agrippa II. After giving the account of Jesus's coming as the predicted Messiah, Paul then told of how he himself was confronted by Jesus on the way to Damascus (Acts 26:14–18). The Lord had confronted and commissioned Paul, and now Paul's argument was that he was simply being faithful to the heavenly calling he had received. He was not a criminal or insurrectionist.

How did Paul's politically powerful listeners respond?

Well, cloven tongues of fire didn't drop from the sky, like at Pentecost. There wasn't a revival among the Roman leadership. Instead, Festus said with a loud voice, "Paul, *you are out of your mind*; your great learning is driving you out of your mind" (Acts 26:24; emphasis added).

Festus thought Paul was a crazy person. That was kind of rude, especially with King Agrippa present. But yes, even in the ancient world, people recognized a place for insanity in their understanding of the human condition. It has always been clear when someone is insane, losing it, with some screws loose, a madman, coo-coo-snaz.

Paul replied to this charge by saying, "I am not out of my mind, most excellent Festus, but I am speaking true and rational words" (Acts 26:25). Paul understood exactly what Festus was saying and countered by arguing that his words were *true* and *rational*. Therefore, he could not be out of his mind—he was not out of touch with reality.

As you'll recall with Clifford Beers, the mental health crisis of our day actually began with more of an emphasis on insanity than it did with ambiguous categories of "mental illnesses." Remember that Beers had jumped from a fourth-story window in an attempt to take his own life. He was hospitalized for both the medical damage he caused to his body as well as for his perceived insanity. And, to be fair, he would be perceived as insane today if he continued to believe his entire family were assassins wanting to kill him, or that a gathering of people in a neighboring field were preparing to take his life (both things Beers actually believed at one point).

Mental health treatment started with more of a focus on insanity, rather than speculative mental illnesses. Beers wanted to see reform in the care of those who showed signs of insanity, which is a real issue. In fact, the treatment and reforms that he brought about for the genuinely insane are actually good. Thanks to Beers, people still maintain their basic, fundamental human rights while placed into psychiatric care.

Yet we would not say that mental illnesses are insanity, would we?

In fact, it seems insulting to imply that a person with depression is crazy. "Hey, you with ADHD, you're insane."

It seems insulting because inwardly we have a different tier for those whom we deem as truly crazy people. This is the guy barking in front of the public library whom I mentioned back in chapter 3. It's the lady dancing in the middle of the street. Recently, while driving, I watched a homeless man yell at the cars that were going forward on a green light. One time a gentleman told me he was running for president, and that to prevent him from winning, the government was sonic-booming his house. I was like, "Uh huh. And the neighbors don't hear it?"

All of us have encountered a person who seems to fit the bill of insanity. What Beers did was open the door for anything to be considered a mental illness, and now legitimately insane people are lumped into a category of mentally ill in the same way as a person with changing moods. Mental illness is a broad, sweeping category that actually flattens the needs of those with insanity. In this way, mental illness is hurting the care of the genuinely insane.

As we've seen a bit already, the Bible shows that insanity is real. We see it multiple times from multiple authors of the Bible, each of whom demonstrate that when a person's senses do not match reality, they are "out of their mind." They are losing a grip on what is true. Mental illnesses are largely speculative, but insanity is a real anthropological category. Perhaps there are medical issues related to this, or perhaps it is a person's faulty worldview that contributes to inaccurate interpretations of the world. Scripture does not explain the causes of insanity, but it is a reality the Bible describes.

In this chapter, we are going to analyze the different instances of insanity in the Bible. In doing so we will see that throughout the Bible it is understood that a person can be insane. Then we will investigate whether the Bible ever provides a reason for insanity, and whether it is a brain issue or a mind issue.

Old Testament "Madmen"

In the Old Testament, the term *shga* (i.e., שׁגע), which literally is translated as "madmen" or to be "mad" in terms of driven to insanity, is used seven times to refer to a person who is acting crazy, or in warnings that certain actions will make you crazy.[1]

David is one of the clearest examples of this in 1 Samuel 21. In this account, David is seeking refuge from Saul, who maliciously intends to harm him. When he meets the Philistine ruler King Achish, the Philistine servants rightly recognize David as a great warrior. David is fearful of Achish, seemingly because he doesn't want to be seen as a rabble-rouser. Furthermore, do you know where Goliath was from? Yes, you guessed it—Gath of the Philistines (1 Sam. 17:4). And whose sword was David carrying? Right again: Goliath's (1 Sam. 24:9). David would not have been the most popular person in town. So, in order to conceal his appearance, he acts insane (1 Sam. 21:13). He drools down his beard and makes some types of random marks on the doors. (Apparently, this is what insane people did back then. I guess the Philistines didn't have public libraries for them to go to.)

It worked. King Achish said, "Behold, you see the man is mad. Why then have you brought him to me? Do I lack madmen, that you have brought this fellow to behave as a madman in my presence? Shall this fellow come into my house?" (1 Sam. 21:14) The king of Philistia understood what insanity looks like, and apparently this wasn't the great warrior David. It was some madman that he didn't need to bother with.

In the Old Testament, there are other instances of people being accused of insanity:

- Elisha is said to be a madman (2 Kings 9:11).
- Shemaiah is told to be a ruler over the madmen (Jer. 29:26).
- The prophets of Israel are madmen (Hosea 9:7).

A New Testament Idiom: "You're Out of Your Mind"

In Mark 3, Jesus was teaching in the synagogue, healing on the Sabbath, and rebuking religious leaders. Many people were eager to hear His teaching. In fact, the crowds were so great that Jesus and His disciples headed to the sea for a potential escape route (v. 9).

Jesus's family was not so enthralled, however. According to verse 20, Jesus returned home to Nazareth, and His family seemed to think He had lost touch with reality. Verse 21 says, "And when His family heard it, they went out to seize Him, for they were saying, 'He is out of His mind.'" Instead of believing Jesus's teaching, believing in His miracles, His family accused Him of being "out of His mind." *Can you grab your brother? He's losing it!*

In the Greek, "out of your mind" is an idiom that is really one word: *existemi*. It's a word that means that your senses don't match reality. It means "inability to reason normally, *lose one's mind, be out of one's senses.*"[2] In this state, you are not utilizing your senses to think correctly. Interestingly, *existemi* is where we get the English word *ecstasy*. It could also be translated as "astounded, shocked, amazed." Semantically, it could refer to being in a state that makes little or no sense.[3] It is similar to those utilizing hallucinogenic drugs, where a person under the influence is in a state where their senses do not seem to comport with reality.

Needless to say, it is not a compliment.

As we saw earlier, Paul was also accused of being "out of his mind," but not just in the book of Acts. The Corinthians accused him of just about everything under the sun: *not being a real apostle, being weak in person but strong in word, not being as cool as Apollos, oh yeah, and being crazy.*

"For if we are beside ourselves, it is for God; if we are in our right mind, it is for you," Paul writes in 2 Corinthians 5:13. Some translations, such as the NIV, will translate "beside ourselves" as "out of our mind." When Paul is accused of being crazy, he says, *if I am crazy it is for God, but if I am sane, it is for you.* "Beside ourselves" is the same term that Jesus's family accused him of: *existemi*.

But note, the idiom *existemi* speaks of your senses not comporting to reality, rather than directly referring to your mind. So we have to be careful about drawing too many conclusions about the mind, because the term could just as well be translated "you're out of your senses."[4]

Also, *existemi* does not mean that you are out of your *brain*. In fact, that statement (hopefully) seems a bit odd because when we are out of our brain, we are no longer alive.

The authors of the Bible understood, through the inspiration of the Holy Spirit, that the mind is the center of cognition. If your mind or sensory perception is off, then you must be insane. Jesus's family thought He was losing His grip on reality.

But they weren't the only ones. The Jews also accused Him of being out of His mind:

> There was again a division among the Jews because of
> these words. Many of them said, "He has a demon, and is
> insane; why listen to him?" Others said, "These are not the
> words of one who is oppressed by a demon. Can a demon
> open the eyes of the blind?" (John 10:20; emphasis added)

In John 10, Jesus says that He is the Good Shepherd, and that He has sheep He is gathering and guiding. He works intimately in the will of His Father, and He will lay down His life for His sheep (v. 17). After hearing this, the Jews could not figure out why He was talking like that, so they began to look for the most likely explanation. He's got a demon. Or wait, maybe He is just flat-out insane? Anyone who believes their actual father is God must have a demon or be insane, right? "But if he really was crazy and demon-possessed," one person objects, "how could he open the eyes of the blind?" Good question.

This time, unlike in His family's accusations, the Jews use the term *mainomai*. It means to "be mad, be out of one's mind."[5] Almost all English translations are going to translate this word as "mad, out of your mind" or "insane." The Jews thought Jesus was acting in a way that was bizarre and saying bizarre things. In all fairness, in modern times we seem to think very similarly. Except we would primarily focus on insanity, since the secular world doesn't believe in demons.

In describing this accusation, one author said, "In the NT, then, μαίνεσθαι [*mainesthai*] expresses the judgment of unbelief on divinely filled witness, on the inconceivable act of divine salvation."[6] In other words, insanity is a common accusation when a person cannot believe something divine has occurred. In this way, a person can default to accusing another of being insane because what they're doing doesn't seem sensical—it is nonsense. The Gospel is said to be "foolishness" to those who don't believe (1 Cor. 1:18), in part because it is seen as nonsensical.

Paul says this is one of the reasons why sign gifts should have been practiced with discernment. Sign gifts are the supernatural gifts given by the Spirit to Christians for the purpose of authenticating the Gospel message and the authority of the messenger (1 Cor. 14:22). Apparently, the Corinthians were using the sign gifts in a way that was chaotic. One person would stand to prophesy, another would have the gift of tongues, and there was no one to interpret the tongues. Thus a stranger would go to the church service and think the Corinthians were crazy. Paul says, "If, therefore, the whole church comes together and all speak in tongues, and outsiders or unbelievers enter, will they not say that you are out of your minds?" (1 Cor. 14:23).

I'm sure the outsider would think that. I've seen videos of sign gifts being abused in modern times, and I think the people doing so are out of their minds. The sign gifts were to be practiced with discernment so that you wouldn't communicate that your church was filled with insane people. Paul is saying that sign gifts were to be governed in part by the way they would have come across to an unbeliever who was visiting. Thus one person should speak in tongues and the next person should interpret. Then sign gifts won't make it look like you're out of your mind.

In Acts 12, Peter's deliverance from jail was such an unlikely reality. Heavily guarded, with Herod attempting to gain political favor with the Jews, Peter was guarded by "four squads of soldiers," which is the equivalent of about sixteen soldiers.[7] Yet the believers prayed for his release, and God miraculously sent an angel to *walk Peter out of the jail*, past two guards and an iron gate (Acts 12:10–11). Peter's first destination upon his release was to John Mark's mother's house, where the believers were praying for him. A servant girl named Rhoda heard knocking at the door and was surprised to hear Peter's voice! In her joy, she turned back to tell the others—while leaving Peter at the door—and no one believed her! What did they say? Rhoda, you are *mainomai*, or "out of your mind" (Acts 12:15).

How could Rhoda be out of her mind? From their perspective, she must have some sensory issue and she is obviously acting bizarre because of course Peter *is in* jail, protected by sixteen Roman soldiers. Rhoda's senses must not be working correctly. But then they went to the door and realized that Peter was standing there, having been delivered by the Lord. Rhoda wasn't out of her mind after all (Acts 12:19).

An insane person can exist, according to the Bible, but when something is difficult to understand, miraculous, or supernatural, a response can be to accuse a person of insanity. That is what Rhoda was accused of, and that is also how Festus understood Paul's testimony.

Is Insanity a Spiritual or Physical Problem?

Insanity can have many causes but can be said to be present when:

- A person is using words that are irrational because their words do not comport with reality, and thus truth;

- A person's senses are malfunctioning and creating wrongly perceived interpretations of reality (i.e., Rhoda);
- A person's senses are malfunctioning and instigating bizarre behavior (i.e., fake-David);
- A person lives according to their faulty perceptions yet genuinely believes them to be true (i.e., accused of Jesus).

Because God defines reality, an evaluation of truth and rationality must involve God's perspective on the matter offered in the Bible. Now, some of you inevitably are asking whether physiological triggers contribute to insanity. Namely, do the brain and body contribute to insanity in any way? Is it possible for a known biological reason for insanity to be the reason why a person is acting bizarrely?

That is important to ask. My answer is yes, because the senses are not functioning as they should and they will in turn affect a person's behavior. For instance, consider sleeplessness. A person who goes long enough without sleep will start to hallucinate, struggle to discern between reality and nonreality, and even begin to hear things.[8] Sleep is a physiological issue, even though sleep is given from the Lord (Ps. 127:2). Now, sleep is not exclusively physiological because we know that a person can be worried and thus suffer with insomnia. However, for you to be sleepless might mean that you are going to struggle with your body and senses not functioning as they should. The failure of your senses is not necessarily a sin issue, or merely a mind issue. And if you're still seeing things after you get good sleep for a period of time, let's get your eyes checked. Again, there can be a biological reason for your sense of sight breaking down, so treat that physical problem. It's that simple.

Here is where it gets messy. Insanity is also related to your mind when you begin to live in a false reality. We might call this type of a person a "paranoid schizophrenic" because they are living in a false sense of reality. One gentleman who had been labeled schizophrenic talked with me at church, per the request of his family. When I spoke with him he was 1) running for president of the United States, 2) living off his disability money, 3) being "sonic-boomed" by the government in his sleep, 4) thinking his phone was being tapped, and 5) believing that the government was spying on him.

As we talked, it was apparent that he could see me and hear me, and we even shook hands (so I'm guessing he could feel me?). His senses were all working but his *reason* was distorted. He drove himself around, shopped for himself, and led his own independent life—which tells you he could see, hear, touch, and smell mostly accurately. Yet he still lived in this alternate reality that he had constructed for himself in his own *mind*. His insanity didn't seem to be a physical issue, but an issue of the mind. You cannot take a pill to believe differently about the government. You cannot take a pill to change your thoughts. This gentleman had an issue of insanity as it pertained to his *mind*, not his brain/body.

How then should a Christian, who is committed to understanding people biblically, approach a scenario like this? Well, if there are sensory issues, then let's address those with medical treatment. However, if there are times when a person seems to have their senses functioning correctly, yet their rationale is wacky, then you need to focus on the renewal of the mind through the truth of Scripture. In other words, get your ears and eyes checked, but if those senses are seemingly healthy then this is most likely a matter of the mind that is encouraging insanity. You don't need word puzzles if it's your mind—you need the truth of Scripture to bring you back to reality, and to have a sound mind.

Malfunctioning senses may correspond to a mind that is darkened and genuinely cannot (or refuses to) understand the truth. "Seeing they do not see" (Matt. 13:13). You're not going to fix that with word puzzles, medication, yoga, or sudoku. This is because the brain, as an organ, cannot make the immaterial mind well or sick. Clifford Beers missed that and began to conflate the mind with the brain, and vice versa. The darkened, futile mind needs repentance, and that repentance is the first step toward having a transformed mind that functions as God designed it to.

CHAPTER 12

Disorder, Disease, or Disobedience— Addiction and Mind

Addiction is a neurobiological disease—not a lifestyle choice—and it's about time we start treating it as such.

—JOE BIDEN[1]

I'm convinced that calling addiction disease is not only inaccurate, it's harmful.

—MARC D. LEWIS, *THE BIOLOGY OF DESIRE*[2]

One of the last bills Joe Biden sponsored as a US senator was the "Recognizing Addiction as a Disease Act of 2007." It called for changing the name of the National Institute on Drug Abuse to the "National Institute on Diseases of Addiction." The bill also would have changed the name of the National Institute on Alcohol Abuse and Alcoholism to the "National Institute on Alcohol Disorders and Health."

It might seem like a small thing, just to change a few words in a government agency's name. But the worldview significance is huge. The term *abuse* was seen as pejorative, thus the replacement of *addiction* was closer to what Senator Biden thought represented the research. By changing the terms, it would lower social stigma and personal shame.

Biden had come to these conclusions based on what he regarded as scientific findings—empirical research:

> Addiction is a chronic, relapsing *brain disease* that is characterized by compulsive drug seeking and use, despite harmful consequences. It is considered a *brain disease* because drugs change the *brain's* structure and manner in which it functions. These *brain* changes can be long lasting, and can lead to the harmful behaviors seen in people who abuse drugs. The disease of addiction affects both *brain* and behavior, and scientists have identified many of the biological and environmental factors that contribute to the development and progression of the disease.[3] (Emphasis added)

Four times in this quote from the Senate's meeting in 2007, Biden used *brain*, not *mind*. Addictions are an issue of the *brain*. If you call it "abuse," you're missing the point because the *brain* is causing this. *Abuse* connotes personal responsibility. It implies that someone has made choices, and poor choices at that.

In instances like addiction, it really does come down to what caused what. Does the brain cause addiction, or is the brain affected by the abuse of illegal substances? The Recognizing Addiction as a Disease Act of 2007 did not pass, but the worldview behind it is still prevalent today.

The American Medical Association has considered alcoholism as a disease for decades,[4] while the American Psychiatric Association calls it a disorder.[5] And this isn't only a position taken by Democrats like Joe Biden. Chris Christie, the former Republican governor of New Jersey whom President Trump appointed in 2017 to be chairman of a White House commission to combat drug addiction, made "addiction is a disease" one of his main talking points.[6]

But what leads a person to use illegal substances in the first place? What leads a person to reach for their *first* illegal substance, before they have ever tried drugs of any type? You can probably guess: it's the *mind*. Can the brain be damaged because of drug use? Of course! But what started it all? The mind.

Though they might never say it out loud, "my brain made me do it" is a common attitude people have when they're struggling with pornography, drug abuse, or alcoholism. Many take on the identity of "addict" or "alcoholic" and go through life as if there is no hope for freedom.

It is true that pornography rewires the brain,[7] some foods and drugs contain chemicals intended to cause the body to crave them more,[8] and genetic and metabolic factors can make alcohol easier to get "hooked" on for some people.[9] But some treat these issues only as brain problems, rather than moral problems with roots in the mind. By changing nomenclature, people remove any sense of responsibility and wrongly use clinical terminology to remove shame and guilt. But the Bible addresses these problems as issues of the mind, not the brain.

The brain cannot make you think impure thoughts. The brain may cause you to experience symptoms of withdrawal, but it cannot make you call your drug dealer. These are sins, motivated by deep desires and idols in your mind, to be repented of, not sicknesses in need of mere medical treatment.

In counseling, addiction is a difficult reality. By *addiction* I mean that a person has used chemicals/substances in their body that have affected the way they express their mind, *and* they have a strong physiological craving for those substances. At my church, I once cocounseled (along with a female colleague) a lady whom I'll call Sarah. She had been addicted to methamphetamine, and one time when she had meth in her system, she got into a car accident with her four-year-old son in the vehicle. As you might guess, the state took her son from her.

It was tragic. Sarah was in rough shape when she came to the church. She came to us because the state's social worker required that she go to counseling.

In our counseling sessions, I wasn't too sure how recently Sarah had last used meth. She would come to counseling looking high. Her hair was usually disheveled, and her eyes would wander during conversation. Yet Sarah could interact and answer questions. She would be spacy, but it was hard to tell if these were the aftershocks of using meth, or if she was still using meth in some way (she insisted she wasn't). Sarah held down a part-time job though, so she was being at least somewhat responsible.

Regardless of whether she was genuinely clean or still using meth, counseling was a means to seeing her son. We understood that, so we gladly met with her to try to help from a biblical perspective.

But it was hard to break through. Sarah's brain was so affected by the meth's damage to her body, it sometimes felt like we were counseling a wall. Imagine counseling a person who is severely sleep-deprived: yes, you can read the Bible with them, but the greater issue is there are some physiological problems that need to be addressed to help them be coherent. Substance abuse is the same way. (I will not counsel people if they are high during the counseling session.)

Did Sarah have a disease called "addiction," or is using meth something she needed to repent of? The way you answer this question affects the treatment of the issue. Joe Biden was a senator from Delaware when he pushed for the Recognizing Addiction as a Disease Act of 2007. His exact reason for doing so? "By changing the way we talk about addiction, we change the way people think about addiction, both of which are critical steps in getting past the social stigma too often associated with the disease."[10] Change the terminology and you remove stigma, like shame and moral responsibility.

The question is still this: Is what we are calling an addiction really an issue of disobedience?

Throughout this book, we've seen how the mind is the source of cognition and the seat of the intellect (Rom. 12:2). When you make a decision, it is a combination of thought and volition—both of which are inner-man realities (cf. Gal. 5:17). In this way, we can say that you choose what you choose because of what is happening in your mind. Throughout Scripture, we see many instances where a person is told to choose: Joshua tells Israel to choose (Josh. 24:15), we are commanded to not choose to be like an evil man (Prov. 3:31), Jesus chose the twelve disciples (John 6:70), the early church chose Barnabas and Paul (Acts 15:22), and Paul says it's hard to choose between being in Heaven with Jesus and ministering to the Philippians (Phil. 1:22).

What you choose may be influenced by your brain, but not determined by it. The Christian, through the freeing work of the Holy Spirit, can choose to live a life that is honoring to God (Rom. 6:19). What does this have to do with addiction? The first time a person uses addictive substances, they are making a *choice*. They do not yet have a physiological craving for these substances, because they've never tried them. Furthermore, their brain has not yet been warped by these substances.

When someone starts using drugs, it is because of their mind. They might think drugs will give them an escape, a sense of acceptance with a friend group, a relief from earthly troubles, or some other supposed benefit. Then, after the utilization of the drugs, they begin to develop the physiological side effects of drug use.

Psychosomatic Effects

The National Institute on Drug Abuse says that some of the side effects of drug use are "lung or heart disease, stroke, cancer, or mental health conditions."[11] If you use methamphetamine long enough, it begins to affect your body, including your brain. "When people refer to substance use-related 'brain damage,' they may be referring to a brain injury due to the destruction or alteration of cells in the brain," according to American Addiction Centers. "Such injuries may happen either as a direct result of the toxic effects of drugs and alcohol or as a consequence related to drug use. . . ."[12]

However, a damaged brain is not *why* a person started using drugs in the first place.

> Brain damage related to substance abuse
> is a side effect of a mind's decision to use
> drugs, and thus a person is damaging
> their body, which includes their brain.

Marc D. Lewis is a clinical psychologist, neuroscientist, former professor at the University of Toronto, and former drug addict. He's not a Christian, but he wrote a book titled *The Biology of Desire*, which says, "Brain disease may be a useful metaphor for how addiction *seems*, but it's not a sensible explanation for how addiction works."[13]

Lewis cites two primary examples as reasons why the "addition-as-disease" model is inadequate: 1) brain change does not equal disease and 2) drug abusers often change without treatment.[14] If the brain is causing the "disease," as Lewis points out, then why would a person quit cold turkey? The addiction-as-disease model has no substantive answers for this.

Christians, we must be discerning. Just because the brain is damaged by drug abuse does not mean the brain is the reason why a person is abusing drugs in the first place. You can study the CT scans of all the drug addicts in the world but they won't tell you why the drug addict called their dealer in the first place. The brain and mind influence each other (Ps. 32:3–4) but *the mind* is the source of cognition.

In this way, it is totally reasonable to say that a brain has made it more difficult to choose what is right, but the mind is still the source of cognition and volition. Thus you never "have" to choose substance abuse as a Christian. Short of being tied down and forced to take drugs, you have a choice. Even if you were raised in a household of drug addicts, you still had and have a choice. Your environment can absolutely encourage you to use drugs, but the choice comes from your mind.

Drunkenness, Substance Abuse, and Sexual Addiction

The Bible often speaks about the drunkard. Proverbs 20:1 says, "Wine is a mocker, strong drink a brawler, and whoever is led astray by it is not *wise*" (emphasis added). The Bible says that intoxication shows that a person lacks wisdom, not dopamine. In the New Testament, we see that drunkenness is a marker of a non-Christian's life (1 Cor. 6:10; Gal. 5:21). It is strictly forbidden in Romans 13:13 for the Christian.

What the Bible would call drunkenness, the secular therapeutic culture would call alcohol use disorder (AUD). According to the DSM-V, AUD is a mental disorder, and you qualify for it if you meet at least two of these symptoms:

- Had times when you ended up drinking more, or longer, than you intended?
- More than once wanted to cut down or stop drinking, or tried to, but couldn't?
- Spent a lot of time drinking? Or being sick or getting over other aftereffects?
- Wanted a drink so badly you couldn't think of anything else?
- Found that drinking—or being sick from drinking—often interfered with taking care of your home or family? Or caused job troubles? Or school problems?[15]

After reading these criteria, is this a disorder, disease, or actions based on desires in disobedience to God? To call drunkenness a disease or disorder is not only unhelpful, it is patently false. Your brain doesn't make you drive to the liquor store. Your brain doesn't make you "want" a drink so badly that you cannot "think" of anything else, as the DSM states it. Your mind does the wanting and the thinking.

Drunkenness is an issue of your mind that results in damage to your brain. As a Christian, you must remember that no sin must rule you (Rom. 6:6). You are able to resist drunkenness through the work of the Holy Spirit in your life. Yes, you can have physical cravings for alcohol, but no—your mind doesn't have to choose it over honoring the Lord.

Although it is similar, substance abuse warrants its own category for the examples of so-called addictions. There is another "mental disorder" to articulate so-called addictions to substances: "substance abuse disorder (SUD)." Similar to AUD, SUD has symptoms to help a person know when they are supposedly bordering addiction/disorder. According to the National Library of Medicine, these symptoms can include:

- Consuming the substance in larger amounts and for a longer amount of time than intended
- Persistent desire to cut down or regulate use. The individual may have unsuccessfully attempted to stop in the past.
- Substance use impairs ability to fulfill major obligations at work, school, or home.
- Recurrent substance use in physically unsafe environments
- **Tolerance**: Individual requires increasingly higher doses of the substance to achieve the desired effect, or the usual dose has a reduced effect; individuals may build tolerance to specific symptoms at different rates.
- **Withdrawal**: A collection of signs and symptoms that occurs when blood and tissue levels of the substance decrease. Individuals are likely to seek the substance to relieve symptoms. No documented withdrawal symptoms from hallucinogens, PCP, or inhalants.[16]

Note: Some of these symptoms are for different categories of SUDs. SUDs are diagnosed with entirely social or immaterial symptom-based diagnosing. Apart from tolerance and withdrawal, the symptoms listed here are primarily nonphysical. There is no discussion of the components of the brain that, if damaged, indicate you have an SUD. A CT scan is not even mentioned by the DSM diagnostic criteria for SUD.

So what about Sarah? Did she have a mental disorder? No, she didn't. She *chose* to use meth, and that usage undoubtedly damaged her brain. But SUD is not a brain disorder.

An extremely hot topic these day is "sexual addiction." According to *Psychology Today*, "The concept of 'sex addiction' is under heated debate. However, in a controversial decision, compulsive sexual behavior disorder was added to the World Health Organization's International Classification of Diseases."[17]

However, sexual addiction is not accepted as a disease/disorder by the American Psychiatric Association and was rejected as a mental disorder in the DSM-V. The term that is being used for sexual addiction—though not adopted in the DSM-V—would be *hypersexuality disorder*. The fear in adopting that term is that it "regulates behavior" or pertains more to "impulse control problems."[18]

People don't like this. A total creeper who has spent years using his power and money to take advantage of others in a sexual way could now claim that he "cannot help it." He is an "addict." In the book *Behavioral Addictions*, two academics write, regarding hypersexuality, that "these terms have been criticized for their focus on excessive sexual behavior, which remains undefined . . . and holds the risk of pathologizing normative patterns of sexual behavior."[19] In other words, the American Psychiatric Association could not find a consensus on what normal sexual behavior looks like, and didn't include hypersexuality as a disorder.

Now, you might be thinking, Can't we just look for a problem with a person's brain to determine whether it's an addiction, disease, or disorder? If these are true medical issues, can't you do a study of CT scans from those who seem to be hypersexual and identify brain patterns? *Ha! Busted.* If these were medical issues, then the medical proof of their existence would determine whether inclusion to the DSM-V was permissible . . . but they're not medical issues. They are moral issues.

Sexual addiction demonstrates that some issues will not be called disorders if the culture doesn't want that. We don't want to exonerate the sexually abusive man—and rightfully so. Still, there is also no medical evidence for AUD or SUD, yet we include them. Sexual addiction is an issue of the mind, not the brain, just like AUD and SUD. The Bible, however, consistently treats these issues as matters of sin.

At What Point Is It a Sin?

Just to be clear, the habitual use of something doesn't necessarily mean that you are an addict or substance abuser, let alone that you have a disease. Nor is the habitual use of something *always* sinful. If this were so, many of us would have to repent of drinking coffee!

Let me provide a few theological parameters that shed light on how to know that you are dealing with a sinful issue rather than stewardship by a faithful consumption issue.

First, *when you are using something that is illegal, damaging to your body, or forbidden in Scripture,* then you are entering into sin.

All illegal drugs are easily categorized this way because Christians are called to submit to and obey governing authorities (Rom. 13:1; Titus 3:1). This is an easy delineation to make. You might ask, "What is something damaging to my body?" Tobacco use would be an example. If you are habitually using tobacco through cigarettes, chewing tobacco, or some combination, then you know that it is damaging your body and becoming an issue of sin though poor stewardship. And while certain drugs are legal (for example, marijuana), the Bible forbids the use of things that lead to a loss of self-control (Eph. 5:18).

If it is illegal, damaging to your body, or forbidden in Scripture, then it is a sin issue.

Second, *when you are willing to sin to get it, use it, or taste it,* then you know it has become an issue of sinfulness. Ken Sande calls this "Sin to Get" in his excellent book *The Peacemaker*.[20] If you are willing to sin in order to fulfill your desire for something that you use habitually, then this is becoming an issue. So, if you're using painkillers and sin to keep using them, it is becoming a sin issue.

Third, *you are willing to sin to keep it.*[21] This means that you are using some form of substance and it *must* stay that way, or you will dishonor the Lord by losing it. In this way, coffee could become an issue of sinful, habitual use if you sinned against others to maintain your coffee in the morning. Sorry to break it to you.

Finally, *when you are willing to sin if you don't get that substance,* you know this is a sin issue.[22] Coffee didn't happen this morning and you snapped everyone's head off? Yep, sin issue. Coffee is becoming too important to you if this is the case.

Using these four criteria can help you identify what is an issue of the mind and disobedience, rather than calling everything we don't like an issue of disobedience.

The way this would look practically is that it is possible for a person to drink a glass of wine (less than five ounces; I know I have to be specific for some of you!) without sinfully using alcohol. Someone is not a drunkard for having a glass once in a while. If they have wine, that's no problem, and if they don't have wine, that's no problem either. They don't care that much about it. This would *not* be an issue of sin. Disobedience comes when a person begins to use wine in a way that dishonors the Lord by drinking too much of it, sinning to get it and keep it, or if they don't get it. The disobedience starts not necessarily at consumption, but rather when consumption leads to dishonoring God or the consumption of a substance inherently dishonors God.

How do you know this is really an issue of sin as opposed to you being dependent on something to live? You can use these four criteria to help you work through that. The bad news is, yes, *anything* can move into this habitual use that errs toward sinful behavior—that includes coffee. (I'm sorry, truly, I am. At least it's not a disease too.)

My guess is that you cannot go more than a few minutes without breathing oxygen (and no, don't try timing yourself; that's dangerous). Just because you depend on sleep, food, and oxygen doesn't mean that you are sinfully "addicted" to them. God is the only independent being, meaning He does not depend on anything outside of Himself to exist.[23] Yet you and I depend on many things to exist. Food. Water. Sleep. Oxygen. Each of these is essential to keep our physical lives going. However, we do not worship these things—we worship God. So with or without food, I can still trust the Lord. Just because God has created us as dependent beings does not mean that we are habitually using something to the point of sin. Rather, we are trusting God for these provisions (Matt. 6:33).

Many of us know the sad reality that some mothers use illegal drugs while pregnant. As a result their unborn baby can be physiologically dependent on these substances. Some children are born with drugs in their systems, affecting their development and general physical health. Neither Christians nor secular therapists would say this baby is a drug addict or they have SUD. Why not? Because they didn't *choose to use the substance.* Choice is an overflow of the mind, not the brain. The child didn't sin, even though they were on drugs. The mother sinned in using drugs and endangering the life of her child. She not only rebelled against God for herself, but also endangered the physical well-being of her child, which brings greater accountability (cf. Exod. 21:22–25).

This means that not all habitual uses of something are sin issues. *But most are.* If we are talking about drunkenness, or what secular therapy would call AUD, it is an issue of disobedience. If we are talking about SUD, it is an issue of disobedience. These problems are rooted in a rejection of God's plans for one's life.

What Is the Source of Most Physiological Cravings? The Body

The Bible does speak about having physical cravings. For instance, in Jesus's sinlessness, He still had cravings like hunger, thirst, and even tiredness (John 19:28; Matt. 4:2; Matt. 8:24–25). We know that Jesus "knew no sin" (2 Cor. 5:21) and yet he experienced physiological, human cravings like you and I do.

What does this tell us? That a physiological craving is not inherently sinful. Just because you crave rest, food, and water does not mean you are sinning and need to repent. Now, you may let the desires of your body actually move you to a place of sin (Eph. 2:3), but that does not mean that a physiological craving is inherently sinful.

As a college professor, I try to remind students that if they are not resting well during finals week, then their body will catch up—sleeplessness doesn't go away. A person's body needs rest, and those all-night study sessions can be very shortsighted.

However, there is one more nuance to consider. Your inner person, like your mind, can influence your body to crave something. Don't believe me? Just watch the food commercials. The juicy burger is flipping through the screen. Cheddar cheese slaps itself onto the burger, then fresh lettuce and tomato top it all off. All of a sudden, you went from not thinking about eating to seeing a commercial and then moving to the kitchen to eat. How did that happen? Your mind influenced your body. So not every physiological craving comes from the body. The mind can incite these cravings as well.

Biblically, we have seen how the body and soul are interconnected (1 Kings 19:4–8; Ps. 32:4; Acts 27:33–34). The drunkard's brain can absolutely be affected by the use of alcohol, and bring with it brain limitations and capacity issues. For instance, according to the National Institute on Alcohol Abuse and Alcoholism, "Alcohol interferes with the brain's communication pathways and can affect the way the brain looks and works. Alcohol makes it harder for the brain areas controlling balance, memory, speech, and judgment to do their jobs, resulting in a higher likelihood of injuries and other negative outcomes."[24] If this is true, then the brain can influence an inclination to use alcohol. Most theologians I know agree with this.

We should also consider the plasticity of the brain, how it physically changes over time in both positive and negative ways. The website Very Well Mind says, "Neuroplasticity is the brain's ability to change and adapt due to experience. It is an umbrella term referring to the brain's ability to change, reorganize, or grow neural networks."[25] That means the physical structure and functioning of your brain changes over time. So if you have a darkened mind that habitually abuses alcohol, the structure of your brain will literally change—for the worse.

But ask any former "addict" about how they changed after they stopped using drugs and you will see that a changed mind (perhaps a transformed mind?) leads to the brain being healed and being restored to higher physiological capacities. The brain changes and the mind helps shape the capacities of the brain.

So for a Christian, what does renewal of the mind also bring with it (Eph. 4:23)? A healthier brain.

Can a Christian "Lose Control" in Addiction?

In meeting with many Christians for counseling, I can say that a person who has repeatedly misused drugs or alcohol will have stronger cravings that really do affect the choices they make. The Bible would definitely support the idea that the body can influence the inner person, to include that of physical cravings for substances. In this way, a brain is making it hard for the Christian to say no. If Sarah were a Christian, and I'm not sure she was, then her getting clean from meth definitely brought physical cravings that had to be denied.

However, as followers of Jesus we know that we never *have* to sin.

I have mentioned Romans 6:6; consider verse 14: "For sin will have no dominion over you, since you are not under law but under grace." Biblically, we cannot think that we are "addicted" to sinful actions, even if we have strong physiological compulsions and cravings for them. The Christian cannot be addicted to sin because through conversion, the power of sin is broken for the Christian.

This is not to say that the Christian cannot have strong physiological cravings for substances. Alcohol. Meth. Nicotine. Yes, each of these creates a physiological craving for a substance, but no Christian is forced to sin by their body—they willingly submit themselves to sin (Rom. 6:19). What if there is a really, really strong physiological craving toward alcohol, which often leads to drunkenness? Can that Christian still honor God? Yes, there is no instance in which a Christian must sin (1 Cor. 10:13).

Our culture *currently*—and this may change—knows that a "sex addict" can resist the temptation and we still hold the hypersexualized responsible for their actions. The same is true for the drunkard and drug abuser. Yes, they have potentially trashed their brain so much that it is hard for them to choose what is right, but the reality is that if a person is a Christian, they never *must* sin.

A Word of Caution, and Encouragement

It pains me to write this.

Sarah slowly stopped coming to counseling. She had made very few changes when she was there. After the sessions ended, I would still see her at church once in a while, and she always graciously addressed me as "Pastor Greg."

I was headed to church one Wednesday when I got a call from Sarah's mother. Sarah had been found dead. After her son was taken from her indefinitely, she went back to meth. We are not sure how she died, but it most likely was connected to her use of the drug. When she had lost all hope of getting her son back, she gave up all restraint and went "all in." She went back to the streets.

The English theologian John Owen wrote, "You need to be killing sin, or it will be killing you."[26] In this he echoed the warning of Scripture: "for the wages of sin is death" (Rom. 6:23). Sarah didn't repent of her sins in using meth, and it killed her. I don't know if Sarah was a Christian, as I saw very little fruit in her life, though I know she heard the Gospel before she died. It was such a sad turn of events, because we loved her and wanted to see her get clean. But she didn't.

Let me tell you a happier story.

Another lady I was counseling—we'll call her Mary—was abusing alcohol. She would drink every day after work to the point of inebriation and the alcohol was taking its toll on her marriage, her body, and her parenting. On some days she would consume a whole bottle of wine.

Mary was a gracious Christian, but she refused to let go. Her non-Christian husband was patient, but obviously sick of it. He didn't want to abandon her, but he also was starting to say she needed to get help "or else." In counseling, I could never persuade Mary to forsake drinking. I remember countless times of telling her to get it out of the house. We talked about going to rehab, and of taking her sin seriously. We talked through how she was worshipping escape and comfort in the bottle, when she should be finding refuge in Christ. Her husband was supportive of change. I tried to both warn and encourage her to obedience, but she wouldn't let go. She was unwilling to totally get rid of wine from the house, and there was no real change. It was sad.

Counseling eventually stopped due to lack of progress, and we lost touch for a season. It wasn't until she came to church one day, after returning from a rehab center, that she shared the news about being clean from alcohol. Her marriage had been disintegrating, and her daughter was getting older and noticing her issues, so Mary finally *chose* to let go. Going to rehab was a way of letting go of control. When she finally chose to honor God, she was able to get clean. She repented in her mind of the use of alcohol, and rehab helped her body and brain to detox.

Mary repented, and it led to life. Sarah didn't repent and it led to death. If you don't know the difference between the mind and the brain, you will approach these circumstances all wrong. Call it a disease instead of disobedience and a person needs treatment, not repentance. Sarah needed repentance—she had access to all the treatment resources she could desire through the state. Yet without repentance, her sin killed her. Of course, the brain can be affected through substance abuse. However, the mind is free in Christ to honor Christ. *The Christian never has to give in to sin.* The Christian does not have to choose to sin, not even once. If you are struggling with a besetting sin, something the world calls an addiction, you do not have an incurable illness. You can be set free.

CHAPTER 13

Questions, Objections, and Clarifications

As I have tested these ideas at speaking engagements and conferences, and in conversations with Master's University faculty, I have received similar questions, most of which have helped me clarify or adjust my positions.

Many people want to know the ten-second answer. I understand that—people are busy. This chapter is just that, a quick reference guide to the questions that are addressed throughout the book. If you're turning here because you just want the bottom line up front, that's great, but if you are intrigued by these answers, then you must read the rest of the book because I will explain them in greater depth.

What if there is mental illness, but the science isn't advanced enough to study it?

First of all, we have to acknowledge that science is—in amazing ways—developing and advancing. If the Lord does not tarry, then in the near future doctors may complete surgeries with robots while being in another part of the world.[1] Wow! Three cheers for scientific advancement!

There will always be limitations on what science can do. One limitation will be the psychosomatic illnesses that seem to actually stem from nonphysical sources. Stress, anxiety, depression, and so forth have immaterial and material stimuli. While a person might not only be depressed because of his thoughts, if he meditates on the woes of his life instead of that which is true and honorable (Phil. 4:8) then it will inevitably affect his mood. In this way, science will not be able to—now or ever—change a person's thinking. Why not? Because thoughts are immaterial. They come from the mind.

Is it possible, then, that the science will become so advanced that we will be able to more accurately identify physiological versus immaterial etiologies? Yes, absolutely. Science and medical care can continue to advance so that matters of the body become even better understood and treatable by medications. But remember, MRI results do not tell you *why* something in the brain happened in the first place. Yes, you will be able to accurately understand the body, but you will not necessarily understand the etiology of that issue. It could come from sin, in all seriousness (cf. 1 Cor. 11:30). A medical test will never be able to identify that. So medical science will continue to progress in amazing and profound ways to better help us understand what is happening in the body.

Will medical science ever advance to the point where it can examine the "mind"? No, it won't. The mind is immaterial. You cannot place it in a beaker or under a microscope. No matter how far it advances, the medical sciences by their very nature require observability, repeatability, and verifiability. This will *always* make the study of the mind within the natural sciences evasive. Ontologically, the immaterial will never be observable.

So I do expect that medical sciences will continue to advance to be able to more accurately identify the brain's and body's responses to the mind. In the same vein, I do not expect medical or natural sciences to ever be able to observe the unobservable immaterial mind. The broken promises of psychiatry since the 1980s further remind us of the perennial limitations of medical science.

Are psychotropic medications helpful? Are they wrong to use?

I've met with people who have been on psychotropic medications for years and are stable, and in some way the medication seems to help their brain. Now, neither I nor they may be totally sure about *how* that medication is helping, but the person has fewer mood swings, doesn't experience as many low points, or has attempted going off the medication years ago and experienced significant disruptions to their mood and thought life. They do not place their hope in the medication to save them, so to speak, and are not legitimizing sinful behavior on or off the medication.

In that case, I recommend that if it seems the medication is helping, then *stay on the medication*. I've counseled enough and pastored for a long enough time to say that if a person isn't placing their hope in their medications, sees their medications as helpful but not their god, and doesn't legitimize sinful behavior, then they do not necessarily have to be weaned off them. This principle is summarized by saying that a person can take psychotropic medications in a legal, God-honoring way.

However, a person must utilize that medication while acknowledging that the medication is not treating their mind, but rather is influencing their brain (or body) in such a way that it seems to be immediately helpful, making it easier for them to glorify God with their mind. The end. It can be as simple as that.

It's important to note that for every person who is helped by psychotropic medications, there is another who is hurt by them. The *Wall Street Journal* published a scathing review of online clinicians who prescribed a stimulant for a man whose online prescription contributed to a drug relapse.[2] It takes only cursory research to find that those who go on antidepressants and stimulants often experience the negative side effects of suicidal ideation, mood dysregulation, sadness, insomnia, and lethargy, all of which wreak havoc on their personal wellness.[3] I have had both friends and counselees start antidepressants only to experience the damage they can cause in either their side effects or their combination with other medications. The psychotropic isn't always helpful, so proceed with prayer, caution, and close advising from a physician. Do labs, scans, X-rays, blood work, allergy tests, and check on the quality of the thyroid, diet, sleep, and exercise. If those results are inconclusive, then focus on the mind. Meet with an experienced biblical counselor who can help you unpack your struggles through the lens of Scripture. Try to evaluate, biblically, what is happening in your life. Consider how your mind is playing a part in this.

Biblical counselors should *not* dabble in adjusting medications, and it is not inherently sinful to take legally prescribed psychotropic medication (1 Tim. 5:23). Sure, it may not always be of help if the primary issues are of the mind, but if a person is taking psychotropic medication legally, with God-honoring motivations, it does not mean that they are in sin and need to drop the meds. Some biblical counselors have communicated that any such use of meds is a compromise of one's faith, and that is not true. Sure, in some cases people are making medications their god. But in other instances it's much more pragmatic: The med seems to help. A person can *finally* sleep again.

How should I respond to my child's mental illness label?

The school psychologist is using the terminology based on secular interpretations of symptoms and you need to work through the diagnosis with what those symptoms mean according to the Bible.

For instance, if your child is diagnosed with ADHD, you have a child who has a unique type of giftedness that doesn't lend itself to sitting still or focusing on a particular subject. That's not a disease or illness. Your child doesn't have some incurable condition. However, your child may be struggling with these things. So ask good questions, or get a qualified, experienced biblical counselor to help ask good questions. Learn what is happening and then discern from God's Word what to do in response to this.

My child's school would like to "test" them for a mental illness or impairment. What should I do?

If you sense this is the only way for your child to get helpful resources, then allow for the testing while reinterpreting what diagnosis is offered. Most likely, your child will be told they have a learning disability. Help your child see that these are arbitrary diagnoses and to *not* view themselves through the lens of the secular therapeutic terminology. Rather, equip them to think biblically about the label. But get tested to access the resources that the school would gladly provide—tutors, smaller classes, quieter learning environment, and so forth.

I see no problem with accepting some of these benefits while reinterpreting the secular therapeutic. In fact, I have many students at The Master's University who have educational accommodations, and I'm perfectly supportive and fine with that. The reality is that you can benefit from some of these resources, but that doesn't mean you have a learning disability. You may benefit from a tutor, but that doesn't mean you have an illness called ADHD.

Should I use the term mental health?

I've stopped using the term *mental health* because it is confusing. As Christians, we should use biblical terminology to help us think about things biblically. That means when we knowingly use terms that don't accurately capture the way the Bible speaks of something, we are being needlessly vague. Don't use *mental health*; say *mind renewal*.

Are so-called mental illnesses real?

There is truth in that what is being called a mental illness may exist, but usually, it is not physiological illnesses. So you can easily say that ADHD exists, but it's not an illness or disorder. This is why I wrote a book titled *Helping Your Family Through PTSD*. I do believe that PTSD can exist, but it is not a mental illness. When a person uses the term *PTSD*, they are describing a group of symptoms. The term alone doesn't tell you why you are struggling; it only describes what you are struggling with.

So the only truth that comes with so-called mental illness terminology is a description of the symptoms that a person is facing.

What is a social problem versus a mental illness?

A person can have certain social struggles because of their body, brain, upbringing, childhood environment, family background, or other reasons, but that does not mean they have a so-called mental illness. If you were raised by drug dealers, of course it would affect your social development. In 2018, a family in California raising thirteen children was abusing them, chaining them to beds, underfeeding them, and preventing them from leaving the house.[4] If you were raised in this home, you might need some time to learn social skills based on a lifetime of mistreatment, but that's still technically different from an illness of the mind.

I'll never forget when I was speaking at a church in central California and one of the attendees at the conference said that he had been released from prison within the last few years and was raised in an awful home, with no father present. He said he had to learn how to be affectionate and hug his kids. He never received affection himself as a kid and so needed to learn these social skills. We were all rooting for him to grow in this area. But just because a person has a social problem does not mean that they have a mental illness.

What does it mean to "renew your mind" (Rom. 12:2)?

Simply put, you don't renew your mind, but God does. The verb *to be transformed* in Romans 12:2 is an imperative, which makes it a command. However, it's in the passive voice. That means you submit yourself to the truth of God and He renews you. This is also true for Ephesians 4:23, where "be renewed" is in the passive voice.

So what does the Christian do? They "think like Christ" (Phil. 2:5) and guard their mind with the truth of the Bible (Phil. 4:8), and God renews their mind as they do this. The renewal means that God is restoring your mind to a mint condition of an image bearer. The more renewal happens, the more your mind is restored, so that it can function more and more as it was originally designed to (2 Cor. 3:18).

Do certain so-called mental illnesses have a biological source? Autism or ADHD, for instance?

Sure, it's possible that autism has a physiological cause. In speaking with parents of autistic children, a common theme emerges, that their kids had light sensitivities, aversion to chaotic schedules, and noise sensitivities, that they loved a structured home and didn't resonate with physical discipline, along with a few other themes "since they were little." Many parents observe that their child has always been that way.

This means that a physiological or genetic factor can underlie autism, and autism can still not be a so-called mental illness. Could the same be true for ADHD? Sure, no problem. Biblically the body can encourage you to have a level of activity that affects focus and being distractable. That is not inherently a sin issue. So a CT scan that shows similarities with children who have ADHD patterns in their brain is not a problem (although it doesn't demonstrate etiology). The Bible makes it clear that your body can encourage you to respond in certain ways, but it never causes you to do so.

The list of so-called mental illnesses is quite long, and the reality is that a physiological trigger may be possible for some of them. In this way, you would want to rethink the role of the brain and the mind. Recall that the brain doesn't cause the mind to do something, even in significant brain impairment. But a biblical worldview is open to finding those physiological sources for so-called mental illnesses, and if one does not seem apparent, then it makes sense to focus on the mind. Autism and ADHD may have a physiological source, yet the brain doesn't control the mind.

If the brain and mind influence each other, wouldn't medications help the mind?

Not necessarily. The medication is affecting the brain, but the mind is immaterial. Think of the brain as the filter through which the mind expresses itself. The mind is affected only by the filter. Thus the mind is influenced because the brain is influenced. However, the mind is not necessarily *helped*.

Remember, we want to have healthy brains, but the mind is really why you think what you think or choose what you choose. The mind is the immaterial seat of your cognition. You cannot take a psychotropic to change your thoughts, but you can take one to slow your brain down, which may help you focus on the mind. Or you can take a psychotropic to help you sleep, and then the refreshed and rested brain can be helpful for when you're renewing your mind to respond more biblically.

Can a person be out of their mind?

Yes, when their senses and mind don't match reality. See the chapter on insanity for the full answer.

Why does a TBI affect cognition?

This is a fair question, and traumatic brain injuries can be anything from a concussion to a full-blown violent blow to your head and thus your brain. Sports, car accidents, fights, and more can severely damage your brain, which affects the expression of your mind. A damaged brain can exacerbate struggles you already had in your mind. You could experience a sense of fogginess in your thinking, or struggle to recall specific details. A police officer I met with for counseling was run over while directing traffic. After the accident, it took him longer to express his thoughts. I honestly had to discipline myself to not finish his sentences. His brain was damaged, and his mind was affected in how it expressed itself.

A person's mind can be vibrant while their brain is deteriorating. After all, that is the promise of 2 Corinthians 4:16: "So we do not lose heart. Though our outer self is wasting away, our inner self is being renewed day by day." Not to minimize the awfulness of a TBI, but all of our brains are wasting away. A Christian's mind is being renewed even while their brain is wasting away. This means that as we get older it will take all of us a bit more to process cognitively and have clear thoughts. However, that is the brain influencing the mind, not controlling it. The brain doesn't make you think thoughts. It influences the expression of them. Thus a TBI affects cognition in this way.

Christ Offers More

All Scripture is breathed out by God and profitable
for teaching, for reproof, for correction, and for
training in righteousness, that the man of God may
be complete, equipped for every good work.

—2 TIMOTHY 3:16–17

Many people I have counseled remind me of the woman in the eighth chapter of Luke who came to Jesus. "As Jesus went," the chapter says, "the people pressed around him. And there was a woman who had had a discharge of blood for twelve years, and though she had spent all her living on physicians, she could not be healed by anyone. She came up behind him and touched the fringe of his garment, and immediately her discharge of blood ceased" (v. 42b–44).

I've spent much of this book arguing that many of our struggles are spiritual issues, not medical ones. So I'm only making this comparison metaphorically. But just as this woman spent so much money looking for physical healing from many physicians and still was not healed, so also many people find that there's a certain hopelessness at the end of the secular therapeutic process.

Perhaps that includes you. You've bounced from therapist to therapist, tinkered with medications, and only become more and more hopeless, drowning in the arbitrary diagnoses and empty promises of secular therapy, which brings "coping mechanisms" and medications.

Couched in seemingly medical terminology—like "mental health professional" and "mental health treatment"—the secular therapeutic is bankrupt. Not poor. Not trending toward bankruptcy. Secular therapeutic is more broke than Enron and Kmart combined. We see all around us that the secular therapeutic defaults on its promise to help.

Perhaps even your pastor shares insights from therapists about good coping mechanisms and how to handle stress. Your family member speaks through therapeutic terminology about themselves and the world. Your kids are imbibing the zeitgeist, seeing themselves as triggered and traumatized. What will end all the craziness and suffering that secular mental health culture has wrought? The answer is simple: recognizing the sufficiency and beauty of the Bible.

You might be thinking, "That's cute, but I need professional help." And I agree that you shouldn't bring your problems to just anyone, without discernment and testing. And of course, if you have a medical issue, you should see a doctor.

My point in all this is not that medical doctors are bad—not even close. Rather, I'm saying that while the world has limits on what it can heal, Jesus does not. Secular therapy, even with all of its confusion between the mind and the brain, can sometimes treat our symptoms. But Jesus can save and completely transform our minds. If He has the power to heal our even outer-man issues when He wills, why should we not trust Him with the struggles we face in our inner man?

Many people think about faith and salvation in a compartmentalized way. "Yes, Jesus helps save my soul, but I need a mental health expert for the day-to-day issues." If this is you, let me challenge and encourage you: your view of salvation is too small. There is so much more that the Bible offers, you can spend the rest of your life discovering it and being transformed by it.

Jesus is not an addendum to your therapist. He doesn't just offer positive encouragement while the psychologist or psychiatrist does the real work. If Jesus's only role in your life is to save you for Heaven

(Acts 4:12) and be worshipped on Sunday morning, then you are missing out on so much more. Consider this description of Christ in Colossians 1:15–20:

> *He is the image of the invisible God, the firstborn of all*
> *creation. For by him all things were created, in heaven*
> *and on earth, visible and invisible, whether thrones or*
> *dominions or rulers or authorities—all things were created*
> *through him and for him. And he is before all things, and*
> *in him all things hold together. And he is the head of the*
> *body, the church. He is the beginning, the firstborn from*
> *the dead, that in everything he might be preeminent. For*
> *in him all the fullness of God was pleased to dwell, and*
> *through him to reconcile to himself all things, whether on*
> *earth or in heaven, making peace by the blood of his cross.*

Jesus created you, and everyone who has ever lived, forming mankind from the dust of the ground, giving the breath of life to what previously had not been alive (Gen. 2:7). Jesus rules over all things, and He upholds the universe by the Word of His power (Heb. 1:3). He has the power to destroy both soul and body in Hell, and He is mighty to save so that the gates of Hell won't stand against His bride, the church (Matt. 10:28 and 16:18). He is the God of all comfort, who comforts us in our afflictions (1 Cor. 1:3–4). He is gentle and lowly, so that a bruised reed He will not break (Matt. 11:29 and 12:20).

He is strong enough to save even you, and not only from Hell, but from the afflictions of depression and anxiety and countless other diagnoses. He is able to bring you through trials of various kinds, so that you can say with the Apostle Paul:

> *We are afflicted in every way, but not crushed;*
> *perplexed, but not driven to despair;*

persecuted, but not forsaken;
struck down, but not destroyed;
always carrying in the body the death of Jesus,
so that the life of Jesus may also be manifested in our bodies.
—2 CORINTHIANS 4:8–10

But whatever gain I had, I counted as loss for the
sake of Christ. Indeed, I count everything as loss
because of the surpassing worth of knowing Jesus
Christ my Lord. For his sake I have suffered the loss
of all things, and count them as rubbish, in order
that I may gain Christ and be found in him.
—PHILIPPIANS 3:7–9A

For I consider that the sufferings of this present time
are not worth comparing with the glory that is to be
revealed to us. . . . For I am sure that neither death
nor life, nor angels nor rulers, nor things present nor
things to come, nor powers, nor height nor depth, nor
anything else in all creation, will be able to separate
us from the love of God in Christ Jesus our Lord.
—ROMANS 8:18, 38–39

Oh, that every one of us had this view of Christ all the time! He is able to meet our every need, no matter how dark a night our souls might be in. Celebrate that, dear believer.

Jesus, in this way, is who we really need for the well-being of our minds. He regulates my wayward thoughts and offers us His own mind! *We have the mind of Christ* (1 Cor. 2:16). If you view Jesus as well-meaning but still not enough, then you don't understand Him as revealed in the pages of the Bible.

Similarly, if you view the Bible as just a great historical writing, one of the great pieces of Western literature with many helpful moralistic ideas, you're missing out on so much more. Listen to Psalm 19:7–11:

> The law of the LORD is perfect,
> reviving the soul;
>
> the testimony of the LORD is sure,
> making wise the simple;
>
> the precepts of the LORD are right,
> rejoicing the heart;
>
> the commandment of the LORD is pure,
> enlightening the eyes;
>
> the fear of the LORD is clean,
> enduring forever;
>
> the rules of the LORD are true,
> and righteous altogether.
>
> More to be desired are they than gold,
> even much fine gold;
>
> sweeter also than honey
> and drippings of the honeycomb.
>
> Moreover, by them is your servant warned;
> in keeping them there is great reward.

Verse 7 says, "The law of the Lord is perfect, *reviving the soul*." God's Word is not a historical snapshot of yesteryear; it is the very light that illuminates our paths (Ps. 119:105). The Bible is not my truth, it is *the* truth (John 17:17). It is the Christian's sustenance (Matt. 4:4). When you read the Bible, you read the very breath of God (2 Tim. 3:16). When you understand this, you can say with Peter, "Lord, to whom shall we go? You have the words of eternal life" (John 6:68).

God's Word is the authoritative guide to understanding our struggles, not the DSM. It is the only lens through which we can truly understand who we are. If secular therapy has become the lens through which you view yourself and this world, and your therapist is your functional savior, then *you* are the one who is missing out. Secular therapy has fallen short of its promises. Promises like finding biological markers for so-called mental illnesses, and to destigmatize those with diagnoses. It has failed. But God's promises never fail. While the methods of psychology and psychiatry might provide some symptom relief, will they ever cause rejoicing in the heart? Can they make the simple wise with the wisdom that is from above? Can they transform our minds to be like Christ's?

After years of working as a biblical counselor, my faith in the Bible's power and application for every issue of life has only grown. It has given me a deep amazement of the Scriptures, which I hope you share and will grow in as well. The Psalmist says, "In the way of your testimonies I delight as much as in all riches" (119:14). Do you know, brothers and sisters, that you can find delight in the Word of God?

The Bible tells us how to change (Eph. 4:22–24). And it may be a surprise to you, but you have all that you need in Christ and His Word to change (2 Pet. 1:3–4; 2 Tim. 3:17). Secular therapy is not helping our nation. In fact, it's causing even more confusion. Instead of seeing the Bible as having some pat Sunday school answers, commit yourself to learning the Bible and how it teaches change. Put off anxiety and put on trust in a sovereign God. Put off hopelessness and put on biblical hope. Through the work of the Holy Spirit your mind is capacitated to know and understand the things of God (2 Cor. 3:17; Titus 3:5). You need a mind that works properly, and that is what happens to your mind at the moment you are saved. Without a renewed mind, your mind is corrupt, darkened, and calloused. The Bible promises that through the Gospel, you can have the mind of Christ. Not a treated mind, but a transformed mind.

Where can you learn the Bible better, hear the Gospel regularly, and be encouraged to grow in sanctification by learning from others how to put on the mind of Christ? At your local church.

Nearly half a millennia ago, Martin Bucer wrote in *Concerning the True Care of Souls*, "All strengthening of the weak and ailing sheep depends on the word of God being faithfully set forth to them, and them being led to listen to it gladly and have all their joy in it."[1] Your pastor is the overseer of your soul (Heb. 13:17) and in your local church you find brothers and sisters who will remind you of the truth of God's Word. We need pastors who are teaching the Bible on Sunday mornings, not sharing psychology insights. Church is not about donuts and chitchat, but about hearing the Word of God and doing it (James 1:21–22). When you are bitter, you need a friend to remind you of the truth so that you don't get poisoned by bitterness. When you grumble, you need a friend to encourage gratitude.

Your mind will only be truly well if you are connected to a solid local church that will help you abide in the Scriptures and draw near to Christ. This shouldn't surprise you after all we have covered in this book. In fact, in my experience, those with the worst counseling needs are often the least connected to a local church. In the process of biblical change described in Colossians 3:5–14, you'll notice that transformation takes place within the context of the local church:

> *Put to death therefore what is earthly in you: sexual immorality, impurity, passion, evil desire, and covetousness, which is idolatry. On account of these the wrath of God is coming. In these you too once walked, when you were living in them. But now you must put them all away: anger, wrath,*

malice, slander, and obscene talk from your mouth. Do not
lie to one another, seeing that you have put off the old self
with its practices and have put on the new self, which is being
renewed in knowledge after the image of its creator. Here
there is not Greek and Jew, circumcised and uncircumcised,
barbarian, Scythian, slave, free; but Christ is all, and in all.

    Put on then, as God's chosen ones, holy and
beloved, compassionate hearts, kindness, humility,
meekness, and patience, bearing with one another
and, if one has a complaint against another, forgiving
each other; as the Lord has forgiven you, so you also
must forgive. And above all these put on love, which
binds everything together in perfect harmony.

How can you grow in compassion, kindness, and patience with others if you're trying to do the Christian life by yourself? We only grow muscles by using them, and so also we grow in the fruit of the Spirit through doing life together with our brothers and sisters in Christ. That's why I say as often as I can:

> The local church is the most important organization on earth.

Not just important for the world, but for you. So join a good local church if you are not already part of one, even if you sense things are going well in your life. Look for a church that loves the Bible, teaches it, and submits to it.

Lastly, when you need help, find a good, certified biblical counselor. Note that I've said "certified," because we need someone who is held accountable. Biblical counselors use the Bible to counsel and reject secular therapeutic models for what they are—a sham. In one of the appendixes, I give practical steps on how to find a certified biblical counselor in your area. Don't settle for the darkened mind of a secular therapist for you or your kids; rather meet with a certified biblical counselor who will use the authoritative and sufficient Bible to truly help you. There are also biblical counseling books, podcasts, websites, and conferences, all of which can help you understand our inner-man issues biblically. You can find many of these resources through Fortis Institute at fortisinstitute.org.

Through His Word and His Church, Christ can transform your mind to be like His own. He calls us to do so much more than what the world offers. And so my prayer is that, as you finish this book, your life will ever more reflect what we are called to in Romans 12:1–2:

> *I appeal to you therefore, brothers, by the mercies of*
> *God, to present your bodies as a living sacrifice, holy and*
> *acceptable to God, which is your spiritual worship. Do*
> *not be conformed to this world, but be transformed by the*
> *renewal of your mind, that by testing you may discern what*
> *is the will of God, what is good and acceptable and perfect.*

And, as you pursue Christ and He transforms you, may your heart also cry out in worship:

> *"To the King of the ages, immortal, invisible, the only*
> *God, be honor and glory forever and ever. Amen."*
> —1 TIMOTHY 1:17

My Visit to the Psychiatrist

January 3, 2023, 8 a.m.

My intention in visiting a psychiatrist was to simply learn about the diagnostic process firsthand. I wanted to know whether a psychiatrist would be willing to diagnose me—though I was healthy overall in body and mind—and prescribe a medication, and how they would arrive at that conclusion. I believed that if I had asked something like this in an interview for a book, I might get a different answer. I wanted to know whether they would empirically test me. How would they know whether I had an inner-person or outer-person issue? I wanted to be honest about who I was and my emotions, actions, and moods during the appointments so as to 1) not create a situation that is unfair for a psychiatrist to treat and 2) ensure I don't create personal problems in the research process (you know, the kind that get the police called on you).

So, I simply answered questions as they applied to me, in all honesty. In December 2022 I reached out to my provider to schedule an appointment with a psychiatrist. Here is how the process unfolded.

First I was screened on the phone for what seemed to be the severity of the problems I was facing. I was asked questions about my emotions, moods, problems, any suicidal or homicidal tendencies, work injuries, workers' compensation claims, or any legal problems. After answering all of them, I was able to schedule another screening appointment with a licensed professional therapist two weeks later.

On January 3, 2023, I met with an LMFT over a videoconferencing app. It was my choice to use the telemedicine option, for the sake of convenience. I was also really hoping to check the box to be allowed to speak with a psychiatrist. I had three more questionnaires to complete for this appointment. They were similar to the first one, asking more about my living environment, family relationships, legal problems, and suicidal or homicidal tendencies (if any!). Naturally, there were many questions about whether I had a desire to hurt myself or others.

Once the meeting started, the LMFT, whom I am calling Mr. Smith, told me this would simply be an evaluation meeting for about thirty minutes. He graciously provided two phone numbers for me as we started, one to reach him and one for a crisis hotline number. He then began to confirm all the data that I provided him in the prior surveys, although he hadn't seen the two recent ones prior to our meeting. He asked the following questions, although this list isn't exhaustive, and I provided my responses in italics.

- Do you have trouble sleeping? *Yes, sometimes I do.*
- Do you have a lack of motivation? *Yes.*
- Do you experience a depressed mood? *Yes, sometimes.*
- Do you lack confidence in yourself? *No.*
- Do you feel guilty? *No.*
- Do you have decreased interest in activities? *Yes, sometimes.*
- Are you able to go to work? *Yes.*
- Do you struggle with worry? *Yes.*
- What do you do when you worry? *I put my trust in the Lord, actively meditate on the truth of Scripture, and attempt to move on with my next activity.*
- Have you ever received mental health therapy? *Depending on how you define that, but yes, through church, since I am a Christian.*
- Do you own any firearms? *Yes, all of which are registered with the state of California and legally owned.*
- Do you believe you have a healthy social support network? *Yes.*
- What is your relationship like with your sons? *Awesome.*

- What is your relationship like with your wife? *Better than awesome.*
- What is your goal in meeting with an LMFT? *Well, I'd actually like to speak with a psychiatrist, which is why I was sent here first. I'd like to get a medical professional's input on my life and I'm not interested in meeting with an LMFT.*

At this point, Mr. Smith seemed perplexed at what I was really reaching out for, which is totally fair. I told him multiple times that there were no acute issues or crises, but that I wanted to speak with a psychiatrist to get their perspective on my life. He said that my anxiety and depression were most likely not severe enough to warrant a meeting with a psychiatrist but he would put in a referral for me nevertheless. He said what I was experiencing seemed normal. At this point, I asked, "How do I know my symptoms are severe enough and no longer normal?" As you may suspect, there wasn't a laboratory or vile of blood that I needed to provide. Mr. Smith said, "when you can no longer function."

The meeting ended after twenty minutes, and he said he would let me know if I can get an appointment with a psychiatrist.

The key takeaways from this meeting:

1. In light of the above, my provider's system is not slap-happy with diagnosing or even granting access to a psychiatrist.
2. Had I merely said that my symptoms were worse and I couldn't go to work, things would have been very different. There is no empirical way to prove I have severe symptoms or not.

Early February 2023

I did get an appointment with a psychiatrist. When I left the meeting with the LMFT, I wondered whether I would, but the health care provider called me to schedule my psychiatrist appointment within three or four days. I then was a slacker and took about a week to call them back, but eventually I scheduled my appointment: Valentine's Day 2023. How romantic.

February 14, 2023, 7:30 a.m.
I received a phone call from my health care provider yesterday saying that Dr. Jones, my psychiatrist, was not going to come into the office. So I could choose between a telehealth appointment or rescheduling. After attempting to reschedule for an in-person visit, I found that the next appointment wasn't for three weeks, so I decided to keep the one I had.

I set up the computer in my dining room while unkempt and still in my pajamas. This is the way I typically am dressed for my early mornings, so I figured a 7:30 a.m. appointment would also get this type of Greg. However, I knew this could be a part of the assessment for my well-being. While not wanting to skew the assessment, I do think a person's appearance can affect a practitioner's assessment. I know it does for me.

Dr. Jones joined me in the videoconferencing room at 7:44 a.m. and asked a great many questions. The first was "What encouraged you to reach out for help?" I answered, "I'd like to get a medical professional's perspective on what I'm experiencing." I appreciated the thoughtful and mostly comprehensive questions she asked. Here are some questions she asked for about thirty minutes, until approximately 8:15 a.m.

- What are you experiencing?
- Do you have depressed moods?
- Do you experience decreased motivation?
- What do you get anxious over?
- What causes anxiety?
- Are there specific themes?
- Why reach out now?
- How long have you felt this way?
- What happened in May when you said this started?

- Does your family have a history of mental illness?
- How frequently do you experience this?
- How are your energy levels?
- How is your focus?
- Does anyone else say you need counseling?
- How have people responded when you told them you were going to meet with a psychiatrist?
- Are you required to come to meet with me?
- How did your wife respond when you told her you were reaching out for help?
- Do you normally take the advice given to you?
- If not, why not?
- Why didn't you listen to your dentist?
- Are energy levels and focus getting better or worse?
- Do you want to hurt yourself?
- Do you have firearms?
- How are they stored?
- What do your work responsibilities look like?
- How many hours per week do you work?
- Have your moods affected your work performance?
- How is your sleep?
- Do you have dreams?
- What are your dreams about?

Dr. Jones then began to describe what she was hearing. She said that it seemed like I was experiencing symptoms of major depressive disorder as well as anxiety. However, she wasn't sure if the anxiety was from the depression or vice versa. She then offered her recommendation of options going forward: either antidepressants or therapy. She said therapy could help with adjustment of my moods and perhaps there would be no need for antidepressants, but I could receive antidepressants if I desired.

"What do you recommend?" I asked. Dr. Jones said, "I recommend

therapy and if that doesn't help you adjust, then trying medication."
I said, "Okay."

We then discussed therapy and she said it was client-centered, where I would help identify the goals of counseling and the therapist would help me reach them. I obviously had no desire to enter into long-term therapy, but I also had genuine questions about the process. "Does the therapist tell me if my goals are bad?" When she asked for an example, I put forth, "If I wanted to become a murderer, does the therapist help me reach that goal or would they say that is wrong?" She smiled and said the therapist would not give me right-or-wrong evaluations, but rather evaluations based on what is achievable.

She then told me of the internal therapists available to me and we then discussed scheduling options. Dr. Jones bid me farewell with a gracious, "It was nice to meet you."

Observations

What's interesting is that Dr. Jones was willing to provide an antidepressant after no blood test, no labs, and never having taken one of my vital signs. However, the medication route was available for me.

Dr. Jones became convinced that my work responsibilities were adding pressure to my life, but she never asked how my youngest child (who was fifteen months old then) was affecting my sleep. She simply noted that my sleep was indeed disrupted. She also never asked what personally changed in my life in the last year, and the reality is I had a family friend stay with us for about five months. In thirty minutes, Dr. Jones gathered what she believed to be enough information to make a diagnosis and recommended steps for care. She was nearly fifteen minutes late to the appointment, asked questions for thirty, and then was able to offer her recommendations.

In all fairness to Dr. Jones, she wasn't on a rampage to prescribe medication. She presented medication or therapy as options and asked

me what I wanted to do. For the sake of this book, I asked for her recommendation. I wonder how another person would respond if they
were facing difficulty? Would they trust the process of therapy, or
would they push for immediate relief from medications? Would they
really want to talk about their life with a therapist for appointment
after appointment, when they had the alternative of the convenience
of the pill? While Dr. Jones wasn't medication-happy, would some
patients be?

Lastly, she was a great data gatherer. In biblical counseling we are
trained to ask questions, and she did that quite well. She rushed and
missed obvious facts about my life, but did ask most of the questions
for thirty minutes. Out of those questions, the interpretation was almost entirely based on her worldview. Remember, no lab results, only
Dr. Jones's perspective of my struggles. While she seemed to be kind
and caring, Dr. Jones was more like a spiritual advisor with the ability
to prescribe medications. And that must be part of the draw to psychiatrists in the first place.

Habits for a Healthy Brain

While I'm not a medical doctor, I do attempt to maintain a personal level of health and nutrition as an act of stewardship and worship (Rom. 12:1–2; 1 Cor. 6:19). This affects my counseling and understanding of people as well. We do present our bodies as a living sacrifice in their totality. Thus you exercise as an act of worship, you eat as an act of worship (1 Tim. 4:3). All of these promote a healthier body and a healthier brain. Conversely, if you are physically run-down, don't be surprised if that influences your mind. Being overweight, eating poorly, and sleeping inadequately are signs that you may need to work on stewarding the health.

Now, before all of the gym bros start citing 1 Timothy 4:7 to argue that everyone should go to the gym, let me be clear: *A good steward of the body doesn't worship the appearance of the body, but seeks to keep it healthy for the sake of the Gospel* (1 Cor. 9:27). The good steward probably has a small belly, or higher level of body fat, but generally sleeps and eats well, and doesn't put harmful things into their system—tobacco, drugs, too much alcohol, three apple pies. A good steward is just that, stewarding their body but not idolizing it. Who is a better steward: the gym rat with six-pack abs and three knee injuries from lifting weights, or the person who only walks, eats in moderation, and sleeps like a baby with no injuries? It would seem to me that some of us even endanger our bodies in the name of "health." Instead we should discipline ourselves for the purpose of godliness (1 Tim. 4:7).

What then are habits that contribute to your health, especially for your brain? Well, diet, exercise, and sleep are a mantra that I will ask about in counseling. I also ask about caffeine use, alcohol use, tobacco use, and drug use for the sake of understanding what's going on in a person's life. If I hear that they are only sleeping three or four hours per night, I will encourage them to go to their medical doctor to get help with the body issues that are hurting their sleep. I'll do the same for caffeine and alcohol: work with a medical doctor so that you only use healthy levels of these substances, or abandon them altogether. You don't need to have caffeine and alcohol, and sometimes it would be wiser to let them go completely, even if only for a season.

Here are the guidelines that I encourage counselees to follow:

- **Restorative Sleep:** Try to get eight hours of sleep. Men need less and women need more. In either case, get to bed on time, turn off your electronic gadgets, and don't take naps if you're struggling going to sleep.
- **Healthy Eating:** Don't obsess about caloric intake, but do seek to have a healthier diet. If you're not good at this, then consider meeting with a nutritionist to help you out.
- **Moderate Activity/Exercise:** Many people in white-collar, sedentary jobs are not physically tired at the end of the day. I do think that physical activity is a great way to help you be rested, have cardiovascular health, manage cholesterol, and be ready to go to sleep at night. In my stage of life, four days at thirty minutes per day with moderately vigorous exercise makes sense, but talk to your medical doctor about what they recommend (not the twenty-two-year-old personal trainer at your gym).
- **Rest:** We simply cannot go-go-go all the time. We need to be engaged in fruitful labor, but also have a sabbath. Burnout will happen if you don't learn how to say no to work. Don't get me wrong: six days a week, you work hard, but you should find a day to take a rest. This is to sleep in, eat well, go slow, and help

your body be restored. In counseling, I advise people to create extra free time in their calendar, so they are not running ragged. Find a day to piddle around so you can be refreshed the rest of the week.

When you go to biblical counseling, the counselor should say, "Hey, your sleep seems really off. You should talk to your doctor." If your biblical counselor says, "Hey, your sleep seems really off. I am going to make it a part of your homework to eat salads, get rid of caffeine, and sleep eight hours per night," then your biblical counselor has just stepped into medical, which is not their lane. This is where the holistic biblical counselors go wrong: they blur their jurisdictional lines with a medical doctor. Steward your brain with wise advice from medical professionals. That is their exact realm of expertise.

Habits for a Biblically Transformed Mind

There are things you can regularly do that help contribute to the renewal of your mind, and things the missing of which will contribute to the spiritual hardening of your mind. Shameless plug: I wrote an entire book, *Heart & Habits*, on this topic.[1]

I want to give you some habits that contribute to the renewal of your mind (Eph. 4:23). Remember, God does the transformation according to Romans 12:2; we work out our salvation (Phil. 2:12). There should be no passive approach to sanctification, even though we know God must bring about any genuine mind transformation. This appendix will give you the downstream tools to help with this.

In the order of importance, here are specific habits that help with the renewal of your mind:

- **Bible Engagement:** I do say *engagement* because I mean more than just reading. All of us should be continually engaged in listening to the Bible, reading the Bible, memorizing the Bible, and meditating on the Bible (Ps. 1:1–2). I recommend setting aside at least thirty minutes each day where you can engage in the Bible without distractions. Even if you have kids at home, or you work evenings, you need a time in the Word. I recommend doing it first thing in the morning, so it *always* happens. I have seen in counseling that those who do their Bible engagement at lunch or in the evening before bed often have a lower-quality Bible engagement time. Not everyone, but most. Do you want to have a renewed mind? Start your day with the Scriptures, not your email.

- **Biblical Thinking:** You may be like, "Hold the phone, Gifford, thinking is a habit?" Yes, I do want you to see that your internal thoughts are part of your habits. You should pursue thinking like Jesus (Phil. 2:5) and that means guarding your thoughts with the Bible (Phil. 4:8). An undisciplined mind will wreak havoc in your life. Think about all the awful things of life every day, all day and watch how it hurts you. God calls us to not think on certain things (Col. 3:2) and to think on certain things (Phil. 4:8). This happens internally in your mind. Practice the process of biblical change by putting off unbiblical thoughts and putting on biblical ones (Eph. 4:22–24).

- **Church Attendance:** If you've seen the *Transformed* TV series, you have seen that with everyone I counsel, I ask them to find a Bible-preaching local church and then get involved. Going to church is a habit (Heb. 10:24–25). Maybe you have never thought of it, but waking up on Sunday and going to a local church is a habit. You need to have this habit baked into your life for the sake of renewing your mind. You need your pastor to preach directly from the Bible. You need other Christians to encourage you and periodically rebuke you. Church attendance facilitates mind renewal.

- **Prayer:** Prayer is simply talking to God. We are commanded to pray (Matt. 7:7; James 4:2) and prayer actually has a renewing effect on the mind. By praying we are seeking God's will, not our own (Matt. 6:10). We are submitting to God's plans when we pray according to His will. That means that if I am praying with God-honoring motivations, in God-honoring, not selfish ways, then I am orienting my mind back to God and His plan.

- **Repentance:** Repentance in the context of progressive sanctification is a means of mind renewal. You are calling sin what

God calls it through confession (1 John 1:8) and then turning from that sin. A hardened and corrupt mind doesn't want to see sin as sin, but a renewed mind sees it as sin and forsakes it. Your repentance during your walk with Christ helps your mind stay renewed.

- **Giving:** I would argue that giving to your local church helps you to value the things of God. Giving orients your mind (Matt. 6:21). Giving orients what you value and see as valuable. It connects you to your local church and the ministry of your local church around the world. In addition, Paul says that the Corinthians not only gave but *wanted* to give (2 Cor. 8:10). Giving changes your mind and helps facilitate a mind that is not set on earthly things (Col. 3:2). So give generously, starting with your local church. A habit of a renewed mind is giving to what God values, starting with the local church.

If you are looking for practical ways to renew your mind, you should start with each of these, one by one. Start with Bible engagement and church attendance. When those are habit, move to biblical thinking and prayer. When those are habits, move on to giving. If you are not strong in these habits, the renewing of your mind will be greatly impaired.

How to Find a Biblical Counselor

I'm often asked if I could recommend a biblical counselor. It is an honor when someone trusts me enough to allow me to recommend a counselor for them. Seriously, I do see this as an honor. While I don't always have the time, or don't know counselors in that area or with that experience, I generally default to an interactive map that has a list of biblical counselors.

The Association of Certified Biblical Counselors (ACBC) is a certifying organization where we are educated, tested, and supervised in our counseling. In the end, you are certified as either a Level 1 or Level 2 biblical counselor. (The primary, if not only, difference is being ordained as a pastor.) This certification is the most rigorous and biblically sound certification that currently exists within counseling. ACBC is the industry standard for people who are committed to the Bible in the counseling process.

If you are looking for a biblical counselor, I would encourage you to start with the ACBC website (www.biblicalcounseling.com) and then navigate to the "Find a Counselor" tab. Under that location, you can enter your location and find people in your area. You can also narrow down counselors by experience or specialties in counseling. This is an extremely valuable resource.

Every ACBC counselor is already certified and required to have a background check and annual pastoral endorsement. This helps prevent renegade counselors who are personally a wreck and not living lives pleasing to the Lord. The only thing I would encourage you to ask is how much experience this biblical counselor has. Some people on the website are newbies and some only counsel periodically. So ask about their experience and, if you're comfortable with the answer, then move forward with starting counseling. If you have a really nuanced and challenging circumstance, then you might want someone who has more experience in that area (for example, in cases of divorce or sexual abuse).

Lastly, be very careful to go to a self-identified biblical counselor. There are many people who claim "years of experience" or that they have "trained hundreds of biblical counselors" yet they themselves are not certified and do not submit to a certifying organization. Furthermore, they might run their own nonprofit where they are the executive director and accountable to no one. Some used to be pastors but aren't anymore, while others have bounced between ministries like a hot potato. I find that such self-proclaimed "experts" are often not experts at all. Furthermore, if you have a grievance with their counsel, there is nowhere to go. It's best to just let these self-proclaimed biblical counseling experts go their way, and instead seek out an actual biblical counselor who submits themselves to a governing body for their counseling. You wouldn't go to a nonlicensed medical doctor, so don't go to a noncertified biblical counselor.

Acknowledgments

Any author knows that they stand on the shoulders of others who helped write, provoke, and sharpen thoughts, and encourage them along the way. I know that this book is the end product of not just my writing, but the support and encouragement of others. To start, Dr. Abner Chou really helped shape my thinking in private conversation. The mind-versus-brain conversations that he and I have had have placed an indelible mark on my own doctrine and teaching. Dr Chou, thank you.

Next, Todd Friel has been a gracious friend and boss in working with Fortis Institute and *Transformed*. Todd has taught me to be clear and confident in doctrine, but that it's okay to have humor—to be myself to a certain degree. This is why I love working with him. It's funny because this book was a simple email I sent to him one day, which turned into an interview with HarperCollins, which turned into what you see here. I asked if Todd would be interested in publishing it, and here we are. God has been very kind to me through Todd and Fortis Institute. Todd, thank you for your support and ministry partnership.

The third person who has been extraordinarily supportive is James Neidhardt. Honestly, I know that a good editor is essential for having a book that you still like when it's done. James's familiarity with the issues, the key players, the Scripture, and sound doctrine have made the book one million times better. His voice echoes in this book both in content and style. He taught me so much, and I cannot help but give thanks to the Lord for providentially allowing me to work with him. James, thank you. Thanks for your careful attention to make me a better writer and care to honor the Lord.

Next, thank you to my wife, Amber. Her patience as I worked

through the summers and school breaks on this project hasn't gone unnoticed. She humbly asks, "What did you write on that day?" or "How is the writing going?" I then spam her with more details than she would like, but she patiently listens! Amber is and will continue to be the love of my life. We met as kids, dated through high school, married in college, and now are serving the Lord together in Southern California. Amber, you are the butter to my bread and the breath to my life.

To my sons: Zane, Finn, and Jett—follow me as I follow Christ. I love you boys dearly.

To my church home, Faith Community Church: You are my family, my friends, and my community. I love you. Thanks for letting me be one of your pastors!

To the students at The Master's University: You are the best and brightest, and I'm truly not worthy to be your professor. I want to spend my one short life serving you.

Lastly, to my fellow counselors at the Association of Certified Biblical Counselors (biblicalcounseling.com). God has given us His sufficient Word, and it is a privilege to lock arms with you in serving our counselees. May we be faithful. May we reject integrating human wisdom into the Word of God. And may we hold fast to the "trustworthy word" (Tit. 1:9). Let's be steadfast in our commitments to the Word of God and reject integrationism simultaneously.

Notes

Foreword

1. Kao-Ping Chua et al., "Antidepressant Dispensing to US Adolescents and Young Adults: 2016–2022," *American Academy of Pediatrics*, February 26, 2024, publications.aap.org/pediatrics/article/153/3 /e2023064245/196655/Antidepressant-Dispensing-to-US-Adolescents -and?autologincheck=redirected.
2. "Mental Health Drug Prescriptions on the Rise," *Insurance Journal*, April 22, 2021, https://www.insurancejournal.com/news/national /2021/04/22/610924.htm.

Introduction: Secular Therapy Isn't Working

1. Dietrich Bonhoeffer, *Life Together: A Classic Exploration of Christian Community* (New York: Harper One, 1954), 118–19.
2. See C. Arbeit and M. I. Yamaner, National Center for Science and Engineering Statistics (NCSES), "Trends for Graduate Student Enrollment and Postdoctoral Appointments in Science, Engineering, and Health Fields at U.S. Academic Institutions between 2017 and 2019," NSF 21-317 (Alexandria, VA: National Science Foundation, 2021), https://ncses.nsf.gov/pubs/nsf21317/. See also Nicole Gull McElroy, "Master's Degree Programs in Psychology Are Seeing a Wave of New Applicants—Here's Why," *Fortune*, 2023, https://fortune.com/education /articles/masters-degree-programs-in-psychology-are-seeing-a-wave -of-new-applicants-heres-why/.
3. "Data and Statistics on Children's Mental Health," Centers for Disease Control and Prevention, June 3, 2022, accessed January 10, 2024, https://www.cdc.gov/childrensmentalhealth/data.html.
4. Ibid.
5. "Data and Statistics on Children's Mental Health," Centers for Disease Control and Prevention, June 3, 2022, https://www.cdc.gov /childrensmentalhealth/data.html.
6. "Mental Illness," National Institute of Mental Health, accessed July 6, 2022, https://www.nimh.nih.gov/health/statistics/mental-illness. "In 2021, there were an estimated 57.8 million adults aged 18 or older in the United States with AMI. This number represented 22.8% of all U.S. adults."
7. "Mental Health," World Health Organization, accessed January 15, 2024, https://www.who.int/health-topics/mental-health.
8. "Mental Health in America—Printed Reports," Mental Health America,

accessed January 15, 2024, https://mhanational.org/issues/mental-health
-america-printed-reports.

9. "Psychopharmacology—At Least One in 10 Americans Are Prescribed
    Psychotropics," American Psychological Association, https://www
    .apa.org, accessed January 16, 2024, https://www.apa.org/monitor
    /feb08/atleastone. See also "Mental Health Drug Prescriptions on the
    Rise," *Insurance Journal*, April 22, 2021, https://www.insurancejournal
    .com/news/national/2021/04/22/610924.htm.

10. "Mental Health," American Psychological Association, https://www.apa
    .org, accessed April 30, 2024, https://www.apa.org/topics/mental-health.

11. Austin Cline, "What Is the Philosophy of Mind?," Learn Religions,
    accessed April 10, 2024, https://www.learnreligions.com/philosophy
    -of-mind-250531.

12. Jonathan Haidt, "End the Phone-Based Childhood Now," *Atlantic*,
    March 2024, https://www.theatlantic.com/technology/archive/2024/03
    /teen-childhood-smartphone-use-mental-health-effects/677722/.

13. Daniel G. Amen, *The End of Mental Illness: How Neuroscience Is
    Transforming Psychiatry and Helping Prevent or Reverse Mood and
    Anxiety Disorders, ADHD, Addictions, PTSD, Psychosis, Personality
    Disorders, and More* (Carol Stream, IL: Tyndale Momentum, 2020), 5.

14. My thanks to David Powlison for this concept as he described the role
    of the Bible with secular psychologies in David Powlison, "Critiquing
    Modern Integrationists," *Journal of Biblical Counseling* 11, no. 3 (1993):
    24–34.

Chapter 1: A Modern Mental Health Epidemic

1. "Allen J. Frances on the Overdiagnosis of Mental Illness," *Big Ideas*
    (podcast), 2012, accessed July 22, 2022, http://archive.org/details/podcast
    _big-ideas-video_allen-j-frances-on-the-overdi_1000339822641.

2. Elizabeth A. O'Connor et al., "Table 1, Primary DSM-IV Depression
    Disorders, Criteria for Adults," Agency for Healthcare Research and
    Quality, December 2009, https://www.ncbi.nlm.nih.gov/books
    /NBK36406/table/ch1.t1/.

3. Lucy Foulkes and Argyris Stringaris, "Do No Harm: Can School Mental
    Health Interventions Cause Iatrogenic Harm?," *BJ Psych Bulletin* 47,
    no. 5 (n.d.): 267–69, https://doi.org/10.1192/bjb.2023.9.

4. Abigail Shrier, *Bad Therapy: Why the Kids Aren't Growing Up* (New
    York: Sentinel, 2024), 8–9.

5. Miriam Grossman, https://www.miriamgrossmanmd.com/, accessed
    May 6, 2024.

6. "White House Conference on Mental Health," accessed February 4,
    2021, https://clintonwhitehouse4.archives.gov/textonly/WH/EOP
    /First_Lady/html/generalspeeches/1999/19990607.html.

7. Ibid.

8. Ibid.

9. "Psychiatrists," Bureau of Labor Statistics, Occupational Employment

and Wages, 2023, accessed July 20, 2023, https://www.bls.gov/oes/current/oes291223.htm.

10. "Products, Data Briefs, Number 377," Centers for Disease Control and Prevention, September 8, 2020, accessed July 20, 2022, https://www.cdc.gov/nchs/products/databriefs/db377.htm.

11. Mark Moran, "Secrecy Charges Rebutted," *Psychiatric News*, August 21, 2009, https://doi.org/10.1176/pn.44.16.0005a.

12. "Allen J. Frances on the Overdiagnosis of Mental Illness," *Big Ideas* (podcast) 2012, accessed July 22, 2022, http://archive.org/details/podcast_big-ideas-video_allen-j-frances-on-the-overdi_1000339822641.

13. Ibid.

14. "Psychiatric Patients Are Being Overdiagnosed and Overtreated with Allen Frances, M.D.," YouTube, 2018, https://www.youtube.com/watch?v=p4Ts_k_H_nc.

15. "The New Definition of a Mental Disorder," *Psychology Today South Africa*, July 23, 2013, accessed May 6, 2024, https://www.psychologytoday.com/za/blog/rethinking-mental-health/201307/the-new-definition-mental-disorder.

16. "Home," Mad in America, May 6, 2024, https://www.madinamerica.com/.

17. "Data and Statistics on Autism Spectrum Disorder," Centers for Disease Control and Prevention, last modified March 2, 2022, https://www.cdc.gov/ncbddd/autism/data.html.

18. Ibid.

19. John Elder Robison Gassner Dena, "There Is No Epidemic of Autism. It's an Epidemic of Need," *STAT* (blog), March 23, 2023, https://www.statnews.com/2023/03/23/autism-epidemic-cdc-numbers/. See also Ralph Moller, "Is Autism Overdiagnosed? Here's the Truth," Above & Beyond Therapy, November 11, 2023, accessed September 27, 2024, https://www.abtaba.com/blog/autism-overdiagnosed.

20. "What Is Autism Spectrum Disorder (ASD)?," Cleveland Clinic, accessed May 6, 2024, https://my.clevelandclinic.org/health/diseases/8855-autism.

21. Jeffery N. Epstein and Richard E. A. Loren, "Changes in the Definition of ADHD in DSM-5: Subtle but Important," *Neuropsychiatry* 3, no. 5 (October 2013): 455–58.

22. "ADHD Throughout the Years," Centers for Disease Control and Prevention, last modified March 31, 2020, https://www.cdc.gov/ncbddd/adhd/timeline.html.

23. "'Psychiatrist's Bible' Changes: Doctor Talks Controversy," YouTube, 2013, https://www.youtube.com/watch?v=SvQI02iZXQg.

24. Substance Abuse and Mental Health Services Administration, "Table 3.15, DSM-IV to DSM-5 Generalized Anxiety Disorder Comparison," Substance Abuse and Mental Health Services Administration, June 2016, last modified June 2016, accessed July 23, 2022, https://www.ncbi.nlm.nih.gov/books/NBK519704/table/ch3.t15/.

25. Ibid.

26. "Allen J. Frances on the Overdiagnosis of Mental Illness," *Big Ideas* (podcast), 2012, accessed July 22, 2022, http://archive.org/details /podcast_big-ideas-video_allen-j-frances-on-the-overdi_1000339822641.

27. Nancy D. Berkman et al., "Table 1, DSM-IV and DSM-5 Diagnostic Criteria for Binge-Eating Disorder," Agency for Healthcare Research and Quality, December 2015, accessed July 22, 2022, https://www .ncbi.nlm.nih.gov/books/NBK338301/table/introduction.t1/.

28. Ibid.

29. According to Frontiers in Nutrition, caloric "averaged 3,400 kcal in 1909 and increased 18% over the century to 4,000 kcal in 2010." Joyce H. Lee et al., "United States Dietary Trends Since 1800: Lack of Association Between Saturated Fatty Acid Consumption and Non-Communicable Diseases," *Frontiers in Nutrition* 8 (January 2022): 748847, https://doi.org/10.3389/fnut.2021.748847.

30. Frances, "Allen J. Frances on the Overdiagnosis of Mental Illness."

31. Thomas Insel, "Transforming Diagnosis," National Institute of Mental Health, April 29, 2013, http://psychrights.org/2013/130429NIMH TransformingDiagnosis.htm.

32. "Your Diagnosis," National Alliance on Mental Illness, accessed December 21, 2022, https://www.nami.org/Your-Journey/Individuals -with-Mental-Illness/Understanding-Your-Diagnosis.

33. P. Cuijpers, "Targets and Outcomes of Psychotherapies for Mental Disorders: An Overview," *World Psychiatry* 18 (2019): 276–85, https:// doi.org/10.1002/wps.20661.

34. Rolfe Winkler, "Harlan Band's Descent Started with an Easy Online Adderall Prescription," *Wall Street Journal*, August 19, 2022, https:// www.wsj.com/articles/harlan-bands-descent-started-with-an-easy -online-adderall-prescription-11660916158.

35. "Working with LGBTQ Patients," accessed June 7, 2024, https://www .psychiatry.org:443/psychiatrists/diversity/education/best-practice -highlights/working-with-lgbtq-patients.

36. Ibid.

37. Pam Belluck, "Many Genes Influence Same-Sex Sexuality, Not a Single 'Gay Gene,'" *New York Times*, August 29, 2019, https://www.nytimes .com/2019/08/29/science/gay-gene-sex.html.

38. Robert L. Kinney, "Homosexuality and Scientific Evidence: On Suspect Anecdotes, Antiquated Data, and Broad Generalizations," *Linacre Quarterly* 82, no. 4 (November 2015): 364–90, https://doi.org /10.1179/2050854915Y.0000000002.

39. Belluck, "Many Genes."

40. "DSM-IV-TR Diagnostic Criteria for Gender Identity Disorder," *Psychiatric News*, July 18, 2003, https://doi.org/10.1176/pn.38.14.0032.

41. Ibid.

42. "Gender Dysphoria Diagnosis," accessed June 7, 2024, https://www .psychiatry.org:443/psychiatrists/diversity/education/transgender -and-gender-nonconforming-patients/gender-dysphoria-diagnosis.

43. Ibid.
44. "What Is Gender Dysphoria?," American Psychiatric Association, accessed January 30, 2025, https://www.psychiatry.org/patients-families /gender-dysphoria/what-is-gender-dysphoria.
45. "DSM-IV-TR Diagnostic Criteria for Gender Identity Disorder," *Psychiatric News*.
46. "What Is Gender Dysphoria?," American Psychiatric Association.
47. "What Is Gender Dysphoria?," accessed June 7, 2024, https://www .psychiatry.org:443/patients-families/gender-dysphoria/what-is -gender-dysphoria.
48. Francine Russo, "Where Transgender Is No Longer a Diagnosis," *Scientific American*, January 6, 2017, accessed June 7, 2024, https:// www.scientificamerican.com/article/where-transgender-is-no-longer -a-diagnosis/.
49. Fabian Fabiano and Nick Haslam, "Diagnostic Inflation in the DSM: A Meta-Analysis of Changes in the Stringency of Psychiatric Diagnosis from DSM-III to DSM-5," Science Direct, accessed April 12, 2024, https:// www.sciencedirect.com/science/article/abs/pii/S0272735820300775 #:~:text=This%20apparent%20broadening%20of%20definitions ,prevalence%20increases%20as%20a%20result.
50. "Mental Health by the Numbers," National Alliance of Mental Illness, July 20, 2022, https://www.nami.org/mhstats.
51. "Mental Health Disorder Statistics," Johns Hopkins Medicine, last modified November 19, 2019, accessed September 2, 2022, https:// www.hopkinsmedicine.org/health/wellness-and-prevention/mental -health-disorder-statistics.

Chapter 2: Incentivizing Insanity

1. "PTSD: National Center for PTSD," Department of Veterans Affairs, accessed May 7, 2024, https://www.ptsd.va.gov/understand/common /common_adults.asp.
2. "Disability Compensation for PTSD," Department of Veterans Affairs, May 3, 2024, https://www.va.gov/disability/eligibility/ptsd/.
3. "Mental Disorders—Adult," Social Security Administration, accessed May 7, 2024, https://www.ssa.gov/disability/professionals/bluebook /12.00-MentalDisorders-Adult.htm.
4. Charles Taylor, *A Secular Age* (Cambridge, MA: Harvard University Press, 2007).
5. Kirsten R. Müller-Vahl et al., "Stop That! It's Not Tourette's but a New Type of Mass Sociogenic Illness," *Brain* 145, no. 2 (February 2022): 476–80, https://doi.org/10.1093/brain/awab316.
6. Ibid.
7. Ibid.
8. "CPT Coding and Reimbursement," Psychiatry.org, accessed September 2, 2022, https://psychiatry.org:443/psychiatrists/practice

/practice-management/coding-reimbursement-medicare-and-medicaid
/coding-and-reimbursement.

9.   Ibid.

10. October Boyles et al., "CPT Codes for Behavioral Health Billing," updated for 2022, ICANotes, last modified February 27, 2019, accessed December 20, 2022, https://www.icanotes.com/2019/02/27/cpt-code-basics-what-you-should-know/.

11. "Allen Frances on the DSM, Mental Illness and Humane Treatment," Psychotherapy.net, accessed May 7, 2024, https://www.psychotherapy.net/interview/allen-frances-interview.

12. "About IDEA," Individuals with Disabilities Education Act, n.d., accessed December 20, 2022, https://sites.ed.gov/idea/about-idea/.

13. "Section 1401," Individuals with Disabilities Education Act, n.d., accessed December 20, 2022, https://sites.ed.gov/idea/statute-chapter-33/subchapter-i/1401/.

14. "Section 504 of the Rehabilitation Act of 1973," Center for Parent Information and Resources, accessed July 26, 2022, https://www.parentcenterhub.org/section504/.

15. Ibid. "Or any mental or psychological disorder, such as intellectual disability, organic brain syndrome, emotional or mental illness, and specific learning disabilities."

16. Corentin J. Gosling et al., "Influence of the Month of Birth on Persistence of ADHD in Prospective Studies: Protocol for an Individual Patient Data Meta-Analysis," *BMJ Open* 10, no. 11 (November 2020): e040952, https://doi.org/10.1136/bmjopen-2020-040952.

17. "About Disability Insurance," California Employee Development Department, accessed May 7, 2024, https://edd.ca.gov/en/disability/About_DI.

18. "If you have a diagnosis of a mental health or psychiatric disorder that needs treatment and arose or worsened due to your work, your employer must provide workers' compensation benefits and keep your job open for you while you recover." In Highrank, "Receiving Workers' Comp for Anxiety or Stress in CA," Mathew & George, May 15, 2018, accessed December 23, 2022, https://www.caemployeelawyer.com/can-receive-workers-compensation-stress-anxiety-california/.

19. California Labor Code, LAB § 3208.3.

20. "Part I: General Information," Social Security Administration, accessed December 23, 2022, https://www.ssa.gov/disability/professionals/bluebook/general-info.htm.

21. I'm sure it's a cash cow in other parts of the world, but medicine is privatized in North America, making the profit for private companies.

22. "The Most Commonly Prescribed Type of Antidepressant," Mayo Clinic, accessed June 28, 2023, https://www.mayoclinic.org/diseases-conditions/depression/in-depth/ssris/art-20044825.

23. All revenue details are cited from these sources: "Bristol Myers Squibb Revenue 2010–2023," BMY MacroTrends, accessed June 8, 2023, https://www.macrotrends.net/stocks/charts/BMY/bristol

-myers-squibb/revenue; "Eli Lilly Raises Annual Profit Forecast on Strength of Diabetes Drug," Reuters, April 27, 2023, https://www .reuters.com/business/healthcare-pharmaceuticals/eli-lilly -raises-annual-forecast-strength-diabetes-drug-2023-04-27/; "Forest Laboratories Revenue: Annual, Quarterly, and Historic," Zippia, December 14, 2021, https://www.zippia.com/forest-laboratories -careers-23761/revenue/. Even if these sources are off by $1 billion, we are talking about some serious money!
24. Gardiner Harris, "Document Details Plan to Promote Costly Drug," *New York Times*, September 1, 2009, https://www.nytimes.com/2009/09/02 /business/02drug.html.
25. Ibid.

Chapter 3: A Confusing New Religion

1. O. Hobart Mowrer, *The Crisis in Psychiatry and Religion* (Princeton, NJ: Van Nostrand, 1961), 60.
2. Clifford Whittingham Beers, *A Mind That Found Itself: An Autobiography* ([Auckland, NZ]: Floating Press, 2009), http://search.ebscohost .com/login.aspx?direct=true&AuthType=shib&db=nlebk&AN=3307 01&site=ehost-live&scope=site&custid=s8898283, 190–91.
3. Ibid., 12.
4. Ibid., 13–14.
5. Ibid.
6. Ibid., 9.
7. Ibid., 21.
8. Ibid., 26.
9. Ibid., 143.
10. Even in modern times, a BHU will say something like "We treat a wide range of acute psychiatric illnesses, including major depression, bipolar disorder, schizoaffective disorder and schizophrenia. Admission to the BHU can be on a voluntary or involuntary basis." Cf. "Behavioral Health Unit," Henry Mayo Newhall Hospital, Valencia, CA, accessed May 7, 2024, https://www.henrymayo.com/medical-services/behavioral -health-unit/.
11. Beers, *A Mind That Found Itself*, 293–96.
12. Ibid., vii.
13. Ibid., 295.
14. Ibid., 325.
15. Ibid., 315.
16. "Beers Founded the Connecticut Society for Mental Hygiene," Mental Health America, accessed July 19, 2022, https://mhanational.org /node/9438.
17. "Mental Illness and the Family: Recognizing Warning Signs and How to Cope," Mental Health America, accessed July 6, 2022, https:// www.mhanational.org/recognizing-warning-signs.

18. "History," World Federation for Mental Health, accessed July 19, 2022, https://wfmh.global/who-we-are/history.
19. "Mental Illness and the Family," Mental Health America.
20. "Allen J. Frances on the Overdiagnosis of Mental Illness," *Big Ideas* (podcast), 2012, http://archive.org/details/podcast_big-ideas-video _allen-j-frances-on-the-overdi_1000339822641.
21. President John F. Kennedy, "Special Message to the Congress on Mental Illness and Mental Retardation," February 5, 1963, American Presidency Project, accessed July 20, 2022, https://www.presidency .ucsb.edu/documents/special-message-the-congress-mental-illness-and -mental-retardation.
22. "Mental Health by the Numbers," National Alliance of Mental Illness, July 20, 2022, https://www.nami.org/mhstats.
23. "Diseases of the Mind," National Library of Medicine, accessed March 15, 2024, https://www.nlm.nih.gov/hmd/topics/diseases-of -mind/timeline.html.
24. Ibid.
25. "History of Psychiatry at Penn," Perelman School of Medicine, University of Pennsylvania, accessed March 15, 2024, https://www.med .upenn.edu/psychiatry/history.html.
26. "Jon Franklin of *The Baltimore Evening Sun*," Pulitzer Prizes, accessed May 7, 2024, https://www.pulitzer.org/winners/jon-franklin.
27. "The Mind-Fixers by Jon Franklin," Tumblr, accessed May 7, 2024, https://raisedonritalin.tumblr.com/post/150647247777/the-mind-fixers -by-jon-franklin.
28. Anne Harrington, *Mind Fixers: Psychiatry's Troubled Search for the Biology of Mental Illness* (New York: Norton, 2020), xvii. Harrington speaks of the "unraveling" of biological psychiatry in the 1990s (cf. ibid., vxii).
29. "Marco Ramos," Program in the History of Science and Medicine, Yale University, accessed May 7, 2024, https://hshm.yale.edu/people/marco -ramos.
30. Marco Ramos, "Mental Illness Is Not in Your Head," *Boston Review*, May 17, 2022, https://www.bostonreview.net/articles/mental-illness -is-not-in-your-head/.
31. Ibid.
32. "What Is Psychiatry?," Psychiatry.org, accessed December 20, 2022, https://www.psychiatry.org:443/patients-families/what-is-psychiatry.
33. Ibid.
34. "Types of Mental Health Professionals," National Alliance on Mental Illness, accessed March 14, 2024, https://www.nami.org/About -Mental-Illness/Treatments/Types-of-Mental-Health-Professionals.
35. "What Is Psychiatry?"
36. It shouldn't surprise you that psychiatry has many opponents in regard to its legitimacy among the other natural sciences. Some believe it to be a speculative and philosophical field rather than one committed to empiricism and the scientific method. Thus the early wars to even define the terms *psychiatry* and *psychology* were intended to claim their

own legitimacy. Cf. William James, *Writings, 1902–1910* (New York: Library of America, 1987). William James was the father of American psychology and an apologist for the legitimacy of psychology as a natural science. What a coincidence that he also was the primary endorser of Clifford Beers's book *A Mind That Found Itself.*

37. Harrington, *Mind Fixers*, xv.

38. Clifford Whittingham Beers, *A Mind That Found Itself: An Autobiography* ([Auckland, N.Z.]: Floating Press, 2009), http://search.ebscohost .com/login.aspx?direct=true&AuthType=shib&db=nlebk&AN=3307 01&site=ehost-live&scope=site&custid=s8898283, 315.

39. "What Is a Psychiatrist?" David Geffen School of Medicine, University of California, Los Angeles, May 25, 2023, https://medschool.ucla.edu /news-article/what-is-a-psychiatrist.

40. Ibid.

41. "20 Most Used Prescription Drugs in the US," Yahoo Finance, May 9, 2023, https://finance.yahoo.com/news/20-most-used-prescription-drugs -195733272.html.

42. For a play-by-play of my visit with the psychiatrist, please see Appendix A. This doesn't mean that psychiatrists never bring relief of pain through the use of medication. It simply means that they are not practicing objective medicine. You and I could study psychotropic medicine and tinker with their use and side effects in just as an effective way as a psychiatrist because they are not employing medical treatment to diagnose.

43. "Psychiatry," Online Etymology Dictionary, accessed March 15, 2024, https://www.etymonline.com/word/psychiatry.

44. Kendra Campbell, MD, "Are We Drug Dealers or Soul Healers?," *Free Range Psychiatry* (blog), March 12, 2021, https://freerangepsych.org /are-we-drug-dealers-or-soul-healers/.

45. Freya India, "Our New Religion Isn't Enough," January 16, 2024, https:// www.freyaindia.co.uk/p/our-new-religion-isnt-enough?publication_id= 192043&utm_campaign=email-post-title&r=q46v7&utm_medium=email.

46. E. Brooks Holifield, *A History of Pastoral Care in America: From Salvation to Self-Realization* (Eugene, OR: Wipf & Stock, 1983), 11.

47. "Clifford Whittingham Beers," Britannica, July 5, 2023, https://www .britannica.com/biography/Clifford-Whittingham-Beers.

48. Manon Parry, PhD, "From a Patient's Perspective: Clifford Whittingham Beers' Work to Reform Mental Health Services," *American Journal of Public Health* 100, no. 12 (December 2010): 2356–57.

Chapter 4: Distinguishing Between the Mind and the Brain

1. *School of Rock*, DVD (Paramount, 2003).

2. The original word within Daniel would have been written in Aramaic.

3. Francis Brown, Samuel Rolles Driver, and Charles Augustus Briggs, *Enhanced Brown-Driver-Briggs Hebrew and English Lexicon* (Oxford: Clarendon Press, 1977), 524.

4. William Lee Holladay and Ludwig Köhler, *A Concise Hebrew and Aramaic Lexicon of the Old Testament* (Leiden: Brill, 2000), 171.

5. *"intellect, understanding,* and its seat, *the heart, the mind,* Job 38:36. Compare as to this passage ʊ‚ חור, page 321," in Wilhelm Gesenius and Samuel Prideaux Tregelles, *Gesenius' Hebrew and Chaldee Lexicon to the Old Testament Scriptures* (Bellingham, WA: Logos Bible Software, 2003), 789.

6. Johannes Behm and Ernst Würthwein, "Νοέω, Νοῦς, Νόημα, Ἀνόητος, Ἄνοια, Δυσνόητος, Διάνοια, Διανόημα, Ἔννοια, Εὐνοέω, Εὔνοια, Κατανοέω, Μετανοέω, Μετάνοια, Ἀμετανόητος, Προνοέω, Πρόνοια, Ὑπονοέω, Ὑπόνοια, Νουθετέω, Νουθεσία," in Gerhard Kittel, Geoffrey W. Bromiley, and Gerhard Friedrich, eds., *Theological Dictionary of the New Testament* (Grand Rapids, MI: Eerdmans, 1964–), 952.

7. William Arndt et al., *A Greek-English Lexicon of the New Testament and Other Early Christian Literature* (Chicago: University of Chicago Press, 2000), 234.

8. Ibid., 675.

9. J. C. Ryle, *Thoughts for Young Men*, 22. Monergism: https://www.monergism.com/thethreshold/sdg/ryle/ThoughtsforYoungMen%20-%20J.%20C.%20Ryle.pdf.

10. Matthew 27:33; Mark 15:22; Luke 23:33; John 19:17.

11. Arndt et al., *A Greek-English Lexicon*, 541.

Chapter 5: The Body Creates the Trial

1. Bessell van der Kolk, *The Body Keeps the Score* (New York: Penguin, 2014), 12–13.

2. Danielle Carr, "Tell Me Why It Hurts," *New York*, July 31, 2023, https://nymag.com/intelligencer/article/trauma-bessel-van-der-kolk-the-body-keeps-the-score-profile.html.

3. Van der Kolk, *The Body Keeps the Score*, 378.

4. Ibid.

5. Ibid., 220.

6. Carr, "Tell Me Why It Hurts." See also Ellen Rolfes, "How 'The Body Keeps the Score' Became a Cultural Phenomenon," *Washington Post*, August 2, 2023, https://www.washingtonpost.com/books/2023/08/02/body-keeps-score-grieving-brain-bessel-van-der-kolk-neuroscience-self-help/.

7. Cf. Anthony Hoekema, *Created in God's Image* (Grand Rapids, MI: Eerdmans, 1986).

8. "Neuroplasticity, also known as neural plasticity or brain plasticity, is a process that involves adaptive structural and functional changes to the brain. It is defined as the ability of the nervous system to change its activity in response to intrinsic or extrinsic stimuli by reorganizing its structure, functions, or connections after injuries, such

as a stroke or traumatic brain injury (TBI). This activity describes neuroplasticity, the evaluation and management of neuroplasticity, and reviews the role of the interprofessional team in improving care for patients." Matt Puderbaugh and Prabhu D. Emmady, "Neuroplasticity," in *StatPearls* (Treasure Island, FL: StatPearls, 2022), accessed March 7, 2023, http://www.ncbi.nlm.nih.gov/books/NBK557811/.

9.   "Neuroplasticity," GoodTherapy, accessed March 7, 2023, https://www.goodtherapy.org/blog/psychpedia/neuroplasticity.

10. Daniel G. Amen, *The End of Mental Illness: How Neuroscience Is Transforming Psychiatry and Helping Prevent or Reverse Mood and Anxiety Disorders, ADHD, Addictions, PTSD, Psychosis, Personality Disorders, and More* (Carol Stream, IL: Tyndale Momentum, 2020), 5.

11. T. Love, C. Laier, M. Brand, L. Hatch, and R. Hajela, "Neuroscience of Internet Pornography Addiction: A Review and Update," *Behavioral Science* (Basel) 5, no. 3 (September 2015): 388–433, doi:10.3390/bs5030388. PMID: 26393658; PMCID: PMC4600144.

12. "Epilepsy: Overview," Mayo Clinic, accessed June 3, 2024, https://www.mayoclinic.org/diseases-conditions/epilepsy/symptoms-causes/syc-20350093.

13. The exact role of medication is going to be addressed thoroughly in a later chapter.

14. This view is also known as Creationism, which says that "God creates *ex nihilo* a fresh soul for each human individual at or after its conception." In F. L. Cross and Elizabeth A. Livingstone, eds., *The Oxford Dictionary of the Christian Church* (Oxford and New York: Oxford University Press, 2005), 433. "The Biblical belief that 'God created all things out of nothing, by the word of His power, in the space of six days, and all very good' (Shorter Catechism). This doctrine of creation is often referred to as creation *ex nihilo* ('creation out of nothing')." In Alan Cairns, *Dictionary of Theological Terms* (Belfast and Greenville, SC: Ambassador Emerald International, 2002), 117.

15. For further study on the use of πυρετός see Matthew 8:15, Mark 1:31, Luke 4:38–39, John 4:52, and Acts 28:2. In each instance πυρετός is used to describe physical illness of the physical body. Furthermore, νόσος is used to describe illnesses that are entirely physiological (Matt. 4:23; Matt. 4:24; Matt. 8:17, 9:35, 10:1; Mark 1:34; Luke 4:40, 6:18, 7:21, 9:1; Acts 19:12).

16. While the reader is not told the exact nature of Hezekiah's sadness, "Josephus says, the reason why he wept so sorely was that being childless, he was leaving the *kingdom* without a successor. How often our wishes, when gratified, prove curses! Hezekiah lived to have a son; that son was the idolater Manasseh, the chief cause of God's wrath against Judah, and of the overthrow of the kingdom (2 Ki 23:26, 27)." In Robert Jamieson, A. R. Fausset, and David Brown, *Commentary Critical and Explanatory on the Whole Bible*, vol. 1 (Oak Harbor, WA: Logos Research Systems, 1997), 471.

17. Of note, Galatians 5:16 says, "But I say, walk by the Spirit, and you will not gratify the desires of the flesh." The physiological σάρξ and the body of flesh representing the old man in Adam (Rom. 5:12) are different. The desires of the σάρξ lead to the works of the σάρξ as evidenced in verses 19–21. But these are different from physical cravings and physical appetites of the body/flesh. Furthermore, ἐπιθυμία (i.e., desire) does not equate to physical craving in Galatians 5:16. According to R. Jewett, "the flesh is Paul's term for everything aside from God in which one places his final trust." In F. F. Bruce, *The Epistle to the Galatians: A Commentary on the Greek Text*, New International Greek Testament Commentary (Grand Rapids, MI: Eerdmans, 1982), 243.

18. This statement warrants clarification. The Bible does not condemn these cravings inherently; rather it assumes them and then guides the expression of them. For a person to crave oxygen does not necessitate sinful action, but the way oxygen is pursued can become sinful, for instance. Thus for a person to be described as "their god is their belly" (Phil. 3:19) is the ultimate expression of physical cravings leading and dominating one's life.

19. This seems to be the misuse of the Corinthian understanding of physical cravings when they were legitimizing their sinful physical cravings in saying, "Food is meant for the stomach and the stomach for food" (1 Cor. 6:13).

20. Paul says this is why some are "weak and ill" (1 Cor. 11:30), because they have taken the Lord's Supper unworthily.

21. In 1 Kings 18:27, Elijah even mocks Baal's lack of response with a consideration that he is "relieving himself," which is another bodily function.

22. This has further consequences as one considers that the body of a person is not the person themselves. This understanding is paramount to understanding physical existence and dignity in human existence. For instance, because the body is not the totality of human existence, this prevents less human dignity for those with amputations and less "physical body." In this way, by understanding the difference between personhood and body, a Christian maintains the dignity of all human life despite the physical body of that person.

23. Mostafa Aboubakr et al., "Brain Death Criteria," in *StatPearls* (Treasure Island, FL: StatPearls, 2023), http://www.ncbi.nlm.nih.gov/books/NBK545144/.

24. Ibid.

25. Gentle Sunder Shrestha et al., "Apnea Testing with Continuous Positive Airway Pressure for the Diagnosis of Brain Death in a Patient with Poor Baseline Oxygenation Status," *Indian Journal of Critical Care Medicine* 18, no. 5 (May 2014): 331–33, https://doi.org/10.4103/0972-5229.132510.

26. Aboubakr et al., "Brain Death Criteria."

27. Ibid.

28. Jay Adams, *Competent to Counsel* (Grand Rapids, MI: Baker, 1970), 31–32.

29. "Seasonal Affective Disorder (SAD)," Mayo Clinic, December 14, 2021, https://www.mayoclinic.org/diseases-conditions/seasonal-affective -disorder/symptoms-causes/syc-20364651.

30. "Steps to Keep Your Mood and Motivation Steady Throughout the Year—Seasonal Affective Disorder (SAD)—Symptoms & Causes," Mayo Clinic, accessed July 8, 2024, https://www.mayoclinic.org /diseases-conditions/seasonal-affective-disorder/symptoms-causes /syc-20364651.

31. Patricia Gracia Garcia et al., "Personality Changes in Brain Injury," *Journal of Neuropsychiatry and Clinical Neurosciences* 23, no. 2 (2011): E14, https://doi.org/10.1176/appi.neuropsych.23.2.E14.

32. William Arndt et al., *A Greek-English Lexicon of the New Testament and Other Early Christian Literature* (Chicago: University of Chicago Press, 2000), 926.

33. While the believer is not a slave to sin, the unbeliever is characterized as being enslaved to the "passions of our flesh" (Eph. 2:3).

34. The mortal body is simply the translation of the phrase "θνητῷ ὑμῶν σώματι," which means "mortal body [of] you." *Mortal* in this context simply means your earthly body that can have death in it.

35. Self-control is "restraint of one's emotions, impulses, or desires, self-control" in William Arndt et al., *A Greek-English Lexicon of the New Testament and Other Early Christian Literature* (Chicago: University of Chicago Press, 2000), 274. Titus 2:11 says the grace of Jesus Christ "train[s] us to renounce ungodliness and worldly passions, and to live self-controlled, upright, and godly lives in the present age,

36. Remember, material responses are "MR" and immaterial responses are "IR."

37. Abigail Shrier, *Bad Therapy: Why the Kids Aren't Growing Up* (New York: Penguin, 2024). Kindle ed., 119.

38. Edward T. Welch, *Blame It on the Brain? Distinguishing Chemical Imbalances, Brain Disorders, and Disobedience*, Resources for Changing Lives (Phillipsburg, NJ: P&R, 1998), 47–48.

Chapter 6: Treatment vs. Transformation

1. Christopher Lasch, *The Culture of Narcissism: American Life in an Age of Diminishing Expectations* (New York: Norton, 1979).

2. R. C. Sproul, "Sin Is Cosmic Treason," *Ultimately with R. C. Sproul* (podcast), Ligonier Ministries, accessed September 12, 2024, https://www .ligonier.org/podcasts/ultimately-with-rc-sproul/sin-is-cosmic-treason.

3. John MacArthur and Richard Mayhue, eds., *Biblical Doctrine* (Wheaton, IL: Crossway, 2017), 573.

4. Cf. ibid., 603.

5. MacArthur, *Biblical Doctrine*, 932.

6. Grudem, *Systematic Theology*, 1522.

7. MacArthur, *Biblical Doctrine*, 936.

8. Ibid., 923.

9. Ashley Olivine, "What Are the Different Types and Benefits of Therapy?," Verywell Health, accessed September 12, 2024, https://www.verywellhealth.com/benefits-of-therapy-5219732?print.

10. Pim Cuijpers, "Targets and Outcomes of Psychotherapies for Mental Disorders: An Overview," *World Psychiatry* 18 (2019): 276–85, https://doi.org/10.1002/wps.20661.

11. William Arndt et al., *A Greek-English Lexicon of the New Testament and Other Early Christian Literature* (Chicago: University of Chicago Press, 2000), 1021.

12. Ibid., 529.

13. Ibid., 932.

14. Ludwig Koehler et al., *The Hebrew and Aramaic Lexicon of the Old Testament* (Leiden: Brill, 1994–2000), 873.

15. Arndt et al., *A Greek-English Lexicon*, 239.

16. Ibid., 650.

17. Ibid., 621.

18. Koehler et al., *The Hebrew and Aramaic Lexicon of the Old Testament*, 456.

19. Ibid., 70.

20. Healthwise Staff, "Stop Negative Thoughts: Choosing a Healthier Way of Thinking," Province of Alberta, Canada, accessed September 12, 2024, https://myhealth.alberta.ca/Health/pages/conditions.aspx?hwid=uf9857.

21. MacArthur, *Biblical Doctrine*, 929.

22. Ibid., 930.

23. Thomas Insel, "Transforming Diagnosis," National Institute of Mental Health, April 29, 2013, http://psychrights.org/2013/130429NIMH TransformingDiagnosis.htm.

24. Philip Hughes, *The True Image: The Origin and Destiny of Man in Christ* (Grand Rapids, MI: IVP, 1989), ix.

Chapter 7: Mental Health vs. Mind Renewal

1. "President Says U.S. Must Make Commitment to Mental Health Care," White House Archives, accessed May 10, 2024, https://georgewbush -whitehouse.archives.gov/news/releases/2002/04/20020429-1.html.

2. "About Mental Health," Centers for Disease Control and Prevention, April 28, 2023, https://www.cdc.gov/mentalhealth/learn/index.htm.

3. Caring for Your Mental Health," National Institute for Mental Health, accessed November 24, 2023, https://www.nimh.nih.gov/health/topics /caring-for-your-mental-health.

4. "Mental Health," American Psychological Association, https://www .apa.org, accessed May 10, 2024, https://www.apa.org/topics/mental -health.

5. "What Is Mental Health?," Substance Abuse and Mental Health Services Administration, accessed May 10, 2024, https://www.samhsa.gov/mental -health.

6. "Can a Christian Have Mental Illness?," Crossway, September 7, 2023, https://www.crossway.org/articles/can-a-christian-have-mental-illness/.

7. David Murray and Tom Karel, *A Christian's Guide to Mental Illness: Answers to 30 Common Questions* (Wheaton, IL: Crossway, 2023), https://search.ebscohost.com/login.aspx?direct=true&AuthType=ip,shib&db=nlebk&AN=3709969&site=ehost-live&scope=site.

8. See the chapter a friend and I wrote in *Think Biblically* titled "Thinking Biblically About Mental Illness" (Wheaton, IL: Crossway, 2024). We address this idea in a much more abbreviated format.

9. "health," Merriam-Webster, accessed November 23, 2023, https://www.merriam-webster.com/dictionary/health?utm_campaign=sd&utm_medium=serp&utm_source=jsonld.

10. William Arndt et al., *A Greek-English Lexicon of the New Testament and Other Early Christian Literature* (Chicago: University of Chicago Press, 2000), 410.

11. William Arndt, Frederick W. Danker, Walter Bauer, and F. Wilbur Gingrich, *A Greek-English Lexicon of the New Testament and Other Early Christian Literature* (Chicago: University of Chicago Press, 2000), s.v. "asteriktos."

12. See Love in Song of Solomon 2:5, 8, Discouragement in Nehemiah 2:2, Jeremiah 8:18 and sin in Jeremiah 17:9 and Ezekiel 16:30; Romans 1:28.

13. See Ephesians 4:17. *Futile* means "state of being without use or value, emptiness, futility, purposelessness, transitoriness." Arndt et al., *A Greek-English Lexicon*, 621.

14. Arndt et al., *A Greek-English Lexicon*, 21.

15. Northcreek Training Conference in Walnut Creek, CA, September 2023 and ACBC Annual Conference in Santa Clarita, CA 2023.

16. You can see the results of this in "Thinking Biblically About Mental Illness," in *Thinking Biblically*, 2nd ed. (Wheaton, IL: Crossway, 2024).

17. "Caring for Your Mental Health," National Institute of Mental Health, accessed November 24, 2023, https://www.nimh.nih.gov/health/topics/caring-for-your-mental-health.

18. "What Is Mental Health?," Substance Abuse and Mental Health Services Administration, accessed May 10, 2024, https://www.samhsa.gov/mental-health.

19. "Caring for Your Mental Health," National Institute of Mental Health.

20. In a later chapter, I will evaluate the secular therapeutic attempts to help the mind through practices like yoga, mindfulness, friendships, CBT, and other secular so-called helps—to include those of coping mechanisms.

21. Jay Adams, "No Joking," Institute for Nouthetic Studies, *Biblical Counseling* (blog), February 8, 2023, https://nouthetic.org/no-joking/.

22. Cf. Greg E. Gifford, *Helping Your Family Through PTSD* (Eugene, OR: Wipf & Stock, 2017).

23. David Powlison, *The Biblical Counseling Movement* (Greensboro, NC: New Growth Press, 2010), 289.

Chapter 8: Medications Cannot Treat the Mind

1. Anne Harrington, *Mind Fixers: Psychiatry's Troubled Search for the Biology of Mental Illness* (New York: Norton, 2020), xviii.
2. *Zoolander,* Ben Stiller (Paramount Pictures, 2001).
3. Andrea Petersen, "More People Are Taking Drugs for Anxiety and Insomnia, and Doctors Are Worried," *Wall Street Journal*, May 25, 2020, accessed September 16, 2024, https://www.wsj.com/articles /more-people-are-taking-drugs-for-anxiety-and-insomnia-and -doctors-are-worried-11590411600.
4. "Number of People Taking Psychiatric Drugs in the United States," Citizens Commission on Human Rights International, May 19, 2014, https://www.cchrint.org/psychiatric-drugs/people-taking -psychiatric-drugs/. The APA argued for one in ten in 2008. See "Psychopharmacology—At Least One in 10 Americans Are Prescribed Psychotropics," https://www.apa.org, accessed January 16, 2024, https://www.apa.org/monitor/feb08/atleastone.
5. P1—Census Bureau Tables, accessed September 27, 2024, https:// data.census.gov/table?q=P1&g=010XX00US&d=DEC+Demographic+ and+Housing+Characteristics.
6. "Mental Health Drug Prescriptions on the Rise," *Insurance Journal*, April 22, 2021, https://www.insurancejournal.com/news/national /2021/04/22/610924.htm.
7. David Murray, *Christians Get Depressed Too* (Grand Rapids, MI: Reformation Heritage Books, 2010), digital edition.
8. Anne Harrington, *Mind Fixers: Psychiatry's Troubled Search for the Biology of Mental Illness* (New York: Norton, 2020), xv.
9. Ibid., xii.
10. Ibid., xiii.
11. Ibid.
12. Thomas Insel, "Toward a New Understanding of Mental Illness," TED Talk, accessed May 15, 2024, https://www.ted.com/talks/thomas_insel _toward_a_new_understanding_of_mental_illness.
13. Daniel G. Amen, *The End of Mental Illness: How Neuroscience Is Transforming Psychiatry and Helping Prevent or Reverse Mood and Anxiety Disorders, ADHD, Addictions, PTSD, Psychosis, Personality Disorders, and More* (Carol Stream, IL: Tyndale Momentum, 2020).
14. WebMD Editorial Contributor, "What Are Psychotropic Medications?," WebMD, accessed September 30, 2024, https://www.webmd .com/mental-health/what-are-psychotropic-medications; "What Is a Psychotropic Drug? Types, Uses, Side Effects, Risks & More," Healthline, November 6, 2019, https://www.healthline.com/health /what-is-a-psychotropic-drug; "The Most Commonly Prescribed Type of Antidepressant," Mayo Clinic, accessed June 28, 2023, https:// www.mayoclinic.org/diseases-conditions/depression/in-depth/ssris /art-20044825.
15. Amen, *The End of Mental Illness*, 14.

16. Kate Allsopp, John Read, Rhiannon Corcoran, and Peter Kinderman, "Heterogeneity in Psychiatric Diagnostic Classification," *Psychiatry Research* 279 (2019): 15–22.

17. "Study finds psychiatric diagnosis to be 'scientifically meaningless,'" University of Liverpool, accessed July 19, 2024, https://news.liverpool .ac.uk/2019/07/08/study-finds-psychiatric-diagnosis-to-be-scientifically -meaningless/.

18. Ibid.

19. "What Is Psychiatry?," Psychiatry.org, accessed December 20, 2022, https://www.psychiatry.org:443/patients-families/what-is-psychiatry.

20. Open Resources for Nursing (Open RN), Kimberly Ernstmeyer and Elizabeth Christman, "Chapter 6 Psychotropic Medications," in *Nursing: Mental Health and Community Concepts [Internet]* (Chippewa Valley Technical College, 2022), https://www.ncbi.nlm.nih.gov/books /NBK590034/.

21. "What Is a Psychotropic Drug? Types, Uses, Side Effects, Risks & More," Healthline, November 6, 2019, https://www.healthline.com /health/what-is-a-psychotropic-drug.

22. Ibid.

23. "In other words, the available psychopharmacological agents offer a great deal of symptom relief, which in turn has the potential to be of life changing importance to many patients—but they are not disease specific and often are used across diagnostic categories, their discontinuation often is associated with disease relapse, and they have shown little evidence related to their ability to change the trajectory of psychiatric disorders (e.g., medications for attention deficits/hyperactivity and autism spectrum disorders are often introduced in early development, but the developmental trajectory of these disorders does not seem to be affected by the pharmacological treatment in the sense of reduced rates of persistence in older age)." Iliyan Ivanov and Jeffrey M. Schwartz, "Why Psychotropic Drugs Don't Cure Mental Illness—But Should They?," *Frontiers in Psychiatry* 12 (April 2021): 579566, https://doi.org/10.3389/fpsyt.2021.579566.

24. Robert Whitaker, "Anatomy of an Epidemic: Psychiatric Drugs and the Astonishing Rise of Mental Illness in America," *Ethical Human Psychology & Psychiatry* 7, no. 1 (2005): 23–35. Richard Sears, a psychology professor, said, "Researchers have noted that in a nine-year follow-up comparing depression patients that took antidepressants versus those that did not, antidepressants appeared to worsen long-term outcomes. This was true even when researchers controlled for depression severity." Richard Sears, "Overuse of Psychiatric Drugs Is Worsening Public Mental Health, Doctor Argues," Mad in America, December 17, 2021, https://www.madinamerica.com/2021/12/overuse -psychiatric-drugs-worsening-public-mental-health-doctor-argues/; Ivanov and Schwartz, "Why Psychotropic Drugs Don't Cure Mental Illness—But Should They?"

25. Luke Andrews, "Expert Says Many Psychiatrists KNEW Theory Was

'Incomplete,'" *Daily Mail*, July 21, 2022, https://www.dailymail.co.uk /news/article-11035903/Expert-says-psychiatrists-KNOW-theory-low -serotonin-levels-cause-depression-incomplete.html.

26. Andrea Kane, "Therapy Is More than Lying on a Couch and Talking. Here Are 5 Ways It Can Boost Happiness," CNN, June 9, 2024, https://www.cnn.com/2024/06/09/health/therapy-benefits-happiness -wellness/index.html.

27. Saul Mcleod, "Maslow's Hierarchy of Needs," Simply Psychology, accessed July 22, 2024, https://www.simplypsychology.org/maslow.html.

28. Ibid.

29. Charles L. Quarles, "Was New Testament Wine Alcoholic?," Southeastern Baptist Theological Seminary, accessed July 22, 2024, https:// cfc.sebts.edu/faith-and-culture/was-new-testament-wine-alcoholic/.

30. M. D. Ronald W. Pies, "Debunking the Two Chemical Imbalance Myths, Again," *Psychiatric Times* 36, no. 8 (August 1, 2019), https:// www.psychiatrictimes.com/view/debunking-two-chemical-imbalance -myths-again. I would encourage you to do your own research about whether or not there is such a thing as a chemical imbalance, which will require determining which chemicals are imbalanced and what normal balancing looks like.

31. "Do Newer Psychiatric Drugs Really Work?," *Psychology Today*, accessed July 23, 2024, https://www.psychologytoday.com/us/blog /your-brain-food/202102/do-newer-psychiatric-drugs-really-work.

Chapter 9: There's No Better Treatment Than the Truth

1. Paul Tripp uses a similar analogy in *Instruments in the Redeemer's Hands* (Phillipsburg, NJ: P&R, 2002).

2. D. David, I. Cristea, and S. G. Hofmann, "Why Cognitive Behavioral Therapy Is the Current Gold Standard of Psychotherapy," *Frontiers in Psychiatry* 9, no. 4 (January 2018), doi:10.3389/fpsyt.2018.00004; PMID: 29434552; PMCID: PMC5797481.

3. "CBT in 2023: Current Trends in Cognitive Behavior Therapy," *Psychiatric Times*, October 10, 2023, https://www.psychiatrictimes.com/view /cbt-in-2023-current-trends-in-cognitive-behavior-therapy.

4. "What Is Cognitive Behavioral Therapy?," American Psychological Association, https://www.apa.org, accessed May 30, 2024, https://www .apa.org/ptsd-guideline/patients-and-families/cognitive-behavioral.

5. Ibid.

6. "In Brief: Cognitive Behavioral Therapy (CBT)," Institute for Quality and Efficiency in Health Care, 2022, https://www.ncbi.nlm.nih.gov /books/NBK279297/.

7. "What Is Humanistic Psychology and Humanistic Therapy?," WebMD, accessed September 19, 2024, https://www.webmd.com /mental-health/humanistic-psychology-and-humanistic-therapy.

8. Bessel van der Kolk, "The Body Keeps the Score," accessed May 31, 2024, https://www.besselvanderkolk.com/resources/the-body-keeps-the-score.

9. "Yoga for Better Mental Health," Harvard Health, June 12, 2021, https://www.health.harvard.edu/staying-healthy/yoga-for-better-mental-health.

10. Bessel A. van der Kolk, *The Body Keeps the Score: Brain, Mind, and Body in the Healing of Trauma* (New York: Viking, 2014). See the chapter on "Letting Go of Your Past: EMDR."

11. Special thanks to Louise Maxfield et al., "Eye Movement Desensitization and Reprocessing (EMDR) Therapy," American Psychological Association, https://www.apa.org, accessed May 31, 2024, https://www.apa.org/ptsd-guideline/treatments/eye-movement-reprocessing.

12. "What Is EMDR?," EMDR Institute, February 15, 2015, https://www.emdr.com/what-is-emdr/.

13. Ibid.

14. Special thanks to Maxfield et al., "Eye Movement Desensitization and Reprocessing (EMDR) Therapy."

15. "Based on behaviorism, behavior therapy aims to replace maladaptive behaviors with more constructive ones through techniques like systematic desensitization, aversion therapy, and token economies. Systematic desensitization helps phobia patients gradually confront feared objects." "Behaviorism in Psychology," February 1, 2024, https://www.simplypsychology.org/behaviorism.html. Behaviorism is reducing who we are down to "maladaptive" behavior when we need to see that without mind renewal, we are exchanging one behavior for another. You can quit smoking and start working out, but your mind hasn't necessarily changed. We need to focus on the mind and help people see the goal of changed behavior that comes from a changed mind.

16. Joaquín Selva, "The History and Origins of Mindfulness," Positive Psychology, March 13, 2017, https://positivepsychology.com/history-of-mindfulness/.

17. There are multiple forms of mindfulness, with MBCT being part of a third wave. Cf. Rachel Churchill et al., "Mindfulness-Based 'Third Wave' Cognitive and Behavioural Therapies versus Treatment as Usual for Depression," *Cochrane Database of Systematic Reviews*, no. 9 (September 8, 2010): CD008705, https://doi.org/10.1002/14651858.CD008705.

18. "Mindfulness-Based Cognitive Therapy," *Psychology Today*, accessed June 3, 2024, https://www.psychologytoday.com/us/therapy-types/mindfulness-based-cognitive-therapy.

19. "Mindfulness and CBT," 2018, https://www.youtube.com/watch?v=E3WPw-a4gBA.

20. "How Does Mindfulness Change the Brain? A Neurobiologist's Perspective on Mindfulness Meditation," Max Planck Florida Institute for Neuroscience, accessed June 3, 2024, https://mpfi.org/how-does-mindfulness-change-the-brain-a-neurobiologists-perspective-on-mindfulness-meditation/?psafe_param=1&gad_source=1&gclid=Cj0KCQjw0_WyBhDMARIsAL1Vz8sltZ-bE3pOmBjOG-GhE_QDsWCN3R48HxPI4eB8T3a8UXhsoKrPNZoaAibBEALw_wcB.

21. "benefit," Merriam-Webster, May 25, 2024, https://www.merriam-webster .com/dictionary/benefit.

22. C. S. Lewis, *The Weight of Glory and Other Addresses* (San Francisco: Harper San Francisco, 2001), 26.

Chapter 10: What Then of Mental Illness?

1. Thomas Szasz, *The Myth of Mental Illness* (New York: Harper Perennial, 1974), xii.

2. Carl R. Trueman, *The Rise and Triumph of the Modern Self: Cultural Amnesia, Expressive Individualism, and the Road to Sexual Revolution* (Wheaton, IL: Crossway, 2020), 390.

3. Frances Hodgson Burnett, *The Secret Garden* (London: Arcturus, 2018), 191–92. Also: "The fact that Colin's fury at Ben Weatherstaff provides him with sufficient strength to stand reinforces the notion that Colin's inability to do so was entirely a product of his negative thoughts. It also underlines the idea that if one only wishes to over-come one's illness, one can." "The Secret Garden Chapter XX–Chapter XXII Summary & Analysis," SparkNotes, accessed September 30, 2024, https://www.sparknotes.com/lit/secretgarden/section14/.

4. Jesse S. Y. Tse and Nick Haslam, "What Is a Mental Disorder? Evaluating the Lay Concept of Mental Ill Health in the United States," *BMC Psychiatry* 23 (April 2023): 224, https://doi.org/10.1186/s12888-023-04680-5.

5. "What Is Mental Illness?," Psychiatry.org, accessed June 7, 2024, https://www.psychiatry.org:443/patients-families/what-is-mental-illness.

6. American Psychiatric Association, ed., *Diagnostic and Statistical Manual of Mental Disorders,* 5th ed. (Washington, DC: American Psychiatric Association, 2013), 20.

7. "The strength of each of the editions of DSM has been 'reliability'—each edition has ensured that clinicians use the same terms in the same ways. The weakness is its lack of validity." Thomas Insel, "Transforming Diagnosis," National Institute of Mental Health, April 29, 2013, http://psychrights.org/2013/130429NIMHTransformingDiagnosis.htm.

8. "Generalized Anxiety Disorder: When Worry Gets Out of Control," National Institute of Mental Health, accessed July 29, 2024, https://www .nimh.nih.gov/health/publications/generalized-anxiety-disorder-gad.

9. Ibid.

10. https://www.psychiatry.org/patients-families/obsessive-compulsive -disorder/what-is-obsessive-compulsive-disorder.

11. "Turning Your Attention to Narcissistic Personality Disorder," Cleve-land Clinic, accessed July 29, 2024, https://my.clevelandclinic.org /health/diseases/9742-narcissistic-personality-disorder.

12. "Table 18, DSM-IV to DSM-5 Oppositional Defiant Disorder Compar-ison," Substance Abuse and Mental Health Services Administration, June 2016, https://www.ncbi.nlm.nih.gov/books/NBK519712/table /ch3.t14/.

13. "Table 21, DSM-IV to DSM-5 Binge Eating Disorder Comparison,"

Substance Abuse and Mental Health Services Administration, June 2016, https://www.ncbi.nlm.nih.gov/books/NBK519712/table/ch3.t17/.

14. Mateusz Gola et al., "What Should Be Included in the Criteria for Compulsive Sexual Behavior Disorder?," *Journal of Behavioral Addictions* 11, no. 2 (July 2022): 160–65, https://doi.org/10.1556/2006.2020.00090.

15. Ibid.

16. "Autism Diagnostic Criteria: DSM-5," Autism Speaks, accessed June 10, 2024, https://www.autismspeaks.org/autism-diagnostic-criteria-dsm-5.

17. "Is Autism a Mental Illness?," Verywell Health, accessed June 10, 2024, https://www.verywellhealth.com/is-autism-a-mental-illness-4427991; "Is Autism a Disability? Medical, Societal, and Legal Viewpoints," Healthline, June 9, 2022, https://www.healthline.com/health/autism/is-autism-a-disability.

18. "Q & A Panel—For the Valley—Jonny Ardavanis, Costi Hinn, John MacArthur, Scott Ardavanis," YouTube, April 20, 2024, https://www.youtube.com/watch?v=SV9Io7r_hGw, 35:24 and following.

19. "Christ Is Sufficient for All Your Crises," Grace to You, accessed June 11, 2024, https://www.gty.org/library/sermons-library/81-180/.

20. "Dispelling Myths About 'Mental Illness,'" Grace Church, accessed September 30, 2024, https://www.gracechurch.org/news/posts/3982.

21. Truth Unites, "John MacArthur on Mental Illness: This Is Bad Theology," YouTube, May 2, 2024, https://www.youtube.com/watch?v=2JFmxGYtEXk.

22. Ibid.

23. Ibid.

24. Ibid.

25. Ibid. (3:35–8:59).

26. Ibid. (16:00).

27. "Antisocial Personality Disorder—Symptoms and Causes," Mayo Clinic, accessed June 11, 2024, https://www.mayoclinic.org/diseases-conditions/antisocial-personality-disorder/symptoms-causes/syc-20353928.

28. These would not be specific to APD, but to other similar symptoms. Ibid.

29. William Arndt et al., *A Greek-English Lexicon of the New Testament and Other Early Christian Literature* (Chicago: University of Chicago Press, 2000), 700.

30. "Antisocial Personality Disorder—Symptoms and Causes," Mayo Clinic.

Chapter 11: Insanity and the Mind

1. Deut. 28:34; 1 Sam. 21:14; Hos. 9:7; 2 Kings 9:11; Jer. 29:26; and two times 1 Sam. 21:15.

2. Arndt et al., *A Greek-English Lexicon*, 350.

3. Ibid.

4. "Of inability to reason normally lose one's mind, be out of one's senses." Ibid.

5. Ibid., 610.

6. Herbert Preisker, "Μαίνομαι," in Gerhard Kittel, Geoffrey W. Bromiley,

and Gerhard Friedrich, eds., *Theological Dictionary of the New Testament* (Grand Rapids, MI: Eerdmans, 1964–), 361.

7. John B. Polhill, *Acts*, vol. 26, *The New American Commentary* (Nashville, TN: Broadman & Holman, 1992), 279.

8. "The Effects of Sleep Deprivation on Your Body," Healthline, accessed September 20, 2024, https://www.healthline.com/health/sleep-deprivation/effects-on-body.

Chapter 12: Disorder, Disease, or Disobedience—Addiction and Mind

1. "Biden Challenges Public Perception of Addiction," ABC News, accessed June 20, 2024, https://abcnews.go.com/Technology/story?id=3445662&page=1.

2. Marc Lewis, *The Biology of Desire: Why Addiction Is Not a Disease*, 2nd ed. (New York: PublicAffairs, 2016), 9.

3. Recognizing Addiction as a Disease Act of 2007, S. 1011, 110th Congress, 1st Session (2007), https://www.congress.gov/bill/110th-congress/senate-bill/1011/text#ID62d1cfb32cac4597b3d337e38daa4e46.

4. Tanya Albert Henry, "Court Listened to AMA on Defining Alcoholism as a Disease, Not a Crime," American Medical Association, accessed July 30, 2024, https://www.ama-assn.org/delivering-care/public-health/court-listened-ama-defining-alcoholism-disease-not-crime?utm_medium=Social_AMA&utm_campaign=amaone_shared_articles&utm_source=email.

5. "What Is a Substance Use Disorder?," American Psychiatric Association, accessed July 30, 2024, https://www.psychiatry.org/patients-families/addiction-substance-use-disorders/what-is-a-substance-use-disorder.

6. Corky Siemaszko, "For Governor Christie, the Battle Against Opioid Addiction Is Personal," NBC News, accessed July 30, 2024, https://www.nbcnews.com/storyline/americas-heroin-epidemic/governor-christie-battle-against-opioid-addiction-personal-n740066; "Chris Christie: Drug Addiction Is a Disease," MSNBC, accessed July 30, 2024. https://www.msnbc.com/morning-joe/watch/chris-christie--drug-addiction-is-a-disease-562584643511.

7. S. Kühn and J. Gallinat, "Brain Structure and Functional Connectivity Associated with Pornography Consumption: The Brain on Porn," *JAMA Psychiatry* 71, no. 7 (2014): 827–34, doi:10.1001/jamapsychiatry.2014.93.

8. Marta Zaraska, "Food Can Be Literally Addictive, New Evidence Suggests," *Scientific American*, September 11, 2023, https://www.scientificamerican.com/article/food-can-be-literally-addictive-new-evidence-suggests/.

9. "Alcohol's Effects on Health," National Institute on Alcohol Abuse and Alcoholism, accessed August 2, 2024, https://www.niaaa.nih.gov/publications/alcohol-metabolism.

10. "Biden Challenges Public Perception of Addiction," ABC News,

accessed February 4, 2021, https://abcnews.go.com/Technology/story
?id=3445662&page=1.

11. "Addiction and Health," National Institute on Drug Abuse, https://
nida.nih.gov/publications/drugs-brains-behavior-science-addiction
/addiction-health.

12. Stacy Mosel, "Brain Damage from Drugs & Alcohol: Are Effects Revers-
ible?," American Addiction Centers, accessed June 20, 2024, https://
americanaddictioncenters.org/alcohol/risks-effects-dangers/brain.

13. Marc Lewis, *The Biology of Desire: Why Addiction Is Not a Disease*,
2nd ed. (New York: PublicAffairs, 2016), 26.

14. Ibid., 20–21.

15. "Alcohol Use Disorder: A Comparison Between DSM–IV and DSM–5,"
National Institute on Alcohol Abuse and Alcoholism, accessed
June 21, 2024, https://www.niaaa.nih.gov/publications/brochures
-and-fact-sheets/alcohol-use-disorder-comparison-between-dsm.

16. Jennifer McNeely and Angeline Adam, "Table 3, DSM-5 Diagnostic
Criteria for Diagnosing and Classifying Substance Use Disorders [Abc],"
Johns Hopkins University, October 2020, https://www.ncbi.nlm.nih
.gov/books/NBK565474/.

17. "Hypersexuality (Sex Addiction)," *Psychology Today*, accessed
June 21, 2024, https://www.psychologytoday.com/us/conditions
/hypersexuality-sex-addiction.

18. Ibid.

19. Megan M. Campbell and Dan J. Stein, "Hypersexual Disorder," in
Behavioral Addictions: DSM-5 and Beyond, ed. Nancy M. Petry (New
York: Oxford University Press, 2015), https://doi.org/10.1093/med
/9780199391547.003.0005.

20. Ken Sande, *The Peacemaker: A Biblical Guide to Resolving Personal
Conflict*, 3rd ed. (Grand Rapids, MI: Baker Books, 2004), 100–9.

21. Ibid.

22. Ibid.

23. Wayne Grudem, *Systematic Theology* (Grand Rapids, MI: Zondervan,
2021), 1511.

24. "Alcohol and the Brain: An Overview," National Institute on Alcohol
Abuse and Alcoholism, accessed July 2, 2024, https://www.niaaa.nih
.gov/publications/alcohol-and-brain-overview.

25. "How Brain Neurons Change Over Time from Life Experience,"
Verywell Mind, accessed July 2, 2024, https://www.verywellmind
.com/what-is-brain-plasticity-2794886.

26. John Owen, *Mortification of Sin in Believers* (Edinburgh: Johnstone &
Hunter, 1656), 15.

Chapter 13: Questions, Objections, and Clarifications

1. "The Daring Robot Surgery That Saved a Man's Life," *Wired*, accessed
August 5, 2024, https://www.wired.com/story/proximie-remote-surgery
-nhs/.

2.   Rolfe Winkler, "Harlan Band's Descent Started with an Easy Online Adderall Prescription," *Wall Street Journal*, accessed August 22, 2022, https://www.wsj.com/articles/harlan-bands-descent-started-with-an-easy-online-adderall-prescription-11660916158.

3.   "What Is a Psychotropic Drug? Types, Uses, Side Effects, Risks & More," Healthline, November 6, 2019, https://www.healthline.com/health/what-is-a-psychotropic-drug; Maria G. Valdovinos et al., "Adverse Side Effects of Psychotropic Medication and Challenging Behavior: Pilot Work Assessing Impact," *Journal of Developmental and Physical Disabilities* 29, no. 6 (December 2017): 969–82, https://doi.org/10.1007/s10882-017-9570-0; G. A. Fava and C. Rafanelli, "Iatrogenic Factors in Psychopathology," *Psychotherapy and Psychosomatics* 88, no. 3 (2019):129–40, doi:10.1159/000500151; PMID: 31085917; "What You Should Know Before Taking Psychotropic Drugs," Verywell Mind, accessed August 5, 2024, https://www.verywellmind.com/psychotropic-drugs-425321.

4.   Research the Turpin family of California when you have a moment, if you'd like to learn more.

Conclusion: Christ Offers More

1.   Martin Bucer, *Concerning the True Care of Souls* (Carlisle, PA: Banner of Truth, 2016), 167.

Appendix C: Habits for a Biblically Transformed Mind

1.   See *Heart & Habits: How We Change for Good* (Fort Worth, TX: Kress, 2021).

Index

Note: Page numbers followed by n indicate notes.

primacy of symptom relief and,
175–177
yoga and self-care, 170–171
see also psychotropic medication
"nous," 72–73, 83
nutrition, importance of, 256

obsessive-compulsive disorder
(OCD), 185–186
oppositional defiant disorder
(ODD), 187–188, 189
Ortlund, Gavin, 192–193
"Overdiagnosis of Mental Illness,
The" (Frances), 10–11
Owen, John, 226
Oxford University Press, 27–28

pain and sickness, Bible and, 96–97
Passions of the Heart (Street), 189
Paul (apostle), xxvii, 82, 156, 168,
185–186
glorification and, 119
inner man and, 95
issues of mind and thoughts,
72–76, 114, 116, 118–120
outer man and, 82, 84
renewal of mind and, 78–79
sanity and, 200–201, 204–205
sin and, 104–105
Peacemaker, The (Sande), 221
Philippians 3:7–9, 240
physical activity, as therapy, 171
physical body
Bible and, 90–97
categories of outer man, 93–101
cravings and, 97, 223–224,
278n18, 19
difficulty of separating mind
and brain, 101–103
dignity of human life and, 278n22
influence on inner person,
103–107
insanity and, 208

physical death and, 87–107
trauma and the mind, 87–90
post-traumatic stress disorder
(PTSD), xviii, 181, 191–192
EMDR and, 172
financial incentives for
diagnosis of, 23–25
results of diagnosis of, 197
Powlison, David, 140–141
prayer, importance to renewal of
mind, 260
pride, narcissistic personality
disorder and, 187
Priolo, Lou, 188
Proverbs 12:25, 164
Proverbs 23:29–33, 98
Psalm 19, 178, 241
Psalm 119, 179
Psychiatric Times, 157, 166
psychiatry
arbitrary diagnosis methods and
drug prescriptions without
diagnostic testing, 59–63,
247–253, 275n42
defined, 56, 274n36
early hospitals for, 53–54
medical training and neurology
versus mental issues, 53–59
as soft science, xxv
see also secular therapeutic
culture
Psychiatry Research, 150
Psychiatry.org, 29
psychologist, 56, 274n36
Psychology Today, 160
psychotropic medication, 145–163
Christian perspectives on, 145–147
defined, 151
financial incentives for
diagnoses and, 38–40
God-honoring motivations and,
229–231
legality and, 153–154

About the Author

GREG E. GIFFORD is the host of the *Transformed* podcast and television series, the chair of the School of Biblical Studies at The Master's University, and a fellow at Fortis Institute. He is also the pastor of counseling at Faith Community Church in Santa Clarita, California. He holds a PhD in biblical counseling from Southwestern Baptist Theological Seminary, an MA in biblical counseling from The Master's University, and a BA in pastoral ministry from Baptist Bible College. He served as a captain in the United States Army from 2008 to 2012 and is the author of *Helping Your Family Through PTSD* and *Heart & Habits*, which was the 2021 Biblical Counseling Book of the Year. He is married to Amber, his high school sweetheart. They reside in California with their three sons.